Getting Your Manuscript Sold

By

C. L. Sterling & M. G. Davidson

Barclay House
New York

A BARCLAY TRADE PAPERBACK
Published by
Barclay House
a division of the
Zinn Publishing Group:
ZINN COMMUNICATIONS / NEW YORK

ISBN: 0-935016-09-0

Printed in the United States of America

Library of Congress Cataloging-in-Publication Data

Sterling, Cynthia.
    Getting your manuscript sold: surefire writing & selling strategies that will get your book published / C.L. Sterling & M.G. Davidson – 1st ed.
      p.   cm
    Includes bibliographical references.
    ISBN 0-935016-09-0
    1. Authorship–Marketing. 2. Authorship. 3. Manuscript preparation (Authorship) I. Davidson, M.G. (Megan G.). II. Title.
PN161.S74   1994
808'.02–dc20
                                 94-39165
                                     CIP

Dedications

Always first, my husband, Tom. To my mom, for making me read books from the moment I opened my eyes. To all the new writers who have taught me so much over the years. I hope that I serve you well.

— _Cynthia Sterling_

To my husband, Cliff, who has patiently put up with a lot of creative tantrums over the years.

—_Megan Davidson_

____ *Acknowledgments* ____

As is always the truth, no book comes together through the effort of only a single person. Those who have assisted in this book and who have helped me refine my own writing and those who have shared their knowledge of the publishing industry include: My co-author, personal editor and close friend, Megan, whose firm editorial advice makes me look good. To Patrick Freeman, a top editor. I see a book in your future. To Anna Aivaliotis, whose numerous corrections and computer entries made my life easier. To my first editor, Lyn Cryderman at Zondervan/HarperCollins, for giving me the confidence to follow my instincts. To Jim Van Treese at Northwest Publishing, who set me free to write a book with heart and purpose. To David Zinn, my publisher for this book. I admire your vision and am grateful for your confidence in me.

— *Cynthia Sterling*

I'd like to thank my friends and relatives, who have been very supportive; Cynthia, a talented writer and a dedicated agent, as well as a good pal; Denise Little, my editor at Zebra Books, who has been instrumental in getting my fiction published; Jaqueline Shank, my seventh grade teacher in Portland, Oregon, who first nurtured my fierce love for writing; Lewis "Buddy" Nordan, a great writer and a wonderful teacher; and all the writers whom I hope will benefit from this book.

— *Megan Davidson*

CONTENTS

Introduction

Introduction

Writing is hard work that requires extreme dedication. It is not a vocation that a coward would choose. Every step of the writing process – from the first stirrings of the character and story, through the numerous drafts, the cut of the editor's pen, finding an agent, marketing and rejections, to acceptance by a publisher and the resultant publicity – demands nerves of steel. Although we can, with a high degree of confidence, tell you about the various stages you will go through and what you can expect during those stages, for each writer there will be unforeseen twists and turns. These "unseens" may add to the difficulty of achieving your dream.

A little story comes to mind about a friend who was at the crossroads of her life. Annie was sitting in her car waiting for the light to turn green. She was struggling with the idea of leaving her present career to do the thing she always wanted to do – write. Her mind was tired of logically looking at her options and weighing the risks of a career change. Numerous times she looked at the realities of a safe career in the medical field. It paid the bills, even allowed her some luxuries. The white lab coat gave her instant respectability. On the other hand, the job afforded her little time to do anything else. The hours were long, the work stressful, and the truth of the matter was that she was tired of seeing people sick and dying. But following her heart was very risky and filled with unknowns. On the other hand, not doing what she yearned to do was slowly killing her.

"Okay, I give up," she said to no one in particular.

She gazed out the open window and stared down an unpaved side road that curved, then disappeared. *I wonder where that road goes*, she thought to herself. *It goes somewhere*, she reasoned. After all, that was the nature of a road – to take you somewhere. And you trust that it will do its job. You'll end up somewhere. Most roads, Annie thought to herself, take you where you want to go. You just have to want to go there.

Then she realized that that road was the answer. Do I want to travel the road of writing? she questioned herself. Or do I want just to see my name on a book? Both, she decided. "I want both!" she yelled to a passerby who shook his head then quickened his pace. It was at that moment Annie knew what she had to do. She made a sharp turn and took the side road, literally and figuratively.

Annie took a part-time position at a doctor's office while going part time to a local college. She took nothing but writing courses. She started a diary, joined a writer's group, read everything she could about the publishing field, attended seminars and workshops, established some good contacts, hooked up with a great editor, read lots of books and finally started to outline some of her own.

Annie's first work to be published was poetry, then newspaper articles, then magazine articles, until she finally got published by a major publisher, then another, then another.

The time frame from her initial decision to her first major book – six years.

When we asked Annie if it was worth it, she smiled and gently nodded. A quiet satisfaction shone on her face.

Our advice to you is to weigh your options carefully. The writer's road is as dangerous as the yellow brick one that Dorothy traveled. Ask yourself the same questions Annie asked. Do I want to write for writing's sake? Do I want to write for the sake of fame? Answer them honestly. If you find you only want to see your name on a book, forget traveling down the road and hire a ghostwriter to write your story.

If you decide to take the road, then let us be among the first to wish you a safe and speedy journey. We hope this book will answer some of your questions and help you on your way.

CHAPTER ONE

A PROFESSIONAL APPROACH TO WRITING

TODAY'S SOPHISTICATED literary marketplace is often confusing to the new writer. It is also a scary place. Undoubtedly you have heard a few horror stories about the publishing world: the difficulties in securing an agent; the countless rejection slips; the ruthless marketing game to get a book on the shelves; the slash of the editor's pen. Most of what you heard is probably true, at least to some extent.

Most new writers are not deterred by these truths. They know the dangers, yet they push on with their quest of becoming published. After encountering thousands of hopeful writers each year, we have come to believe that it is not what the writer knows that gets him into trouble; it is what he doesn't know.

One of the first points of concern is the writer's lack of understanding about the publishing industry in general. Often writers are so involved in giving birth to their manuscript and nursing the newborn that they have little time to investigate the publishing world. While the actual writing of the story is, for the most part, a solitary effort, the road to publication is not. It takes a group of people working together – a literary partnership – to accomplish the desired end: a successful book.

It's a good idea to know who the partners are and what roles they play. This understanding will help alleviate the tensions that new writers experience and will help make their journey toward the world of publishing a more satisfying experience.

The primary partners in the literary relationship are the writer, the agent, the editor, the publisher, the distributor, the bookbuyer, the bookseller and the reader. The duties that each partner performs are very specific and require a high degree of expertise. A successful partnership requires that each party yield some control to the others, while keeping the lines of communication open. A breakdown in communications between the partners can send a manuscript into a tailspin that may ultimately result in a disaster.

Of all the partners, the one who must surrender the most control is the new writer. This is not to imply that the writer should be out of control; it simply means that the writer must allow his agent, his editor, and his publisher to make certain decisions based upon their experience and in accordance with the restrictions of the marketplace.

Often the writer's expectations are far-reaching and out of step with the realities of the industry. That's where problems may begin. For example, a new writer may feel that his science fiction manuscript is for the mass market. He believes his work should receive an advance on royalties of $250,000 dollars with a matching promotional budget. The agent knows he cannot market science fiction to a mass market publisher. Furthermore, he knows that a publisher of science fiction isn't going to pay that much for a new writer's work in that particular category. Once this is explained to the writer, he has two choices: Get with the program and do what it takes to get published, or believe what Saul Bellow said about the publishing community: "You write a book, you invest your imagination in it, and then you hand it over to a bunch of people who have no imagination and no understanding of their own enterprise." The latter choice will more than likely kill the writer's chance of seeing his work in print.

In addition to learning about the creative and structural aspects of writing, the writer has to be the most knowledgeable of the literary partners. The writer's success is dependent upon knowing the world he has decided to enter. At first the writer will make mistakes, but this is a natural part of starting a new career. Such mistakes are nothing to be ashamed of or to fear. However, not learning from these mistakes can spell failure.

Professional Image

The ancient writer, Epictetus, said, in essence, that a writer, in the simplest terms, is one who writes. An author is a writer who has written a literary work. Usually the title "author" refers to any writer who has been published. To become published, the writer must function on two levels: professional and creative.

Sometimes it is difficult for a beginning writer to take on and maintain a professional image, yet it is essential to do so when dealing with the other literary partners. Publishers are not small, family-owned businesses who love the writer and spend their money publishing books as a sign of their great admiration for the writer's talent. Publishers are corporations. The more well-known the name of the house, the larger the corporation is likely to be. Doing business is the ultimate high, and the bottom line is the main consideration. Publishers understand professionalism, as do the rest of the players involved.

Many times it is the writer's lack of professionalism that stops agents, editors, or publishers dead in their tracks. Regardless of how creative or gifted the writer is, her literary partners will not invest the energy to nurture her professional side if she is sloppy, rude, uncooperative, combative or otherwise problematic. There are lots of other writers whom the literary partners may choose instead.

Some of the common mistakes that writers make come from watching too much television and too many movies. (We will address how these media effect writing style and crafting in later chapters.) Both movies and television have somehow persuaded the writer that he must be one or all of the following: suicidal; depressed; addicted to drugs or alcohol; a recluse; a habitual party goer, or downright crazy.

It is true that the act of writing is basically a lonely job, and some writers have fallen prey to a variety of tragic conditions. This doesn't mean that all writers will do so, however. On the other hand, the successful writer is "crazy," in the sense that logic alone does not drive fiction writing. Creativity, originality, and "irrational" thinking are key tools of the writer's trade.

Through the fantasy world of the movies, the writer comes to believe that he must at all times and at any cost exhibit the three E's of the artistic temperament: emotion, ego, eccentricities. These are accomplished by temper tantrums, a highly defensive attitude, and an air of haughty superiority. Then there is the matter of clothing. There are two popular choices: all black attire, or the "Faulkneresque" ensemble that includes a brown tweed coat with elbow patches, and perhaps a pipe for the gentlemen. (If you are a romance writer, then red is the color and glamour is the goal.)

But "looking the part" only makes the writer appear foolish and amateurish, especially if her writing is not strong enough to back up her elaborate exterior image. The best course is to forget the stereotypes. Simply be yourself, if that includes being professional in approach and demeanor and being knowledgeable about the business you are entering.

What It Means To Be Professional

Manuscript Preparation

Although numerous articles and books have been written on this topic, a startling number of new writers still submit their material in a sloppy, haphazard fashion. We have seen every imaginable form of manuscript, from handwritten documents to yellowed, crumbling pages to sheafs of paper reeking of cigarette smoke. The most common offenses are the following: single-spaced submissions; manuscripts printed on both sides of the page; pages which are not numbered consecutively; bound manuscripts; no name, address or phone number on the work; no synopsis; margins that are too small or too big; type that is too light, and inconsistent typefaces.

To visualize how important these points are, imagine yourself having five minutes to make a sales presentation to the board of a large corporation. The commission you stand to receive is more than a year's salary. You told the boss you could pull it off. You even went so far as to put a down payment on a swimming pool. The kids love you for it, and your spouse is proud of you. This is your moment.

You walk into the room and meet the board. You look good in your Armani suit; you're confident, and you talk a good line. You can see by the look on the board members' faces that they are nearly convinced. Now they want to see it all in writing. You pass out the proposal and, as they open up the folder and look inside, their faces suddenly turn sour. That single-spaced, yellow-paged, hard-to-read proposal printed on both sides of the page has them shaking their heads. They lose interest. You receive a polite "thank you" and are shown the door. As you enter the reception area, you see a dozen other hopeful people, all dressed the part, their proposals clutched in their hands. You try to hide your disappointment, but you're sure they all know you didn't get the deal. One woman nods and gives you a slight smile of compassion. After all, she could be you in a few minutes. "Why does anyone stay in this business?" you hear her say as you walk out the door. "We all must be crazy." Secretly she knows she is one step closer because of your failure.

As John Gardner so aptly put it, "There are other writers who would persuade you not to go on, that everything is nonsense, that you should kill yourself. They, of course, go on to write another book while you have just killed yourself." Don't kill yourself. Instead, next time, correct the mistakes.

The following are not options. They are necessities.

1. Double-spacing. This makes your manuscript much easier to read. Sometimes the person reviewing your manuscript may wish to make a comment. Double-spacing gives them the room to do so.

2. Healthy margins. Margins should be at least an inch on all sides. This gives a neat appearance to your work and, like doubling-spacing, makes the material easier to read and allows room for comments.

3. Number pages consecutively. Often a writer will begin each new chapter with "page one." Therefore, in one manuscript the writer may have twenty-five pages all numbered one. This is very confusing, especially if

the pages accidently get out of order. If you do not know how to program your computer to number pages consecutively, do so neatly by hand.

4. Print on one side only. Double-sided submissions are awkward to handle, since the reviewer must constantly shift his attention from the right to the left. Also, should your reviewer wish to make a comment on one page, it will show through on the other side and interfere with the readability of that side of the page. This is not the time to conserve paper.

5. Do not bind manuscripts. Submit your manuscript in a stationery-size box or padded envelope. You can purchase these for a small sum at your local print or copying shop, or use the boxes which typing paper or computer paper is sold in. Three-ring binders, spiral binders, glued bindings, or paperclipping or stapling each chapter together is not acceptable. Most editors find it easier to "flip through" a loose manuscript.

6. Include a synopsis. Most agents and publishers require synopses. These can be one to five pages long. They give the reviewer a quick idea of what your story is about and a frame of reference for what you hope to accomplish in your novel. Some writers may wish to include a chapter-by-chapter outline which details the central action of each chapter in one to two paragraphs per chapter. (See the appendix for examples of the complete synopsis, the one-page synopsis and the chapter-by-chapter outline.)

7. Provide a word count. The word count should be placed on either the title page or at the right hand corner of chapter one. Both publishers and agents are interested in word count (as opposed to page count) because they relate the number of words to the size of a book. A word count therefore tells the reviewer if you are aware of your market's needs. Example: If you submit a 100,000 word manuscript as a juvenile work, the reviewer will know immediately you've over-written your category by about 65,000 words.

8. Indicate category. This should appear either on the title page or at the right hand corner of chapter one. This lets your reviewer know that you have identified your intended audience – science fiction, contemporary romance, literary, mass market, and so on. It's up to the reviewer to determine whether or not you have accomplished your goal.

9. Include name. Your cover sheet should include your name, address and daytime phone number. Your last name and the book title (or partial title)

should appear in the upper left-hand corner of the back page of the manuscript.

10. Include a cover letter. This is a brief letter thanking the agent for reviewing your manuscript. Since it's a business letter, use the standard business letter format.

11. Include a Self-Addressed, Stamped Envelope (SASE). This is required by most agents. The amount of postage should be the amount it takes to mail the manuscript. This will help insure that, should your manuscript be rejected or require additional work, it will be shipped back to you. If you do not wish for the manuscript to be returned, indicate to the agent in your cover letter that he has your permission to dispose of the manuscript. Most agents prefer to send it back to you.

12. Most important of all, proofread your manuscript. This will help eliminate as many typos and other minor errors as possible. Better yet, have someone else proofread your manuscript. Note that spell-check alone will not catch all minor errors.

Before Submitting Your Manuscript

Finally your manuscript is ready. It has been proofread for errors, all the last-minute changes are done, and the work has a neat, professional appearance. You are one proud parent. If you have not contacted a literary agent by now, this is the time to do so.

Many sources are available to help you locate an agent.

1. *The Literary Marketplace* (LMP) can be found in the reference section of most libraries. This resource book gives an extensive listing of agents; however, there is very little information about each agent or the types of manuscripts the agent handles. It also lists publishers, printers, distributors, and public relations firms. The LMP is mostly used by the other partners in the literary partnership.

2. *The Writer's Market* is a very valuable source of information for the new writer. It is updated yearly, and you can purchase a copy at your local bookstore. Hundreds of agents are listed, and a detailed account of what they handle, their years in business, titles sold, and contact names are all given. This book is strongly recommended to new writers and worth the investment.

3. *The Insider's Guide to Book Editors, Publishers, and Literary Agents*, by Jeff Herman. While the listing of agents is not extensive, it does give well-researched information on each agent. It even makes the agents almost sound approachable and human. We strongly recommend this book, which can be purchased at your local bookstore.

4. *Writer's Digest* magazine is another good source for agents who are advertising for new clients. The magazine intentionally divides agents from literary services in its classified section. The magazine also includes articles regarding publishing and writing, and updates on publishing. Printed monthly, *Writer's Digest* is available at your local bookstore or through subscription.

5. Local writers groups often work with one or more agents. Their members may be willing to pass along their agents' names to you.

6. Attending writing conferences, seminars and workshops are excellent ways to connect with an agent. Of course, you'll want to make certain that an agent will be present before you sign up for the conference.

Contacting an Agent

Once you have obtained some names of agents whom you wish to contact, write the agent to inquire if he is accepting new clients and what his areas of interest are. This letter is called a query letter. (See appendix for an example.) Request a copy of the agent's guidelines. If contacting the agent by phone, remember to keep your conversation professional, courteous and short. Be prepared to answer the following questions:

Is your manuscript fiction or nonfiction?
What category does it fall into?
Is it complete?
What's the approximate word count?
Have you been previously published? (Newspaper articles, poetry, letters to the editor, etc. don't count.)
Can you give the idea of the story in a few sentences?

The question that many writers cannot answer is, "What's the category?" In other words, they do not know who their intended audience is. Are they writing science fiction, fantasy, romance, young adult fiction, mass market or something else? Does the work appeal to young readers, college-educated readers, romance readers, horror buffs, or the sporting crowd? (We will discuss genres and categories at more length in a subsequent chapter.)

It is not solely the job of the agent or publisher to know the audience you are writing for. Before you begin to write, you should be aware of your reader. Not knowing the answer to the question, "What's the category?" is a tip-off to the agent that problems lie ahead. Be sure to have an answer and give it quickly and confidently.

When contacting an agent, you will want to avoid saying or writing statements such as:

This is a bestseller.
Let's make lots of money together.
Send me your guidelines, along with a list of your clients and their phone numbers.
I really don't like agents but....
If you're really interested in representing my work, you won't charge a fee.
I've heard that all agents are crooks, but I need one, so....
My last agent screwed me.
I hope you're reputable.
I don't have any money, so please don't charge me for anything.
I have a real winner.
Thanks, honey (or sweetie, cutie, darling, babe, and so on) or buddy.

Comments such as these only offend an agent and show your lack of professionalism and trust. Be pleasant and polite, and focus on gathering information. Your introduction is most important, so use it to your benefit. (If you need to arrange a fee schedule, most agents will be happy to oblige.)

At the agency, we have seen the entire gamut of what a new writer will request in the way of information, including confidential information. The request that most stands out in our minds comes from a young gentleman who asked for our guidelines, along with a listing of ISBN numbers of the manuscripts that we sold. (ISBNs are numbers assigned to books by publishers and can often be seen on the back jacket of a book. These numbers are for inventory purposes.) He also wanted the names and phone numbers of at least four of our clients, so he could call them for references before submitting his manuscript to us.

An associate agent took the call and explained that our brochure had all the information that the writer needed at this point. The agent also explained that the brochure listed recent titles but not ISBN numbers, and that, while the brochure included client endorsements, the agency did not give out telephone numbers. When the man insisted that we supply the information he wanted, the associate agent put him through to the agent. The agent asked him what he intended to do with the ISBN numbers. The young man did not know what he would do with them. When asked why he requested them, the man simply replied he had read somewhere to ask for them. When asked if we could give his telephone number out to prospective clients should we offer him a contract, his answer was no.

A few days later he re-contacted the agency and requested to speak with the associate agent because he didn't like the agent, who was also the owner. Once again he requested telephone numbers and ISBNs. Once again he was refused.

This is a very good way to make a very bad impression on an agent or other literary partner.

If you receive an agency's guidelines and you still have questions, keep them short and concise. Remember that at some point polite persistence can turn into obnoxious hounding. Most agents are willing to take a few minutes to clarify their requirements or give you a little more information about the agency. However, at this point they are not selling themselves to you: You are selling yourself to them.

After your manuscript has been reviewed and you have been offered a literary contract, this may be the time to ask a few more questions. But keep in mind that the agent is not your enemy; he is your new partner.

CHAPTER
TWO

THE LITERARY PARTNERSHIP: WRITER & READER

THE ROLE OF THE WRITER is not only to be knowledgeable of the marketplace and professional in his approach, it is also, as Anais Nin put it, "not to say what we can all say, but what we are unable to say." Sound impossible? Not so for the skilled writer.

THE WRITER: A BREED APART

One day, while waiting to board an airplane, a writer struck up a conversation with a pleasant gentleman. The man revealed he was a surgeon. "And you?" he asked the writer.

"I write novels," she replied.

"That's interesting," said the doctor. "You know, someday I'd like to write a novel, too."

The writer nodded. "Yes," she sighed. "I know what you mean. Someday I'd like to perform a coronary bypass."

This story illustrates a fact that people often ignore, overlook or even refuse to believe: Successful fiction writers are a very exclusive, very special breed. Not everyone can, should or ought to try writing fiction, at least with publication in mind. Writing takes skills which are learned over time, as well as incredible dedication and commitment.

This notion, of course, flies in the face of a popular belief which holds that everyone should "try writing a book someday." This belief implies that something which is written on a whim by a person with no writing background or skills stands as good a chance at being published as a piece carefully crafted by a skilled writer.

To better understand why this simply is not true – so as to put this misconception to rest for good – let's probe a little further into the writer's psyche.

Writers are often thought of as existing primarily to entertain the reading population. Therefore the writer must believe that her work has value and that others want to read it...or at least need to read it. Writers have traditionally had an enormous influence on culture and trends, leading George Bernard Shaw to remark, tongue in cheek, on their ability to "corrupt" the reader and broaden his world.

No writer is so expert that he cannot improve his writing. In some ways, the writer is an eternal apprentice, always seeking to improve his work.

Most writers have many shared traits that lead them to personal satisfaction regarding their work, as well as commercial success. If you are lacking any of the following, do not despair. Remember, most writers are created, not born.

1. Writers are ill with the writing sickness. Writers are driven to write. To them, writing is a sickness, and the only cure is to write, to paraphrase Anne Rice. Now and then a writer emerges who has but one success; perhaps it is his only work. This is a rarity, since most good writing is not a fluke or a one-time inspiration. Rather it is an unstoppable flood, a constant outpouring, sometimes improving, sometimes declining, but always ongoing. Most fiction writers cannot will themselves to stop writing...nor do they wish to. Writing is virtually an obsession. If allowed to get out of control, it can be destructive. But, once the writer learns how to focus his power, there is nothing more beautiful and uplifting.

2. Writers find people fascinating. That's why successful writers are able to create fascinating characters who are paradoxically often both realistic and larger than life. The writer is such a keen observer of human nature that she will sometimes pause in the middle of a meal or conversation to jot down or make a mental note of some detail or insight on the human condition that she has just witnessed.

A keen sense of observation helps a writer create realistic details and express believable emotional reactions. A good story, told well, goes a long way to capturing and holding a reader's attention and – this is of primary concern to any writer – keeping the reader turning the pages.

Developing the protagonist is crucial to a novel, and the writer understands this. In fact, he knows everything there is to know about his main character, including what flavor of ice cream she likes best. Of course, such details might not show up in the novel, but the writer realizes that he has no excuse for not knowing them anyway.

The writer also understands his characters and knows what they would or would not do in any given circumstance. For example, one writer created a strong secondary character who was a midwife and herbalist. At one point the writer thought of having this character induce her own abortion, then realized that she would never harm a child, even an unborn one. Instead the writer had the midwife use her knowledge of herbal medicine to induce her own sterility.

3. Writers know the mechanics of writing. While writers may manipulate grammar to make a point, they value clear communication and concise writing. This does not mean that every comma will be in exactly the right place according to your 7th grade English teacher. However, the careful writer will vary sentence structure, break long paragraphs, combine short paragraphs, avoid incorrect punctuation and take all other pains to deliver a highly readable piece.

4. Writers care about their readers. One often hears writers making statements to the effect that they "write for themselves" and "don't give a damn what anyone thinks" about their writing. Such statements are probably exaggerations. It's true that a writer must feel free to choose his own subject matter and develop a style that seems natural to him, without being swayed by literary trends or fads. On the other hand, most successful fiction writers take the reader into account because they know their success depends on the reader.

How do writers show concern for the reader? First of all, they do not intentionally confuse or frustrate the reader except for a very specific purpose, perhaps to build suspense. For example, Flannery O'Connor, in the story "Good Country People," reveals very little about the intentions of her secondary character. By doing so she creates a level of tension and suspense that gently but forcefully compels the reader to keep reading. In the end, O'Connor rewards the reader for his patience with a brilliant "sprung" conclusion, that is, one which cannot be anticipated.

Most successful fiction writers strive to create a feeling of trust between writer and reader. The writer trusts the reader to keep reading; in return, the reader trusts the writer not to let him down by unnecessarily misleading or frustrating him or talking down to him. It is never the job of the fiction writer to educate or change the reader, although a reader may indeed learn much from fiction and may change her outlook on life as a result.

5. Imagination and control. Part of the attraction of writing fiction is the sense of power it conveys to the writer. And what a mind-boggling power writers can possess! They can create entire worlds and all the creatures that inhabit them. Furthermore, the writer is capable of changing everything at the slightest whim, erasing people, places and events.

One key to wielding this power is imagination. When most non-writers speak of creativity, they usually speak first of imagination as the ability to picture fictional events, characters and so on. They tend to forget that creativity in fiction writing also means the ability to put all this material down in a cohesive, readable way, using only the written word.

At least on some level, a writer understands that with the power of imagination comes the responsibility to communicate to the reader. He understands that creativity without structure is chaos. Therefore, the writer also understands that creative fiction writing is a sort of dance between imagination on one hand and structure on the other hand. How these two elements combine to form a novel is the essence of writing fiction.

Physiological studies have borne out this theory. Writing is one of the few human endeavors which necessitates rapid back-and-forth communication between the left hemisphere of the brain (which governs logic, language and linear thinking) and the right hemisphere (the source of creativity, inspiration, imagination, random order and holistic thinking). In other words, a person actively engaged in writing is actually balancing organizational skills with nonlinear thinking almost at once. Anyone who has ever composed an outline for a novel is probably acquainted with this mental state.

6. Persistence, Persistence, Persistence. Persistence and resilience are two of the most valuable assets a writer can have. Anyone who is serious about writing fiction either has these resources or soon develops them. There is no room for beginning writers with fine sensibilities and artistic temperaments in the sweaty arena of fiction writing. Competition is extremely fierce. Once a writer has established herself as a valuable commodity, however, she may find herself in a much better position to negotiate and to stand up for her opinions.

The road to becoming a writer, as you can see, is long and hard. Unfortunately, if you have the "illness" you have no other choice but to travel down that road. Many beginning writers are dismayed to find that, once they have put years of hard effort into writing a novel, they have months if not years of work still ahead of them before it is actually sold. If it were only true that novels were produced in mere months and snapped up by publishers in a few weeks. Alas, it is only a myth.

While writing is not that easy, beginning writers should take comfort in the following good news.

1. The more you write, the more your writing will improve...assuming

that you are committed to improving your writing. To polish your work, read it over often to see where it is lacking and how you can make it better. Remember, all but the best writing can be improved.

2. Publishers are always looking for powerful, insightful books that look at an old subject in a fresh, new way. When you write, ask yourself: What is my work bringing to the table? How is it new, different or better than other fiction on the subject? Why would anyone want to read my book instead of another book? The answers to these questions should be included in your cover letter to the agent or publisher.

3. Writing is the ultimate forgiving medium. Like a loving dog, writing will let you shove it about as much as you wish, yet always do as you ask of it. Certainly James Joyce proved that in *Finnegan's Wake*. Unlike speech, writing allows a person to go back and correct mistakes as often as desired. Computers have made writing even more malleable and supremely easy to change.

4. Models for intriguing protagonists and striking plots are all around. People are fascinating, and so are the lives they lead, whether they are hermits or adventurers. The more you write, the less time you will have to watch TV or movies, which interferes with fresh, realistic, "uncanned" ideas for fiction.

5. No art form gives the artist more power to create more freely and extensively than writing. If you have ever dreamed of setting your imagination free, then writing is the medium for you. There is nothing you cannot put down in writing. Raw, unguided writing is a wild horse, beautiful but unapproachable because it kicks and bites. In time the writer learns to gentle the magnificent wild horse of his imagination and train it to perform for the delight of others, willingly and easily, without restraint of a harness.

6. In writing there is no right or wrong, only that which works and that which does not. Most people can learn the conventions of fiction writing, and those who do will develop the skills to make their writing stronger and more readable...in short, they will learn to make their writing work. All the effort you put into learning how to write more effectively will show up in spades in your writing.

7. Publishing what you write is not the be-all and end-all of the writer's

existence. Although we all hope to be rewarded financially for our efforts, writing has intrinsic rewards that go beyond making money. Surely there are few better ways to access your deepest feelings, to express your creativity or to communicate with relatives and friends. Many writers we have worked with have discovered that they are wiser for having written their work. They have received many insights into the human condition and learned much about the power of communication and language.

8. Many, many sources are available to help you learn how to craft your writing. Writing classes, workshops, seminars, retreats and home study are all available to the beginning writer.

A Writer's Worst Fear

Writers often experience fear when the time comes to let go of their work. After all, they are sending their child out into the world to see if he can make his living on his own, and they exhibit all the anxieties of a concerned parent. Will the work be rejected? Will it succeed? Will it travel far before it does succeed? And what will people think of the "parent"?

A writer's fear is usually exhibited in two ways: sheer terror or over-confidence. We find the first type of reaction the easiest to handle. Because the writer is new to the business, he quite naturally may feel unsure of himself and even the quality of his writing. A few reassuring, kind words go a long way to calming the writer, although of course, there are no guarantees.

Over-confident writers are a bit more difficult to manage. These writers usually have a difficult time accepting constructive criticism, and will often become quite defensive of their manuscripts. By defending their work against criticism intended to improve it, they become like over-protective parents with a severe case of nearsightedness. When this happens, such writers have a hard time improving their manuscripts...or seeing the need to do so. Yet, when finally forced to send their manuscripts into the hands of publishers, the over-confident writer normally does so with great fear of rejection and disapproval. This moment is the true test of a writer's trust in the value and competence of his work.

THE READER

The reader is the Supreme Court, the philosopher's stone, the crucial ingredient, the moment of truth of the book writing process. Without the reader, writing is nothing. A novel sitting on a shelf benefits no one. It is only when the novel is read that it springs to life in the mind of the reader.

The Writer/Reader Collaboration

A written piece is a connection between a writer and a reader. In fact, it can be seen as a collaboration between those two people. While the writer creates the novel, the reader gives it her own unique interpretation. Even a simple sentence, such as "The messenger entered the tent," invites a world of interpretation regarding the age, sex, clothing and appearance of the messenger, as well as the size and general appearance of the tent. What the reader "sees" will largely depend on the context of the sentence and the reader's experience with messengers and tents.

Unlike a movie, which visually presents a "canned," one-sided view of a story, a novel is an intellectual process constantly open to different interpretations based on individual readers' imaginations, backgrounds, and intellects. Two people watching "Rambo" are likely to walk away from the theater feeling that they have both passively experienced "the same thing." We know, for instance, that Rambo is the "hero" of the movie; we must root for him, for we are not given any opportunity to view him as anything but noble and praiseworthy.

However, reading is an active process. Two readers of a probing, creative novel such as *Lolita*, by Vladimir Nabakov, may have different, even conflicting views on the very meaning of the work and may experience the novel in very different ways. For example, they may view Lolita as a victim or a vamp; Humbert Humbert may be a sick, perverse criminal...or a sensitive but disturbed hero...or a brilliant man ruined by a destructive obsession. The reader is somewhat at liberty to "devise" the story as it unfolds before him, and a good writer knows this.

What is a fiction reader looking for when she picks up a novel? Perhaps escapism, perhaps a sense of romance or adventure, perhaps insight into the human condition or a specific historical era, perhaps the beauty and power of the language...or perhaps just a pleasant way to while away a few hours. Reasons for reading vary almost as much as the readers themselves.

As mentioned earlier, the writer and reader unwittingly share a pact of trust and mutual respect: The writer trusts the reader to read his book, and the reader trusts the writer to present her with material that is both readable and interesting, and preferably powerful, insightful, moving or enlightening.

The onus of this pact is on the writer. After all, if the reader has invested in a book and has set aside time to read it, she has fulfilled her part of the bargain. The writer's part is more complicated. He must be true to his craft, his content and his own imagination, and still fulfill his commitment to the reader.

What the Reader Wants to Avoid

Of course, tastes will vary, and not all writers' works will appeal to all readers. In addition, writers often go through several stages in their writing careers, and what appealed to one group of readers may not appeal to another. Still, there are some things a reader does *not* want from the writer:

1. Confusion. Who is the main character? Is he sympathetic? Where and when is the novel set? Are there sufficient physical details to make the reader feel as if he has stepped into the fabric of the fiction and become part of it?

2. Boredom. Is the pace of the story sufficiently brisk so that the reader does not doze off while reading in bed at night? This does not mean that the plot has to be larded with action scenes, but it does mean that fiction has a very strong element of storytelling. Novels often include a sense of forward progression and rising action which either make the reader curious about what happens next...or care enough about the protagonist that he feels compelled to read on to discover what happened to her.

3. Jaded Language and Plots. Originality counts where the reader is concerned. People who read tend to read a lot, and they do not take kindly to reading the same plot over and over. While it is true that "there are no new stories under the sun" and that most subjects have already been explored in fiction, it is still the writer's obligation to the reader to provide some original insights along well-trodden paths. Whatever the genre or target audience, originality and fresh ideas tend to captivate and enthrall the reader.

Hackneyed language is almost as deathly as hackneyed storylines. If a reader wished to hear cliches, he would watch television. Because of its half-hour segments and its need to appeal to a wide audience, television deals primarily in cultural cliches and stereotypes. But in writing, cliches stand out like dead roses in a bouquet of fresh flowers.

4. Unreadable Language. If the reader has to read the novel with a thesaurus and a dictionary propped up beside him, then the writer has a problem. One beginning writer used the technical term "orts" to describe plain old crumbs in his writing. This turn for the obtuse only frustrates the reader.

There is no place in published fiction for incomprehensible sentences, yet readers sometimes find themselves deciphering such passages as this: "He signaled for the flagman for the truck to proceed, standing in the road-way with his jacket inside out."

Writing like this stops the reader abruptly, and it usually takes some time for him to recover and continue reading (if he wishes to). Clear, precise, direct language and powerful but simple words allow the reader to access the writing and interpret it effectively.

5. Insults. A reader can tell when a writer is talking down to him and will not put up with much abuse. Patronizing takes many forms, including direct or indirect references to a reader's inability to understand the writing, and an obvious attempt to "explain" or "define" terms or actions. One beginning writer created an obnoxious protagonist who proclaimed that readers would not be able to comprehend the full range of his knowledge. Unless such a remark is obviously an attempt at humor, it is best omitted.

6. Gaffes and Poor Writing. For some reason, the agency receives a lot of material from writers who objectify body parts to ridiculous extremes. Poor writing can produce peculiar sentences, such as:

— "He continued to hold her eyes with his."
— "His eye fell from Jones, followed down his arm and dropped into the lake."
— "Jackson summoned the officer of thick blond hair."
— "Julia carried her head with pride."
— "He crossed his feet and poured them both a mug of tea."
— "Meandering down the street, her feet slipped out from under her."
— "Philip glued his astonished face to the wall."

Reading suspect passages aloud may help prevent awkward noun, verb and preposition combinations and misplaced modifiers.

Another common mistake is the direct use of onomatopoeia, or the attempt to mimic natural sounds. Thus we sometimes get such awkward sentences as:

— "Twang! The arrow sailed through the air."
— "Gloria heard someone rap at the door: knock, knock, knock."
— "BOOM! roared the explosion."

Onomatopoeia is best used indirectly (She heard the twang of the bowstring), and then sparingly.

Sometimes writing is simply confused and confusing. Consider this sample from a beginning writer. It is the first paragraph of a novel.

> The speaker's words were assaulted by the gun-fire blasts of a 25-year-old Volkswagen van that appeared to have no muffler. The driver swerved into Beauman's limited access lane smack-dab ahead of him, without an inch of leeway. Beauman cursed as the van sped away, then bent down toward the radio.

Anyone who reads this paragraph is likely to have many questions about its meaning: Where is the speaker? Is he or she standing on a street? Is it important that the van is a Volkswagen and is 25 years old? If we assume the driver is driving the van, who is Beauman? Is he the speaker? Is he also driving? What is a "limited access lane?" Where is the radio that Beauman is bending toward?

The writer's editor had to read the above paragraph five times before the answers to all those questions became clear. The speaker's voice is coming from the radio in Beauman's car. This is the radio he bends toward. The age and make of the van are unimportant, as is its driver. We learn later that the "limited access lane" is a futuristic freeway lane in which speeds are strictly controlled. Beauman is driving his car on this freeway, listening to an announcer on the radio.

A successful writer knows he cannot lead his reader on such a dance between words and meaning *unless he has a specific reason to do so*, perhaps to indicate the chaotic mind of a person with a mental disease. In this case, however, the writer was neither innovative nor creative, but simply lazy. He was not concerned about his reader and did not realize the importance of clearly setting scene and character. Here is one way to rewrite the paragraph to make it more understandable.

> Beauman turned up the volume of his car radio. As he hurtled down the new, 30-lane controlled speed highway, a rattletrap van swerved in front of him, cutting off both him and the voice of the radio announcer. "Damn, what was that?" grumbled Beauman, leaning forward to catch the announcer's next words.

Reading What Your Write

A writer would do well to also be a reader.

Once you've written a piece, it is no longer yours. It belongs to its readers. Therefore, if you wish to evaluate something you've written, you can't read it as a proud new writer would, blind to its flaws. You must put on your reader's hat and read the work fresh, as a reader would, demanding clarity, accessibility and originality. Those parts which are not clear, accessible or original will probably be obvious.

Once you have read it to yourself, read it again, out loud, chapter by chapter. This is the best way to honestly evaluate your own manuscript, as even small details that don't work will be very apparent once they are voiced.

As the temperamental Samuel Johnson once wrote, "Read over your compositions and, when you meet a passage which you think is particularly fine, strike it out."

CHAPTER THREE

THE LITERARY PARTNERSHIP: AGENT, EDITOR AND PUBLISHER

THE AGENT

A LITERARY AGENT, normally the first partner with whom the writer comes in contact, represents authors to publishers and/or movie producers. He is a liaison between the writer and whoever buys the writer's work. Agents sell the author's work, negotiate contracts, see that contractual obligations are being met and, to a limited extent, perform some public relations for their clients. To become a literary agent is simply a matter of calling yourself one. At this time there are no licensing requirements, no tests, no special training or education. Several organizations do exist for agents, and, should an agent decide to become a member, he must agree to adhere to that group's standards. The penalty for not complying could result in loss of membership. The standards of required business practices vary depending on the organization. Most of these organizations require a minimum number of manuscripts sold and the backing of several members in good standing before allowing membership, thus barring most newer agents. Once an agent becomes established and is successful in operating his business, he is probably no longer in need of the support that the organization has to offer.

This lack of quality control is of concern to some writers and sometimes causes the beginning writer to be a bit wary of agents. However, we think it is safe to say that the majority of agents are hardworking and upfront in their dealings with writers. And, like it or not, without an agent most publishers will not even consider a new writer's work.

Since the agent plays a vital part in the success of your manuscript, let's take a good look at exactly what an agent is. First, an agent is a businessperson. Business requires overhead such as advertising, phone bills, office rent or mortgage, staff, taxes, office equipment and so on and so forth. The agent is not immune to the cost of doing business. His first concern is staying in business so that he is able to perform many services for his clientele.

An agent must be flexible and willing to adjust to the demands of the marketplace. Until recently the agent's primary job was to "sell" writer's works, a task he could accomplish from his home. But a salesperson working out of the home cannot usually compete successfully in the present market of highly trained professionals of the corporate world, nor withstand the increasing competition among literary agents for quality manuscripts. Also, ever-tightening tax laws strongly dictate a businessperson's course of action regarding how her company will operate.

Some writers, especially those who don't conduct themselves in a professional manner, demand that the agent be a professional. In the writer's mind, this involves an extensive staff, a nice office and the latest equipment, as well as up-to-date contacts at all the houses and production companies. The agent should also be well-read in both classic and contemporary literature, return all the writer's phone calls in ten minutes or less and have the answers to all questions regarding writing and marketing.

If a literary agent, or any other businessperson, is to reach that degree of quality, she must be one thing above all else: a businessperson. Hopefully, an agent is in the literary field because a love of writing is in her blood. However, a writer shouldn't believe for one moment that the agent isn't always looking at the bottom line – because she is. The agent who does not put business first will probably not possess all those qualities that the writer has the right to demand from the person representing their work.

The agent's ability to take care of business first actually sets the foundation that supports the needs of the writer. How agents structure their business and the reasons they enter the literary field vary, but one element is always involved – money. No business operates without it.

Some agents inherit an established agency from a family member; these are the few and lucky ones. Others have worked for an agency gathering experiences, contacts and the loyalty of established authors, then have opened their own agency, taking with them some of the clientele. Some agents have worked for publishers or book distributors, gaining first-hand knowledge of the publisher's and distributors' needs...while establishing very important contacts in the industry. A few are attorneys who have either worked for a publisher or who have fallen into the business when a client came to them with a manuscript and the attorney landed a publishing contract.

Then there are those agents who start from scratch. They learn both the rules of business and the rules of publishing as they go. This is where the majority of agents start. This is also one of the reasons that many agencies are out of business within six months to a year.

It is difficult to establish any business without expertise, unless one has a very healthy bankroll. However, the need for new professionals with a fresh outlook on the industry is necessary for the writer. Why? Because many established agencies will not take on new writers at all, nor are they set up to handle the needs of the new writer. On the other hand, many upstart agencies simply do not have the resources to become successful, even though they understand the writer's plight. The lack of resources and the need for new agents probably started the practice of charging reading fees.

Reading Fees

The reading fee is one of the most touchy subjects among writers and agents. On one hand, the writer wants an agent's professional attention. On the other hand, the agent wants to help, but knows he must satisfy the costs of doing business first. So the agent charges a fee to cover editorial costs. The writer believes the agent should give his time for free. The agent's business sense tells him that he should not give something for nothing. The battle is a never-ending one, and the loser depends on whom you ask – the writer or the agent.

Trade magazines geared for new writers still warn against reading fees and sometimes agenting fees in general. They believe that endorsing fees will open a floodgate, encouraging a tidal wave of unscrupulous agents who will appear from nowhere to take advantage of the new writer. We have yet to see, however, a magazine publisher give away a subscription or one of the many books he publishes on writing and marketing to the new writer, free of charge. Recently, publications geared for new writers that criticize reading fees have come under heavy fire from both agents and writers.

Literary organizations have somewhat adjusted their viewpoint on reading fees. For their members who charge a fee, these organizations have established a set charge that member agencies are not permitted to exceed.

A question the writer may wish to ask herself before deciding to pay or not to pay is, "What can I expect to get for nothing?" If the answer is nothing, then pay the fee.

It is the writer's responsibility to find out what he can expect to receive for his investment. Most agents are willing to send writers information or answer brief questions regarding their review policies and their charges. Policies, fees and what the writer receives for his fee vary greatly from agent to agent. Some agents give comprehensive reviews, some only a few remarks.

The whole matter of reading fees has been debated for years and will probably continue to be debated for more years to come. As more agents continue to charge fees, the debate will not be as heated, simply because the writer will have little choice.

Marketing Fees

How agents arrive at a marketing fee also varies. Some charge a flat rate of, say, $250.00. Ostensibly, this is to pay for postage, phone calls and related marketing costs. Before agreeing to pay this charge, ask exactly how that money will be spent. Then get the answer in writing. Some questions you may wish to ask are: Will a synopsis of your manuscript be one among many others that are being sent to publishers? If so, how many other projects are being offered at the same time? How many publishers will your manuscript be sent out to? Are synopses arranged according to category? What is the success ratio of this method? Will there be any additional charges, such as for postage or copies, if a publisher requests the manuscript? How long will the agent continue to market in this fashion? Will he continue to represent you once he has completed his mailing?

Most agents charge what they term "out of pocket expenses" for items or services purchased without your direct permission. For the established author, this charge is normally minimal and usually deducted from the advance royalty payment. However, the agent normally bills new writers when the expenses have been incurred. Before agreeing to pay this fee, ask what you can reasonably expect to pay in the normal course of marketing. It is a good idea to put a limit on the amount the agent is permitted to incur without first asking your permission. Have your agent put this figure in writing.

Editing Fees

One result of a healthy business is growth. Recently, publishing companies have been growing in leaps and bounds. Already big businesses have become bigger as a result of mergers with other publishing companies, both domestic and foreign, and with movie production companies. The bigger the publishing industry becomes, the more strongly the focus is on the bottom line, now more than ever before. Accordingly, publishing corporations have been eliminating less profitable lines, laying off staff they consider unnecessary, and redefining the duties of existing staff.

One department heavily affected by the new bottom line emphasis was editing, a change that only further added to the problems that the hopeful new writer must face. An already over-burdened editorial staff and the discontinuation of certain lines resulted in more rejections for the writer. Simply put, editors do not have time to help craft the work of every talented writer hoping for a publishing contract. Editors are looking for manuscripts that will give them the least amount of trouble while satisfying the line or category of the publisher.

So who is left to assist the writer in learning his craft and bringing his manuscript up to publishing standards? In answer, many editing and literary services have started up in the last few years. However, as beneficial as these services are, most editing services and literary services do not market the manuscripts they edit; also, they do not usually work with publishers closely enough to fully understand the needs of the market. To help fill this gap, some literary agencies have begun to offer editing services. Now, in addition to paying reading and marketing fees, the new writer must consider editing fees. Another charge to the writer, another battle for the agent as he tries to explain why editing fees are necessary.

Editing is an extremely difficult, time-consuming job. Some manuscripts require only the lightest of edits, which sometimes the writer may easily undertake himself. However, some manuscripts with a great deal of potential nevertheless require a comprehensive edit from a professional editor. We will deal with edits more thoroughly in another section of this book, but suffice it to say that a professional edit may be invaluable in terms of getting your manuscript ready to market.

Literary Contracts

The days of a "handshake deal" are more or less gone. Therefore, most agents have developed their own standard literary contract, which both agent and writer must sign before the agent will begin to market a work. Normally, publishers do not request to see a copy of the literary agreement; however, should any disputes arise, a signed contract will help settle the problem.

There are basically three types of contracts:

1. *The time contract* states the time period in which the agent has to sell a particular work. This is usually on the low end of six months to the high end of two years. After the stated time, the writer is then free to seek the services of another agent.

2. *The per project contract* states that the agent has the right to represent a said work. This contract may or may not state a time period. If there is no time period in the contract, check to see how you can break the contract in the case that you feel your agent has not been effective in selling your

manuscript. If there is neither a time clause or another means to terminate, you may wish to have one included.

3. *The exclusive contract* states that the agent has the right to represent all the literary works of a writer. Like the per project contract, this may or may not have a time clause or another means to terminate. You should be wary of this type of contract, especially if there is no means for getting out of it. Agents have been known to make writers pay their way out of such a contract.

All contracts should be carefully reviewed. If you do not understand any of the points, ask questions. Get clarifications and all changes in writing.

As a new writer, you're likely to experience some degree of difficulty and frustration in both securing the services of an agent and working with an agent. Do not be discouraged. There is a common thread that binds agents and writers together: getting the manuscript sold.

The final decision to accept an agent's terms is totally up to the writer, no one else. If a writer pays a reading fee or editing fee without first learning what he can reasonably expect for that fee...or if a writer signs a literary contract without understanding the terms and a problem arises in contractual issues, the writer must realize that he is ultimately responsible.

Finally, after all is said and done, the deciding factor in choosing an agent (either to send your manuscript to or to sign up with) is usually your gut feeling. Can you work with this agent? Do you trust him?

Keep in mind that most agents are not high-powered salespeople, nor is every writer a literary genius. Respect for each other's position and a desire to see a good manuscript get into print will go a long way in determining each other's success.

THE EDITOR

Writers must learn many writing skills, and not all writers will be able to juggle all their skills effectively at any given time. They may become carried away with a plot, bogged down in description, or simply fall into some lazy grammatical habits. It is not always easy for writers to see these problems in their work, and to help them, God (some would say the devil) invented editors.

H.G. Wells once remarked that no passion on earth equaled the "passion to alter someone else's draft." Indeed, the best editors are often those who approach a work with passion and spirit – not to destroy the piece or lambaste the writer, but to point out the weaknesses in a manuscript. Dedicated editors will note their concerns and make suggestions, trying to help a writer make a good manuscript better.

One particularly distraught writer, upset by an editor's rather comprehensive edit of her rambling but promising work, cried, "Don't you understand? I've been working on this piece for years. This novel is like my child."

To this the editor replied, "I know, ma'am. Why don't you consider me a surgeon operating on your child? He's sick, but I can help him."

Types of editors

Whether or not they are as precise as a surgeon, editors come in all stripes, from editorial assistants who review unsolicited manuscripts at publishing houses, to publishers' editors who work with the writers of accepted manuscripts, to editors who work for literary agencies or literary services. Many have a background in teaching, journalism, publishing, writing or related professions.

While most editors are skilled professionals committed to helping writers, not all are always in a position to edit a piece as thoroughly as they might wish. This is especially true of manuscripts from first-time writers, who represent something of a risk to publishers, since they do not have an established following. Because many publishers have greatly reduced their editing staff over the years, the remaining editors are often hard-pressed to handle the enormous workload that needs their attention. As implied earlier, this is perhaps the single largest reason why so few fiction publishers today accept unsolicited or unagented manuscripts. In many cases, agents' editors now do the work once reserved for the publishers' editors, i.e., selecting promising writers and helping them polish and present their work.

A subjective task

Regardless of their employers, editors know that their work is highly subjective. What the beginning writer might consider an innovative technique (such as the use of first and third person points of view in one manuscript) an editor might consider simply sloppy or confusing.

Skilled editors read a manuscript for much more than technical competence. They are looking for style, for content, for originality, for wit or humor, for the ability to move the reader's emotions, for realistically developed characters, for excruciating attention to detail and imagery, for concise writing, for readability and plot integrity – in short, for all the signs of a skilled writer.

While their comments appear critical, they are usually intended to improve the writing, not ridicule it. In general, the more a beginning writer can swallow his pride and at least consider an editor's suggestions, the better off he will be. Defensive skills are fine for sports teams, but beginning writers should try to cultivate an open mind about their manuscripts.

About 25% of the writers who query the agency claim to have a best-seller, the Great American Novel, or a book that publishers will be ripping each other apart to handle. None of these claims have yet proven true. While it is good to be confident, it is unwise to demand too much. In any case, a good editor can improve most well-written novels, let alone poorly-written ones.

(Can some writers afford to ignore their editors' remarks? Yes, very popular writers whose works are read regardless of their merit, or very skilled writers whose most pedestrian work is still quite marketable, can often get away without extensive editing. Alas, few writers live in this rarified atmosphere. Certainly this does not apply to beginning writers.)

Looking for Mr. and Ms. Write

Just what do editors look for when they read a manuscript? While edits vary from one editor to another, depending on their backgrounds, personal tastes and priorities, fiction editors are generally looking for novels with:

1. Interesting, well-drawn characters, including a sympathetic protagonist who develops or changes over the course of the story and has a distinctive, intriguing "voice."

2. A point of view which is consistent and helps the reader delineate and explore the main character(s).

3. A plot which quickly captures the reader's attention and holds it throughout the course of the story.

4. Writing that is literate, colorful, compelling to read, powerful and fairly easy to understand.

5. A strong visceral and/or emotional appeal. (This is what many editors mean when they say they want a "sexy" story. They don't necessarily want to read sex scenes, but they do want to see sensuality, physicality and passion in the writing.)

6. A fascinating setting. Details about an unusual place or time period will intrigue the reader and give him the impression he is learning a little history or geography in the most pleasant way possible. (The setting needn't be exotic, just enthralling.)

If the work is genre fiction, the editor will also look for category-specific qualities. For example, if the piece is a romance, the editor will probably look for a sympathetic female protagonist, a third person point of view that is primary attached to the protagonist, a conflict that puts considerable pressure on the principal characters' budding relationship, and other time-tested romance conventions.

Of course, a romantic novel intended for a broader, mainstream market need not follow these conventions. By the same token, a literary novel will be evaluated according to a completely different sets of standards. (See Chapter Four for general qualities relating to various categories of fiction.) In all cases, character, plot and style will no doubt figure prominently in a thorough edit.

Note that the editor will probably not rewrite much of the manuscript, though she will indicate errors and often suggest how to correct them. Sometimes she will rewrite a few sentences as examples of how the writer should approach his work, but the editor will not do the writer's work for him.

What will the editor query?

Editors will question many minor, specific problems in a manuscript. Some of these errors, such as spelling or grammatical mistakes, will be easy to correct; some, such as missing transitions, will take more work to address. While one problem alone is unlikely to sink your chances of publication, you may need a major rewrite if your manuscript exhibits a large number of the following problems.

1. Paragraphing errors, such as when to break a large paragraph or combine several. Do not be like the beginning writer who resented being told to break her two-page paragraphs into several smaller ones. A paragraph is like a hemline: just long enough to cover the topic and just short enough to be interesting.

2. The need for transitions between chapters, scenes, paragraphs and sentences, when necessary. An editor will indicate when one of these units does not flow smoothly into the next. Sometimes a transition may be as

simple as adding a space break. Other times, you may need to write an entire scene or even a chapter to bridge gaps in the story and allow the reader to progress through the story without undue disruption or confusion.

3. Technical inaccuracies, such as the use of inappropriate or incorrect words or imagery. For example, one writer habitually used the word "okay" in her 16th century historical novel, although the word did not appear until the 19th century. Another writer referred to "female oxen," which do not exist in any century.

Also, editors will question cultural or moral considerations which seem to be in opposition to the setting of the novel. For instance, it is highly unlikely that 18th century women would gather together to discuss their orgasms with the freedom and frankness of 20th century women.

4. Mixed imagery, especially in terms of sensual stimuli. For example, one beginning writer set his protagonist in a bath where "cold water rushed over her skin like thunder." Such conflicting sensual terms are confusing to the reader.

5. Awkward or ungrammatical writing, which is so unclear that the editor simply does not understand what the writer is trying to say. Either the passage is completely out of context, or it is written so clumsily or ungrammatically that it fails to make sense. Falling into this category is the common mistake of using ellipses (...) and m-dashes (—) in place of commas. Exclamation points are also frequently abused, and erroneously appear in clusters of two or more (!!...!!!!!!), as if their presence alone adds excitement to the writing. Tension, fear, excitement and other emotions should be woven into the fabric of the novel, not tacked on with punctuation.

6. Imprecise writing, which is ambiguous, misleading or inexact. For example: "George sat alone in the room, thinking of Amelia. He grew excited at the mention of her name." Of course her name wasn't mentioned; it was thought of.

By the same token, the editor will question such bizarre wording as the following: "William's eyes flew ahead of him," or "David's eyes rested on the bookshelf." (For some reason, beginning writers often insist on making eyes do the impossible, instead of using simple words such as "look," "gaze," "stare," "glimpse" or "glance" to indicate the act of seeing or watching.)

Poorly-worded writing need not involve body parts, of course. Consider this sentence: "The house sheltered them from nature's rough weather." (And where would the weather originate, if not from nature?)

7. Unrealistic actions, reactions or events, when realism is clearly intended. For instance, if a character does not seem to register any emotion at the death of her friend and this situation is not explained, an editor might query the writer about this apparently unrealistic behavior.

8. "Show" versus "tell" situations. Writers often compress information in summary narration, when they should construct scenes, perhaps complete with direct dialogue, that will dramatically demonstrate feelings or events to the reader. On the other hand, less significant information should not normally be handled in a scene, but worked organically into the manuscript in narrative form wherever it seems to make sense.

9. Wooden, stilted, melodramatic, or verbose narrative or dialogue.

10. Heavy-handed narrative or dialogue which has no purpose but to relay a lot of background information at one time. For example, many beginning writers start their novels with a physical description of their main character instead of simply getting on with the character's story and working in details in a natural way throughout the manuscript. (See the chapter on dialogue for more information.)

11. The use of passive voice. The passive voice forms weak sentences. It occurs because the writer is timid or uncertain about approaching the action in his story; thus he "backs into" events in the passive voice, rendering those events distant and obscure. The passive voice tends to obliterate characters. A sentence such as, "A scream was heard," has no subject, no actor. It is much stronger to write, "Jonathan heard a scream," or even, "He heard a scream."

In some cases, the passive voice is necessary to avoid naming specific individuals, e.g., "Some objections have been raised," and of course characters may use passive voice in dialogue.

12. Other weak wording, such as "there is" or "there are," or the frequent use of -ly adverbs (slowly, inexplicably, wearily, ridiculously) in place of strong verbs.

13. Switching from one tense to another – present to past, past to present, often within the same paragraph. Many switches in tense indicate more serious faults in a manuscript, including point of view (POV) problems,

undeveloped characters and plotting difficulties. Shifts in tense occur when the whole fabric of the story is falling apart because the POV, structure and characters are failing to develop properly.

14. Inconsistencies in style, speech, names, scenes, descriptions, and so on. A story set in a European forest, for instance, is not likely to feature raccoons. A character who is supposed to be absent should not suddenly appear without explanation. A character who knows fluent French in once scene should not plead ignorance of the language in the next, unless he's lying.

15. Inappropriate pacing – too slow or neurotically fast – which could cause a reader to lose focus or interest in the piece.

16. Overuse of sentence fragments, which tend to create a choppy, disjointed read.

17. Inappropriate beginnings and conclusions. For example, it is rarely necessary to begin a novel with the birth of the protagonist. In all likelihood, this is not really the "start" of her story. By the same token, most successful novels do not simply come to a halt, as if the writer has run out of things to say. Most novels end when conflicts have been resolved and the pressure which has driven the character to act has been removed.

18. Lack of tension in the plot or lack of pressure on the protagonist.

The above points are guidelines and are not meant to be all-inclusive of the work involved in any edit. A given editor may be looking for all, some or a few of the above points, and indeed may have other valuable information to offer.

The Joys of Devastation

After a professional edit, a writer may feel she has just been run over by an International Harvester combine. Her writing is in shreds, her pride and resistance are crushed, and her beloved manuscript which took five years to write may be bleeding red ink from the numerous slashes of the editor's pen. It is no wonder that many writers have little love for editors – at least before publication.

This feeling of devastation isn't unusual; in fact, it's probably very helpful. A devastated writer is far less likely to pick up the pieces of the manuscript and immediately set to work on the rewrite. To do so would be to court disaster. The writer would probably react to the edit, not respond to it, swallowing advice whole instead of allowing it to sit and digest. As a rule of thumb, we advise writers to wait at least ten days before they begin their rewrite. That way they will have had some time to think about how to proceed with it.

A beginning writer should keep in mind that the fewer edits he makes to his own work, the more edits his editor will make. Therefore, it's never a good idea to send a first or even a second draft of a long piece of fiction to an agent or publisher. It's likely to be dismissed out of hand. Go over the work carefully, weeding out typos and obvious grammatical, structural and compositional errors before submitting it for critical review.

"But Is It Really Still My Work If I Have to Make So Many Changes in the Rewrite?"

Many beginning writers ask this question after an edit, and we suppose it is a rather valid question from a person who is still somewhat in shock after learning that his "bestseller" still needs a lot of work.

It's important for a writer to remember that a novel in manuscript form is less a "thing" than it is a process. When it is in print and being read, a novel is something like a photograph of a dance taken at a certain point in time. Many writers of published fiction, re-reading their older works, shudder at some of their writing and wish they could revise it.

A fiction manuscript is in process and under construction, much like an artist's unfinished oil painting or a composer's initial version of a symphony. Unlike the artist and the composer, however, who usually struggle alone to improve their work, the writer has an ace in the hole: the edit. The edit provides professional opinions on the writer's work. The best editors will make many changes, suggestions and recommendations, not all of which they expect the writer to agree with. They are simply letting the writer know what does work (for them) and why, what doesn't work and why, and how the writing might be improved.

Since a writer rewrites and rethinks his own piece, of course the rewritten novel will be "his," even if it incorporates an editor's suggestions. Skilled writers don't fear rewrites: They welcome them. Sidney Sheldon, the popular author of romantic thrillers, once claimed to rewrite his novels at least 12 times. If Sidney Sheldon can admit to so many drafts, then surely a beginning writer should not worry about recrafting his own novel several times until it is as successful as he can make it.

Defending the Improbable

After receiving their edit, new writers often seem to be taken aback by any editorial remarks which question the veracity, authenticity or likelihood of a particular event, especially if the event really took place. The writer frequently defends unrealistic scenes or events in his manuscript by announcing that, "But they really happened. They happened to me," or to a brother or friend, or were discovered during the writer's research on a specific topic.

Fiction is not concerned with "what really happened." That's the job of nonfiction and textbooks. Fiction is concerned with "what would happen if...?" If a writer created a scene around a well-documented fact, such as the assassination of President Lincoln, it could still be written in such a way that the reader would never believe it. For example, Lincoln might be presented as a heartless buffoon and John Wilkes Booth as a brave patriot and hero. Not many writers could present this material in such a way that readers would "believe" it. Conversely, a skilled writer could persuade his readers (at least within the context of the novel) that hostile Martians were landing in New Jersey. (Orson Welles did this to perfection when he presented H.G. Wells' *The War of the Worlds* as a radio drama in the 1930s.)

One editor tells a story that illustrates how self-defeating it is to defend the unbelievable in fiction – even if it's the truth. The editor, also a budding writer, took a fiction writing workshop and presented a short story about an isolated woman who finds a kitten with its head stuck in a jar. None of the other workshop members believed the scenario. When the editor defended it by stating that "it really happened," the teacher explained the difference between truth and fiction, which the editor never forgot. "Whether or not something is actually true is unimportant in fiction writing. Just because something is true doesn't necessarily mean that the reader will think it's true. And that's what's important – making your writing ring true, whether it's true or not. It's the writer's job to make the improbable, even the absurd, seem realistic."

No one expects a beginning writer to churn out a masterpiece – or even a marketable piece – on the first or second try. Editors bring impartiality, distance and professionalism to your writing, pointing out what isn't working, why it's not working, and how to correct it. It's important to take their comments, suggestions and advice seriously if you hope to have your fiction published.

A Sample Edit

Many novice writers don't fully understand the work that is necessary to make a manuscript successful. They have been taught that rewriting involves "cosmetic changes" – a nip and tuck here, a change in wording there or an extra paragraph or two. They often fail to understand that a revision is exactly what the word implies: a new vision for the book.

We receive many manuscripts here at the agency that are nothing more than an author's notes to himself. Still others are first drafts. There is little that we can do with such manuscripts except politely decline to represent them and provide some direction should the writer decide to undertake a rewrite.

Many good writers still need an experienced editor's touch to raise their work to another level. The editing process is extensive and can often seem overwhelming, but the end result is a stronger manuscript.

On the following page is an excerpt of a promising manuscript in the young adult category, *Otters on the Loose* by Louis Dorfman – which was edited by the agency.

[handwritten top annotation:] Put us directly into Petey's thoughts. A young adult book relies on close identification with the characters. This is best accomplished by showing their thoughts and feelings on a frequent basis. Show any thoughts of Petey's that might show that this morning is special to him. Give some other details, like a twitching nose or wagging tail (some otter-like mannerisms). Maybe he's dying to snack on fish or jump in the water.

Dorfman-Otters

[handwritten left margin:] *He wanted to shout, "Wake up, time's a' westin'" but Penny was notoriously cranky in the morning. (or some such detail)*

As the early morning sun filtered into their room, Petey slowly raised his head, *and* yawned, ~~looked over at~~ *His friend slept in a basket bed still snoring soundly.* Penny *beside him,* ~~and~~ casually, started *to* ~~grooming~~ *he* her neck in an attempt to awaken her without any quarrel. *[¶] he opened one eye and regarded* Penny ~~looked at~~ Petey with *a* raised eyebrows, ~~as~~ *she* *but let out a deep sigh, opened her other eye and* ~~reluctantly~~ returned the grooming procedure. ~~which~~ *This* was *every* the accepted method of greeting they gave each other *day* upon awakening.

[handwritten left margin:] Condense the background information. Weave as much exposition into the narrative as possible. For example, you might want to have a scene with Eric playing with the otters and say something about the divorce. Exposition takes the reader out of the story (the fictional dream) in order to explain what is going on, and should be kept brief.

Petey and Penny were two North American River Otters ~~that~~ *who* lived in Dallas, Texas, with their friend, Eric Hodges, and his father, Steve. *Insert from the bottom of pg. 2 & top of pg. 3*

Petey came to live with Eric four years ago. Penny followed two years later. Petey felt very close to Eric; until Penny's arrival Eric had been his only companion. Petey enjoyed their lengthy play sessions, as Eric learned Petey's otter games quickly. Eric always told Petey that the games were *(word choice)* helpful to him; *they* ~~helping~~ *ed* Eric forget something called a divorce between his father and mother. Eric told Petey that his mother lived somewhere far away, just like Petey's mother, and he and Petey were dependent on each other. Eric told Petey two years ago that he didn't want Petey to be sad, like his father, and he brought Penny to live with

Dorfman-Otters   2

them.

✻ Insert dialogue

Petey looked around the quarters he and Penny

shared. He was pleased with the amount of space Eric

and his father had given them. They had two spacious

rooms at the western end of house, with plenty of

privacy, and they had an otter door leading out to a

Good detail! | patio with their very own (small swimming pool situated

on a redwood deck....)

"What shall we do today?" Petey asked Penny.

✻ Insert this dialogue at the top of the page.

Awkward wording. At first glance, it sounds like a snap of the fingers.

With a snap, Penny replied, "Pete, it's barely

daylight. You know that I need to sleep till at least

9 o'clock if you don't want to be grumpy all day."

~~Petey~~ He _looking for an idea_ surveyed their room. ∧ The room in which

they had their bed was twenty feet long and fifteen

feet wide. ~~Their~~ Next to their bed, consisted of six large towels _which_

✻ Knowing that Penny would be annoyed if he played in front of her, Petey

gathered in a corner of the room, ~~surrounded by~~ _were_ a dozen

stuffed animals which they used as pillows as well as

playthings.... ~~He~~ decided ~~that he would~~ _to_ go into their

adjoining ~~second~~ room, ~~of their quarters, which was about the same~~

~~size as the first room.~~

Sequence. You describe the room, then have the dialogue, then more room descriptions. You should keep the descriptions together.

✻ Insert on pg. 1

Petey was the steadfast, dependable, and lovable

friend that Eric could count on to brighten up even his

worst moods. Penny, on the other hand, was a much more

Dorfman-Otters   3

complicated individual. She was a spry, mischievous

little imp that could always be counted on to do the

unexpected. She was the exact counter to Petey's

consistency.

> Consider a transition here, something to the effect of "Petey's belly was growling when he heard a rumbling at the door."

"Good morning, Petey," Eric exclaimed as he

entered the room with breakfast. ✱

✱ The young boy set a tray with two bowls full of ___ down on the nearest table and took a seat on one of the benches.

Petey ~~delightedly~~ squealed his chirping greeting

to Eric which they both knew meant "I'm happy to see

you." Petey jumped into Eric's lap and ~~lovingly~~ gave

Be careful in your use of adverbs.

Eric his traditional good morning kiss. Petey looked

at Eric with gratitude for the love they shared. He

Generally, they are weak, descriptive words. The "squealed" and "kiss" show the delight and love.

saw in Eric's blue eyes a great deal of concern for

How old is he? Isn't this a little large for a young boy?

their welfare. While Eric, at 5'10" tall and 160

pounds, looked huge compared to their twenty pounds and

three foot length, he always treated them with a

Good

gentleness that made his size unimportant.

"You sure are happy this morning, Petey," Eric

observed. "I don't know why I feel so strange today,

like something bad is going to happen...."

Too blatant foreshadowing? If you decide to keep it, precede with a change in expression on Eric's face.

We asked another editor to rewrite the first page. This example of the rewrite, which can be seen below, incorporates the editor's notes from the first three pages.

The early morning sun filtered into the room and through the heap of towels in the corner where the otters slept. Petey slowly raised his head and yawned. He heard the songs of birds outside the window and the delicious smell of his breakfast -- raw fish -- coming from the kitchen. In an instant he was wide awake, ready to take on the day.

Petey nuzzled Penny, sound asleep next to him, and started to groom her neck in an attempt to awaken her as gently as possible. She could be pretty cranky in the morning.

Penny opened one eye and regarded Petey with raised eyebrows. He grinned at her, his whiskers bristling out into a huge fan. "Awake yet?" he whispered.

"What do you think?" she snapped, then opened her other eye and gave his shoulder a half-hearted lick. "I don't want to get up. I'll be grumpy for the rest of the day," she whined. "I was having such a good dream, too. I'd caught a trout and was just about to bite into it when you woke me up."

"Smell that?" said Petey, sitting up on his haunches and sniffing the air.

Penny breathed in deeply. "Breakfast! Smelts, I think."

"So your dream will come true after all!" said Petey, crouching low. "Eric will be in here in a minute or two. Tell you what -- I'll get your mouse, okay?"

"Well...okay," Penny mumbled, still half asleep.

Shoving her playfully with his nose, Petey leaped up and ran out of their towel nest, his paws scrunching on the gravel floor. He zoomed into their second room and found Penny's favorite toy, a black plush mouse, under the pile of branches they loved to play in. Petey nabbed the mouse in his jaws and brought it back to Penny. "Here, catch!" he cried, tossing the toy high.

Penny stretched out her muzzle and seized the mouse in midair.

Just then Petey heard the door to the room open, and there stood Eric, holding two bowls full of little silver fish. "Here you go, guys. Now don't shove! There's plenty for everyone."

Eric set the bowls down, and both otters tore into the fish. When Petey was done, he brushed against Eric and squirmed into the boy's arms. He rubbed his whiskery face against Eric's and licked his cheek. How he loved his human! Penny was still a little wary of Eric, but she had only been in the house for two years. Petey had come to live with Eric four years ago, when he was just a pup.

Eric was young for a human, only thirteen, but he was smart and had caught onto the ways of otters very quickly. He loved to play tug-of-war, scratch-your-belly, and slide-along-the-floor-together as much as Penny and Petey did.

But today something was wrong. A tear glistened on

Eric's cheek. The boy gave Petey a big hug. "Gosh, I love you and Penny!" he said. "Don't ever go away, like Mom did, okay?"

Petey knew that Eric's mom lived far away, ever since the "divorce," whatever that was, which Eric spoke of so often. Now and then Eric would talk to his mother on the hard noisy thing Eric called a "fone" that Petey had seen in the kitchen. Probably that's why Eric was crying now; he'd talked with his far-away mother on the fone. "Don't worry," Petey wanted to say. "I love you. I'm not going anywhere." He licked away Eric's tear, and the boy smiled.

"Hey, that tickles!"

The opening of the book now works on a number of different levels: The exposition has been woven naturally into the course of the narrative; the characters of the two otters and their owner have been more clearly drawn; and the setting is clearly established.

THE PUBLISHER

Publishers range in size from huge mega-dollar international corporations; to medium-sized, mostly private-owned companies; to small publishers who may only publish a few books a year. Writers are always asking what publisher is best for them. The answer is never simple.

While many authors would prefer to work with a large, prestigious publisher, getting a book published should not become a matter of ego-building. Large, medium and small publishers have all had their share of both successes and failures.

The author accepted by a large publisher has the prestige of being associated with a readily recognized name. This is helpful to the author's reputation, especially when a writer is trying to break into the seminar or workshop scene as an invited guest and lecturer. Having a large, well-known publisher also helps in getting your book reviewed.

Even more important, a large publisher has solid sources of book distribution. The large bookstore chains, such as B. Dalton and Waldenbooks, like to do business with large companies because they usually have an inventory varied enough to meet the chains' needs. Also, a large publisher has its systems for ordering and making payments firmly in place. On the other hand, your book may be treated as just another book among the many that the large publisher is releasing. Many worthy books get lost in the barrage of works turned out each year by the bigger publishers.

The medium and smaller publishers are frequently limited in the types of books they publish. Some may handle only nonfiction, some only children's literature, some only one or two categories of adult fiction. (There are even very small publishers which handle only nonfiction computer books or other very limited markets.) These small publishers know their markets very well and are usually better at marketing to their specific niche than the larger houses. However, there are obvious drawbacks to the smaller publisher. Since the large publishers have the best-selling titles and a proven, dependable track record for ordering and payment, national bookstore chains find that doing business with these houses is smoother, more efficient, and often more profitable, compared to working with the smaller publishers, who may not have the most efficient inventory system. The national bookstore chains, therefore, often do not like working with small publishers and make it very difficult for such a company to distribute its titles through their bookstores.

Nevertheless, the small publisher may be the best publisher for your particular book. At the small publishing house, every single title is important and is treated like a bestseller. What monies these companies have are normally put into the promotion of the books they handle, to help ensure the success of each book. They have varied means of distribution, and are often looking for more.

Smaller publishers are hungry. As a result, they tend to be more creative about doing business, taking more risks than the larger companies. Such risk-taking can have both good and bad effects. A marketing move which is too risky can ruin the success of a given book, or even the entire company, while the right move can bring untold riches to all involved in the book.

All this discussion of publishers is somewhat academic where new writers are concerned, since in most cases the beginning writer doesn't have much say in who is going to publish his book. Often a book by a new writer receives only one or two publishing offers, even if the book is excellent. As unfair and frustrating as that sounds, it's one of the many sad truths of the industry. The writer shouldn't despair, however, because the final decision to accept or reject a publisher's offer always belongs to the writer, and there is often room for a little negotiation to sweeten the contract.

Publisher's Contracts

Sometimes the new writer confuses the terms of a literary contract with those of a publishing contract. The literary contract, discussed previously, sets the terms for the representation of the writer's work. These contracts do not deal with a number of items, including: the amount of advance that the author feels he should or will receive; publishing deadlines; financial considerations for movie and other subsidiary rights; and the amount of royalties paid. These are publishing concerns and are all addressed in the publisher's contract, which the publisher proffers to the author once he has agreed to accept your work. Publishing contracts vary widely concerning advances, royalties and number of books to be published and must be considered on an individual basis.

(Remember that having a publisher, big or small, will not guarantee your success. That is why you must take steps to create success for yourself. A pattern for building your literary success will be discussed in detail in the chapter on publicity.)

What about Royalties and Advances?

Royalties are monies paid to the author by the publisher, based on the sales of a book. Royalties are expressed as percentages of the sales, and these percentages vary, depending on the publisher and the category. The exact percentages will be spelled out in your publishing contract.

An advance is money paid to the author against the earned royalties. For example, if the author receives a ten thousand dollar advance, he will not receive any more monies until enough of his books have been sold to exceed the advance paid to him. An advance is really a courtesy that the publisher extends to the author and is by no means mandatory.

We have all heard of the multimillion-dollar book deals or the advances ranging into the six figures for a writer's first novel. However, if you stop and think about it, how often does a publisher give these large advances to the first-time writer? The answer is – not often. Since the new writer has never been published before, the publisher has no way to confidently calculate or predict how well the book will sell. He is therefore taking a risk by offering a big advance on the work of an unproven writer.

What is the normal advance? The average advance varies from publisher to publisher and from category to category. These figures change so frequently that it is hard to pin them down long enough to answer the question above. The whole issue of advances never fails to surprise us. We have seen advances close to six figures for books that we did not believe were going to sell over a thousand copies, to disappointing advances as low as a few thousand dollars for manuscripts that were exceptionally well-written and/or timely. In general, however, expect a lower advance for nonfiction than for fiction, except in the area of celebrity biographies or other very timely topics.

What if the books sales are not sufficient to recoup the advance? In your contract with the publisher, the advance is normally protected against this possibility. That means you get to keep the money from the advance, even though technically the book did not earn you the money.

In the unlikely event that the publisher folds just before or just after your book is published, your advance may still be protected and you may be eligible for some compensation. This contingency should be thoroughly explained in your publishing contract.

The most important thing to remember when dealing with the publisher is that you both want to sell books. Combining your own efforts to sell your book with those of the publisher should make for a more profitable and enjoyable relationship.

Normally you receive half the advance within thirty days of the signing of the contract, and the other half within thirty days of the final draft. The publisher will, in the contract, state all of the terms including the date when the final draft is due at the publishers (deadline).

Deadline

This term indicates the author's due date for the final draft to the publisher. We have seen deadlines as short as two months and as long as a year. It's essential to meet the established deadline. The publisher already has a release date in mind, and your cooperation on the matter of deadlines is important to keep everything flowing smoothing. There have been times in our office when we had to get an extension of a week or two to finish our final editing; however, we anticipated this delay far in advance and cleared it with the publisher a month or so before the book was due. Should the publisher have insisted that we meet the deadline, we would have worked day and night to do so. Keep in mind that when we ask for a small extension, the publisher is familiar with our work and that our extra care makes less work for his staff. As a first-time writer, you are strongly encouraged to meet all deadlines.

Front Cover Artwork

Publishers are generally staffed with their own illustrators or have illustrators of choice. The final decision for the front cover design rests with your publishers. You may, however, be asked for your opinion, but don't be insulted if the publisher does not take it. The publisher knows his audience and what design has been successful in the past. While many new writers want to maintain control of cover design, this simply is not an option. We had a recent release where we were slightly taken aback by the illustrator's choice of design for the jacket of the book. It seemed a little too "tame" for the topic of the book. However, we soon came to realize that, for capturing the attention of the intended audience, it was perfect. In fact, it was so perfect that it stood out among the other titles the publisher was offering. The expertise of the illustrator made money for the author.

Publisher's Edits

You will be assigned an editor who will work with you once your final draft has been submitted. The editorial suggestions may range from a rewrite of a section of your book to a few minor comments on grammar or word choice. Again we must remind you that the editor has much more experience in this area than you do and is really a writer's best friend. Listen carefully to all your editor's suggestions. If you need clarification, do not hesitate to ask.

Also in the editing process you may have to work with the publisher's attorney. This is especially true if you are writing or co-authoring an auto-biography, writing a true story or any other type of book that may include the names of real people. The lawyer's concern of course is that there is no possibility of a lawsuit for defamation of character or slander. If the lawyer is concerned, perhaps you should be too, and make the necessary adjustments if you cannot absolutely back up your writing with solid proof. Often this problem is avoided by using composite characters and by using fictional names for real people.

Galley Proofs

Once your book has been typeset, you will be sent a copy; this is known as the galley proofs and is sometimes referred to as the printer's proof. This is the final chance the author has to make corrections. It is part of your job to check the manuscript for typos, incorrect spellings, or other mistakes that may have occurred during the typesetting process. This, however, is not the time to make content changes, such as rewriting a section of the manuscript that you may find weak. Normally you make the correction on the page and place your initials on the top right-hand corner. If there are no corrections on the page, you still must initial it.

The galleys are then sent back to the publisher.

Bound Galleys

The bound galleys are the uncorrected, bound copies of the manuscript that are sent to book reviewers and trade journals, and often show up at the American Booksellers Association's (ABA) trade show. The distribution of the bound galleys is helpful in obtaining advance reviews, orders, and general interest in your book. Bound galleys can also be used to secure endorsements.

Endorsements

Endorsements are very important selling tools for your book. Obtaining endorsements are normally the responsibility of the author; however, larger publishers will assist you greatly in obtaining necessary endorsements. While most endorsements are given to the author free of charge, don't be surprised if you are asked to pay for the endorsement, especially if you are soliciting a celebrity or other well-known person. Famous authors normally will not endorse your book. The reasons include the following: They don't have the time to read the book; they don't know you from Adam; every new writer wants their endorsement; or their publisher simply does not permit them to give endorsements.

Advertising Copy

The publisher will require you to fill out an author's questionnaire which asks questions about your professional life, such as the clubs or organizations you belong to; the awards or accolades you have received; and the means of distribution you have available to you. This type of information assists the publisher in promotion, publicity and distribution. You may also be asked to supply a 100 to 300 word synopsis of your book for the inside jackets and ten or so bullets, which are short, concise sentences hyping the book. For example, here are some of the bullets used to advertise *The Cross Burns Brightly*, written by Mel Blount with Cynthia Sterling:

- A Super Bowl hero gives something back to society
- Inspiring story of courage, character, and Christian faith
- 16-page color photo section

When, after all this, your book is finally published, you may feel exhausted, exhilarated and at loose ends with yourself. As John Cheever said, "I usually have a sense of clinical fatigue after writing a book." When your book is finished and out in public, you may need to view it as a child who has finally become an adult and is living on his own. He is no longer yours. You'll feel happy to have nurtured him, and sad to realize that he has left the nest. Now it is time to move on to your next book.

CHAPTER
FOUR

CATEGORIES AND GENRES

BASICALLY THERE ARE two types of books: fiction and nonfiction. *Fiction* refers to characters and stories which are made up and are not literally true, although they may be based on true events or even contain real historical figures. Fiction creates an alternate reality, separate from what we call the "real world," but almost always reflecting it. The primary functions of fiction are to entertain and provide insight.

Nonfiction refers to true material, either true stories drawn completely from real life or true material designed to inform, enlighten, persuade or educate. Essays (the candid ideas of philosophers trying to understand and explain certain aspects of the world as we know it) are also nonfiction.

FICTION — CATEGORIES

Both fiction and nonfiction books fall into certain, distinct categories. The largest fiction categories include Mass Market, Literary, Romance, Science Fiction and Fantasy, Mystery, Action/Adventure, Period/Historical, Western, Horror and Young Adult. It is of the utmost importance for the beginning writer to know what category her book falls under (and therefore what market she is writing to).

The most important thing for a beginning writer to know about catego-ries is that a publisher will not create a new category for your novel. If your work is not quite a romance, not quite a fantasy, not quite a horror novel, not quite a mystery, not quite a literary novel – but has elements of all these – expect to have difficulty selling it. It does not fall into a nice, tidy category, and most publishers are in the business of promoting books that fall into distinct categories. New categories are devised *infrequently*. The last new category accepted by the industry was New Age (fiction and nonfiction), which was born about ten years ago. (Of course, popular published authors may mix categories as they wish, since their work is in great demand.)

The following is a brief description of each of the categories listed above. It is in your best interest to research your target category thor oughly, reading several examples from different publishers. This will give you a good idea of what your audience expects *and* what publishers are looking for in each category.

1. Mass Market. Sometimes called "general fiction." These novels have a very broad appeal and usually address a number of aspects of contemporary or historical life. They also often have an element of romance, though romance is not the main focus.

2. Romance. Representing about 40% of the total body of published books, romances are essentially love stories between a man and a woman, although there is also a limited market for gay romances. Normally, the lovers must overcome significant obstacles before their love can be realized.

3. Science Fiction/Fantasy. Frequently considered one category, Science Fiction/Fantasy usually deals with futuristic events, exploration of outer space, invasions by aliens or fantastic events. The last area often involves a pseudo-medieval background usually replete with wizards, dragons and other fantasy icons. (This type of fantasy is sometimes referred to as "Sword and Sorcery.") Alternatively, a fantasy may include material from other myths and even animal tales. Science fiction can be either "hard" or "soft." Hard sci-fi includes very well-researched scientific and technical material, as in the stories of Isaac Asimov. The "soft" variety is more along the lines of Buck Rogers or *Star Wars*, an action-adventure story set in a future time or on another planet.

4. Mystery. One of the largest categories of fiction, mystery novels include many permutations, including detective fiction and murder mysteries, trial fiction, medical thrillers and the latest area, techno-thrillers.

5. Action/Adventure. This category used to be called "men's fiction," since it usually features a strong male protagonist involved in covert, dangerous missions. Military and espionage elements come into play in this category, which also includes books along the lines of the *Tarzan* series and *King Solomon's Mines*.

6. Literary Fiction. Novels that usually provide insight into the human condition. These normally have a contemporary setting and are very carefully written for maximum creative impact and language use. Literary novels are usually serious and dramatic, but may also be humorous.

7. Historical/Period Novels. Really a type of mass market novel, set in a historical time period. May or may not be about real historical events or people.

8. Western. A particular kind of period novel, dealing with real or fictional events and people of the Old American West from pre-Civil War to about 1900.

9. Horror. A catch-all category for all novels whose main purpose is to entertain readers by frightening them. Horror novels may include such topics as vampirism, serial killers, ghosts, the occult, Satanism and so on. There is usually but not always a supernatural aspect to horror novels. For instance, Peter Benchley's *Jaws* was essentially a horror novel, though it was well within the realm of reality.

10. Young Adult. Novels written with a young audience in mind, usually between the ages of twelve and seventeen. These novels are usually shorter and less graphic than adult novels, but are often sophisticated and compelling in their own right. Many YA novels feature humor, historical or fantasy elements, and all are strong on plot and character. Many deal with the strong bonds between young people and animals. (For more on YA novels, read the section on Juvenile Fiction later in this chapter.)

A Word About Syndication

Novels using syndicated characters form a special category. These include *Star Trek* novels, *Beauty and the Beast* novels, and the like. Usually the rights to this sort of material are held by a single publisher or individual, and therefore marketing such works is extremely limited. Normally publishers who hold the rights to this material seek out established authors to write books using syndicated characters. New writers would be well advised to create their own, original characters and steer clear of syndicated ones.

FICTION — GENRES

A category is a broad compartment of fiction and may be broken down into subsets defined by specific content, period or manner of presentation. These various subsets are called genres. Only fiction has genres; nonfiction has only categories.

Most of the categories mentioned are readily broken down into genres, most of which are self-explanatory. We've included a sample list here, for your convenience; a complete list of genres for each category would be too long and unwieldy to include in this book.

1. Romance — Gothic; Regency; Sweet, or Innocent; Graphic, or Explicit; Contemporary; Historical; Time Travel.

2. Science Fiction — Alien Invasion; Alien Partnership; Space Exploration; Futuristic; Space Spoof; Robotics; Sci-Fi Thriller; Astronaut; Nuclear Holocaust.
    Fantasy — Medieval-style Magic and Myth (Sword and Sorcery); Other Culture Myths; Talking Animals; Magic Realism; Time Travel; Modern Magic.

3. Mystery — Hard-boiled Detective; British Detective; Courtroom; Techno-thriller; Woman-in-Danger; Romantic Thriller; Gothic Mystery; Suspense; Espionage; Occult Mystery; Psychological Thriller.

4. Action/Adventure — Military; Mercenary; Intrigue/Espionage; Jungle Adventure; Backwoods Adventure.

5. Western — Gold Rush; Pioneer; Ranchers vs. Sheepherders; Pre- and Post-Civil War; Gunslinger; Women's Western; Indian.

6. Horror — Monsters (Werewolves, Giant Animals, Frankenstein Monster); Vampires; Serial Killer/Psychological Thriller; Occult/Satanic; End of the World.

(Notice that some of these genres overlap. For example, a story about a nuclear holocaust could be a military novel, a horror story, a science fiction thriller, espionage novel or even a satire, depending on how it's written.)
    Once you have established which category your work falls under, try to determine what genre it belongs to. As you can see, one of the most genre-intensive categories is Mystery. You may have a classic detective mystery (which may or may not be a murder mystery)...a courtroom drama...a techno-thriller concerning advanced drugs or technology...a mystery-romance...a gothic mystery...a "woman in danger" novel...a psychological thriller – well, the list seems to be never-ending. Each genre offers the publisher a specific niche under which he can sell your novel. If your mystery novel does not fall in one of the genres above, the publisher may still agree to handle it,

but he is likely to have a harder time promoting and selling it, since its form may not be "familiar" to the audience.

Assume you've written a mystery novel. To determine what genre your novel is, read various mysteries by a number of authors, published by a number of houses. Is your novel like any of them? It's important that beginning writers do their research and study which publishers work with what kinds of genres.

If you have an extremely strong character, you might well consider writing a genre series featuring this character. Certain categories lend themselves to series, particularly Western, Science Fiction, Young Adult and Mystery. For instance, Agatha Christie, Sue Grafton, Dick Francis, Ellery Queen and Ray Chandler have all written mystery series based on strong investigators. A novel without such a dramatic, pivotal character will probably not be suited for serialization.

For more information about genres and who publishes which kinds, consult *The Literary Marketplace*, available in your local library.

A Word about Imprints

Yet another complicating factor regarding genres is the term "imprints." This term refers to certain lines of genre books within a given publishing house. For example, Harlequin is a well-known publisher of romance novels and handles many genres of romance. Each of these genres is published under a specific *imprint*. Consider three of the myriad Harlequin imprints: Harlequin Romance, Harlequin Presents and Harlequin Temptation. Harlequin Romance is the publisher's line of "innocent" romances, i.e., those without explicit sexual description. Harlequin Presents has more explicit language, while Harlequin Temptation is the most explicit.

Beginning writers often confuse the term "imprint" with the term "subsidiary." A subsidiary company is a publisher which is owned by a parent corporation. The subsidiary publishes books under its own imprints. An imprint, as we know, is a specific line of books from one publisher and may include more than one genre of novel. Here's an example of this arrangement: Mysterious Press is an imprint of Warner Books, which is a subsidiary of Time, Inc.

NONFICTION — CATEGORIES

The categories of nonfiction are legion and include: Textbooks; How-To; History; Military History; True Story; Philosophy; Essay; Humorous

Essay; Memoirs; Self-Help; New Age; Sports; Biographies; Autobiographies; Theological Treatises; Sociology; Medicine; Psychology and Psychiatry; Music and Art; Science and Scientific Essays; Cookbooks; Nature Books; Nostalgia and much, much more — virtually as many categories as there are topics of human endeavor.

But category is not key to writing a successful nonfiction book: Format is.

Format refers to the way a writer organizes his nonfiction material. A cookbook, for example, may be arranged by ingredients, courses, ethnic groups, and so on. A self-help book might be structured along the lines of the classic persuasive essay/argument: problem, solution, less effective solutions, history of problem and solutions, the ways your solution works, and anecdotes, case histories and exercises.

There are many ways to format nonfiction, and it's not the purpose of this book to delve into them deeply. However, we will present a few of the most common types of nonfiction formats.

1. Argumentative. Mentioned above, the persuasive argument basically states a problem and offers a solution. The history of the problem and the ways the solution can be put into action are discussed. This form is particularly helpful in a philosophical treatise, a book on psychology, or a self-help book.

2. Concept and Case Histories. Unusual or striking concepts are sometimes best presented by amassing and discussing case histories which illustrate the idea in question. For example, a doctor writing about a new, revolutionary treatment or drug might offer frequent examples of how it has been used and what benefits it has brought to specific individuals.

3. Chronological. Probably the most effective format for memoirs, autobiographies, biographies and histories in general. The writer presents material in chronological order, beginning with a person's childhood, for example, or with a specific historical event, and moving on from that point in chronological increments. This gives the writer a chance to show how experiences "build" on each other in the life of an individual, region or nation.

4. True Story. The true story – a writer's account of an event or series of events which happened to him or which he researched – is also best told chronologically. However, the true story borrows elements from fiction as well: characterization, suspense, pacing and transitions. It may be said of

the best true stories that, if not true, they would be novels.

5. Personal Essay Collection. These can be either serious, humorous or nostalgic, and are often centered around a particular theme: the awkwardness of adolescence; the marvels of nature; the stupidity of politicians; the life of the homemaker, and so on. Usually each essay is complete unto itself, yet ties in to the greater theme. This is perhaps the most informal and least structured type of nonfiction.

The best way to study nonfiction formats is to read many nonfiction works, paying special attention to how they are structured. A rambling nonfiction account that waffles back and forth in time and emphasis is just as ineffective as a poorly plotted novel.

JUVENILE BOOKS

Our agency does not deal with a great deal of juvenile fiction and nonfiction, but it is an extremely fast-growing segment of the literary industry. Therefore, we have included an age breakdown of the market to help writers target their works to the appropriate audience.

1. Infants' Picture Books. These books for very young children feature large, simple, colored illustrations on each page, and perhaps a word or sentence. They are often printed on cardboard or cloth.

2. Read-alongs. For children 3-5. These books have more complicated illustrations on each page, as well as several sentences. Older children will make out a word or two as their parents read them these books.

3. First Readers. For children 5-7. These books have fewer illustrations than read-alongs and use a very simple vocabulary. They usually require a lively story to encourage young readers, and Dr. Seuss's *Cat in the Hat* is a famous example.

4. Juvenile, 7-9. These books may be picture books with lavish illustrations...or chapter books with comparatively few illustrations. Books in this category have more words and more complicated plots and characters, but still incorporate a rather simple vocabulary.

5. Juvenile, 9-12. These are chapter books. What few illustrations they

may have are line drawings. Vivid characters and gripping plots are very important, and the vocabulary is more extensive. No explicit material. From 12,000 to 20,000 words.

6. Young Adult, 12-15. Chapter books; more sophisticated in terms of plot and characterization. They often deal with social themes such as divorce, racism, sexism, war, alienation and abuse, but not in explicit terms. Fantasy themes are also popular. From 25,000 to 35,000 words.

7. Young Adult, 15-17. Chapter books; still more complex in terms of plot and characters, and more sophisticated in terms of theme, vocabulary and advanced writing styles. Not as graphic or explicit as adult books. Up to 60,000 words.

CHAPTER FIVE

FICTION WRITING FOR PUBLICATION

FICTION IS THE craft of telling stories about people. While these stories – anywhere from 5 to 2000 pages long – often seem realistic and reveal general truths about the human condition, they are purely the creations of the writer. The characters and events may be loosely based on truth, but the bedrock of fiction is a child's innate power of make-believe coupled to an adult's knowledge of structure and life. As Mario Vargas Llosa once said, "A wondrous dream, a fantasy incarnate, fiction completes us mutilated beings burdened with the awful dichotomy of having only one life and the ability to desire a thousand."

When one considers how truly difficult it is to write fiction, then adds to that the fact that most people have no formal schooling in writing fiction, it is astounding how many people without any commitment to or knowledge of the craft of writing still insist on writing.

Why do they do so?

Popular wisdom would have us believe that writers create something from nothing, that no special skills or experiences are necessary to write a book that people will love to read. According to this theory, writing fiction is a quick, easy and enjoyable way to gain popularity, fame and admiration. Beginning writers who have swallowed this notion believe that, if only they can get the magic words down on paper, they can entertain, educate and/or enlighten the public and become rich in the process.

Unfortunately, books don't write themselves, and no one becomes a successful writer by simply decreeing that he is one. Make no mistake about it: The decision to become a writer should not be taken lightly. Writing fiction is a hard endeavor, and writing skills are hard to learn and even harder to market. Few public schools include fiction writing in their curricula, and even few college students get a chance to study it in depth. One overly-confident beginning writer, when asked about her writing background, responded that she had "learned to write at school, the same as anyone else. That's good enough."

No, it isn't good enough. Writing for publication just isn't that simple, and the instruction in expository writing one receives in most schools and colleges is woefully insufficient preparation for the tremendous, exhausting task of crafting and writing a novel or even a successful short story. Without comprehensive training in fiction writing, many people develop a romantic passion to write and to publish what they write, but they are often rather unsure how they should proceed to do both. The following chapters are aimed at those writers, with the purpose of helping them achieve their goal of writing marketable fiction – or at least understanding why they don't.

Successful novels often contain specific factors, or elements. Certain writing techniques (also called novelistic conventions) seem to make those elements work more effectively than other techniques. Those writers who are aware of the elements of the novel and the novelistic conventions regarding them often succeed to a greater extent than their less conventional, unenlightened colleagues.

Even writers who wish to create avant garde, innovative, unconventional fiction would do well to become familiar with novelistic elements and conventions. Then they will understand where to twist, bend, distort, omit and add to their writing to get just the effect they desire. Furthermore, they will know *why* they are doing what they are doing.

What are these elements and the conventions which shape them? How can a beginning writer learn them and put them to use? Are there any guidelines for knowing how to use the conventions and how *not* to?

To answer these questions, let's take a look at some of the novelistic elements and conventions and see how they function in the craft of writing fiction.

ELEMENTS OF THE NOVEL

While the act of writing has been depicted as an act of inspiration – romantic, fulfilling and uplifting – there is nothing romantic or particularly attractive about spending hours sitting at a keyboard or staring into space or cringing at words of criticism during a writing workshop. Good writing is rarely produced on a lark or a whim, and while it may be "inspired," it is executed through hard work and perseverance. Writing is a craft that is learned and perfected over many years, and, at its best, it is an art.

Understanding the elements, or building blocks, of the novel provides the basis or foundation for learning the craft of writing. Reading good fiction, practicing writing, and listening to the advice of successful writers and editors help a writer add to that foundation.

Novelistic elements are of great concern to publishers and editors, who often use them as a yardstick to evaluate the prowess of a writer. ("Does she create vivid, believable characters?" "Does she make the reader feel as if he is inside the story?") Editors are usually *not* interested in novels which are devoid of a protagonist or plot...which are so slow-paced that they are lethargic...or which are wordy, hard to understand, rambling or extremely distant in tone. A successful, conventional novel incorporates the elements listed below:

1. A well-developed main character (also called a "round," "changed" or "moved" character)
2. Plot
3. Subplots and secondary characters
4. Setting and sequence
5. Theme, voice and tone

Most novels, including mainstream and literary novels as well as genre westerns and romances, take advantage of these elements in one form or another. Short stories use many of these elements, although few have the "space" to develop more than one character or plotline.

In the next few chapters, we'll examine each element in some detail. In subsequent chapters, we'll also take a look at the literary conventions which help writers craft the elements of the novel.

CHAPTER SIX

ELEMENT: PROTAGONISTS AND CHARACTERIZATION

MANY FIRST-TIME WRITERS believe that characters are merely a means to an end, and the end is the novel. In reality, the characters *are* the novel. A novel is basically an examination of a character's reactions and responses to events in the plot, the consequences of those reactions and their effect on the character.

That having been said, it is odd that, every month or so, the agency receives a manuscript that either has no central character or no plot to speak of. Some manuscripts have neither protagonist nor plot. Apparently, many beginning fiction writers become so involved in developing a style – or aping that of someone else – that they lose sight of an extremely conventional but important concept: A novel is primarily a story about someone, and that person will be central to the novel. Generally, we refer to the "someone" as the protagonist and to the "story" as the plot. The two are intimately entwined and more or less essential to all but the most skilled writers.

A DEVELOPED PROTAGONIST

The protagonist, or main character in a novel, is the person whom the reader is most likely to identify with and sympathize with. This character usually is present for the entire novel, or most of it, and his death sometimes forms the conclusion of the work. Without this main character, the story would not exist.

Graham Greene once remarked, "A novel is a man, and I am looking for him." Of course, the "man" may be a woman, a child...or even a non-human, such as the horse in the novel *Traveler* by Richard Adams, or Gregor Samsa, the former human turned giant cockroach in Franz Kafka's surrealistic novella, *Metamorphosis*. Greene meant that a novel is driven by a main character. A successful novel requires a character who must develop in order for the story to move forward. Interestingly enough, that character will usually develop because of the events that happen in the plot.

What is Meant by the Word "Developed"?

E. M. Forster wrote that "flat" characters are fixed characters, incapable of being "changed by circumstance." "Round," or developed, characters, however, he continues, are moving characters, "capable of surprising in a convincing way." That is to say, developed characters act and react to circumstances and events in the story. Their actions may not be completely predictable because these characters are caught up in the process of change. The fact that the reader cannot exactly predict a character's behavior creates a sense of tension and suspense in the story: What will the character do next? Will he make a wise choice or a stupid one?

In some cases, a main character may fail to develop, even if given plenty of opportunity to do so. Then the story is not about what happens to the character in the novel, but what *doesn't* happen. We see the character's resistance to growth and change, and understand the reasons and ramifications of his resistance. Such a novel often creates a feeling of hopelessness, tragedy or ruination. *The Remains of the Day*, by Kazuo Ishiguro, in which a very proper butler fails to allow passion into his highly structured life, is this sort of novel. Most beginning writers should think twice about attempting to write this kind of story, as it is very difficult to pull off successfully. If not led to believe otherwise, the reader may interpret the character's failure to change simply as the mark of a static character.

Character Biographies, as Opposed to Character Development

Contrary to what many new writers believe, developing a character does *not* mean loading the reader down with a long, involved biography of the protagonist, typically at the beginning of the novel. This material is some- times called the "backstory;" while the writer should know it, the backstory doesn't belong in the book. Biographies (including the character's childhood and early family life, where he went to school, his first love affair, his first job and so on) merely slow down the pace of the novel and encourage the reader to ask, "Who is telling me all this information and why?"

Any important details of the protagonist's past should arise naturally as they impact on the plot. For example, if a character grew up in his grandfather's house, this should be mentioned if the protagonist receives a letter from his grandfather or learns of the old man's death. Similarly, his old school affiliations might come forward if he meets an old school chum or discovers something lacking in his formal education. In nearly every case, details of a character's life should be revealed through events which make the character recall those details.

Static Characters...

Static characters are also sometimes called cardboard or flat characters, which indicates their paper-thin development. Static characters do not change fundamentally over the course of a novel. If they are irresponsible loafers to begin with, they will end up the same way.

One common kind of flat, static character is the "type" or "stock" character, such as the prostitute with a heart of gold or the dashing hero with feet of clay. The type character conforms to an established mold or stereotype and is less a depiction of a real person than a caricature of a kind of person or human behavior. The stern Marine sergeant, the noble American Indian, the conniving *femme fatale*, the crusty backwoodsman, the haughty society dame – these are all type characters, not realistic, developed characters. This is not to say that a novel should not contain Marines, Native Americans, beautiful but shrewd women, woodsmen or wealthy people; they simply must be people, not empty labels.

When readers encounter a type character in a story or novel, they get the impression that the writer did not have the time, talent or inclination to develop a fully rounded, realistic character. The type character comes across as a sort of short-hand or fill-in for more believable characters. Real people rarely fall into neat, immutable categories or stereotypes.

We often see type characters and other flat characters in movies and television, which rarely have the time to develop a realistic character. In a novel, where there is plenty of room to render character through detail, dialogue and the actions of the narrative, static characters are a greater liability. They fail to provoke reader identification. Instead, they move through the story in a predictable way, essentially unchanged from beginning to end. If a flat character suddenly shifts in personality, say from evil to kind or from dull to insightful, the reader is left wondering what caused her to change so suddenly. She had no motivation to change, and her change did not take place in a gradual, believable way as the result of her response to events or other characters.

...Versus Dynamic Characters

A dynamic character who changes and develops is more realistic and believable than a static character. Circumstances do shape the dynamic character. He responds to plot events and is changed by them over the course of the novel or short story. Adults seldom change in terms of outlook or personality, and it may be said that the reason for writing a novel is to show how one individual did indeed change, usually for the better.

Publishers look for manuscripts with developed protagonists who gain insight on life and learn to understand themselves and other people better as the result of confronting events in the plot. This sort of development most closely reflects human growth in real life and thus has considerable power to move the reader. Celie in Alice Walker's *The Color Purple*, for example, is a developed protagonist who moves from semi-literate, downtrodden farm girl to fulfilled woman with a sense of inner wisdom. She grows because she acts and responds to the actions of other characters in such a way that she learns a great deal about the life outside her circumscribed existence and undergoes personal growth because of this knowledge. For example, when her husband takes a lover, Shug Avery, Celie takes advantage of the woman's boundless passion and sympathy instead of railing against her. In this way, Celie gets some inkling of the love and affection that she has missed throughout her early life.

In his book, *Writing in General and the Short Story in Particular*, Rust Hills, former editor of *Esquire* Magazine, writes that, "...in fiction, because of the necessity for something to happen to someone as a result of action, there is perhaps a more-than-normal percentage of forceful, energetic activists who evoke events that cause something to happen. And there seem to be more too of those who are passive and submit to their fate, to drift into situations that cause what happens to them. We tend to encounter characters in fiction at a time of stress in their lives."

Why should this be so? Because it is precisely this stress which both drives the protagonist through the course of the novel and forces him to change and develop into a more complex person. Stress acts to force the protagonist to react to events in the story. For example, in Hemingway's *The Sun Also Rises*, Jake Barnes is under constant stress because, due to a war wound, he is unable to physically respond to Bret, the woman he loves. This frustration causes him to try to wean her away from him. At the same time, he must decide whether or not to stand by helplessly, painfully as she destroys herself and other men...or to interfere with her life.

Sympathetic Characters

In general, successful fiction writers create main characters whom a reader can believe in and empathize with. This means that the protagonist must, on some level, engender the reader's sympathy, even if he is a degenerate psychopath, a murderer or a child-abuser. For the most part, the less sympathetic the character, the greater the difficulty the writer will encounter in making the reader care about what happens to the character.

It could be argued that the reader's urge to find out what happens to the protagonist is the most compelling reason to finish reading a novel. If the protagonist is so unrealistic or unpleasant or unapproachable or devoid of human frailties that the reader *distances* herself emotionally from the character, it is not likely that the reader will care about the fate of the character and even less likely that she will read the entire work.

A first-time writer, for instance, once submitted a romance to us in which the protagonist was a self-serving, obnoxious character who never saw the errors of her ways or changed in any positive manner. Such a negative character might work in a satire, in which the protagonist is being singled out as an object of ridicule. In most works, however, the reader must identify with the protagonist to some extent, or at least be willing to understand and accept her behavior. This character was so repulsive that she resisted all reader attempts to care what happened to her, creating an unbridgeable gap, or distance, between the story and the reader. (We will discuss the concept of distance at greater length in a later chapter.)

By "sympathetic" we do not mean unrealistically wholesome, kind or virtuous. We simply mean that the character has some commanding or endearing quality, be it an admirable nature or an intense, charming personality, that holds the reader's interest and keeps the reader concerned about that character's welfare. In most cases, the main character will probably also be an ethical person, but he need not be. (Neither Humbert Humbert nor Elmer Gantry are ethical, but they are intriguing.)

If the reader does not empathize to some degree with the protagonist and at least understand her position (if not condone it), then a writer is in danger of losing the reader. One writer created a protagonist who thought that a woman who treated a young boy as a sexual pet was merely "weird," not depraved or criminal. The editor pointed out to him that most readers might think the woman was committing child abuse and would therefore think less of the cavalier protagonist.

Can an antagonist also be sympathetic? Of course. Few people are patently evil, although these misfits often make excellent antagonists. As vindictive as he is, Roger Chillingsworth, the cuckolded husband in Hawthorne's *The Scarlet Letter*, has some purchase on our sympathies. After all, Hester's betrayal has incited him to revenge. Sometimes, unsavory characters will even take over the role of protagonist, such as Sinclair Lewis's destructive preacher, Elmer Gantry, and Humbert Humbert, the pedophilic narrator in Vladimir Nabakov's *Lolita*. Sometimes they get their comeuppance, sometimes they don't, just as it is with people in real life. Most of these pro/antagonists have at least some sympathetic aspect to their lives. Gantry, for example, is truly in love with Sharon Falconer, as Humbert is in love with Lolita. Interestingly, their poisoned love ultimately culminates in the destruction of their love objects. Both Gantry and Humbert are complex characters, and though we may not like them, we are fascinated by them nonetheless.

How Does a Writer Develop a Character?

It is not a simple matter to create a rounded protagonist, but two techniques can help. One is by writing a character sketch; the other is by emphasizing your character's reactions.

The Character Sketch

Before actually starting your novel, try writing a detailed description of your main character, including everything you'd like your readers to know about him, assuming you had time and space enough to tell them. Provide an ample "backstory" for your character, relating the details of his life up to the point at which your novel begins. What does he look like? Does he have any pets? What was his childhood like? What incident during his youth had the most effect on his development?

This material is not actually part of your story. It is instead an aid to help you determine the character's personality. Is he sensitive and affectionate...or self-centered and vain? Out-going or withdrawn? Romantic or practical? Well-educated or self-educated? Creative or pedantic? Some details from the sketch may surface at some point in the story, but only if they have a direct impact on the story. If, for instance, your novel is about a woman who must work with children, although she detests them, her own childhood experiences are likely to be an important part of the story.

The character sketch should help you understand your protagonist sufficiently so that you can predict how he would react or respond to various situations. For example, if he is at a party in the company of wealthy, influential people, does he feel at ease...excited to be in the presence of such important people...embarrassed and out-of-place...or downright frightened?

Editors are sometimes reluctant to ask writers to create character sketches, for fear the writer will include the sketch, or a large part of it, in the novel. As we've mentioned earlier, many beginning writers mistakenly feel compelled to begin their works with character biographies instead of a compelling event. Therefore, keep in mind that most if not all of your character sketch is for your edification alone, not your readers'.

Emphasis on Reactions

Say that your protagonist, on his way to lunch at a city bistro, witnesses five police officers beating a man senseless. Not possessing super-human powers, your protagonist decides not to intervene personally, and is unsure whom to summon to the scene. (The police? They're already there.) As he's staring at the men aghast, deciding what to do, a paddy wagon comes and hauls away the stricken victim. Does your protagonist:

A. Proceed with his luncheon date?

B. Return to his office, unable to eat?

C. Take the day off sick?

D. Hire a cab to follow the paddy wagon?

E. Call 911 or the local paper or TV station to report the incident?

How your main character reacts to this scene of violence (or any other event in the story, for that matter) tells a great deal about what sort of person he is. Your readers will feel very differently about the character if he chooses option A as opposed to option D.

Whenever an event takes place in your story, allow your protagonist to react, respond or reflect on it. Even a minor happening, such as a cruel or critical remark made by another character, may deserve your protagonist's response, if it is important to developing his personality or the plot. Like any real person, the protagonist has opinions and feelings. Short of out-right parody, the more we see him respond, the better we will understand his motivations, background, ethics and ambitions.

Take care to ensure your main character is reacting appropriately to specific events. Consider this passage by a first-time writer, for example:

> Walter woke up that morning feeling as if he were lying in a puddle of syrup. Opening his eyes, he saw his wife Angela lying next to him, her face a delicate shade of lavender, her eyes wide open, her mouth gaping in silent surprise. The entire bed was soaked in her blood. Something's very wrong, thought Walter.

One assumes that what follows from this paragraph is a dark comedy or satire. Walter hates his wife and is only too happy to discover her demise. Unfortunately, that is not the writer's intent. Walter loves his wife. The writer has unwittingly given Walter the reactions of a bitter, unhappy man whose subdued mental remark – something's wrong – is so understated as to be humorous.

To make this passage work on the level of serious drama, the writer would have to imagine how a husband would truly react upon finding his wife lying next to him, dead. Would he be horrified? Shocked? Fearful? Irrational with grief? Enraged? All of the above? Would he wonder who had done such a thing, or why? Would he be afraid that the murderer was still in the bedroom, eyeing his next victim?

It is one of the great joys of writing (as well as a necessity) to be able to craft characters, actually *create* complex, realistic, flawed and sympathetic people and their realities. Unfortunately, beginning writers often fail to take advantage of this amazing power to craft a character with depth. In general, when the reader has finished your novel, she should know your protagonist as intimately as she knows a close friend. Only then will the writing achieve maximum emotional impact.

CHAPTER SEVEN

ELEMENT: PLOT AND STRUCTURE

MANY BEGINNING WRITERS cling to the notion one needs only to access his feelings and experiences, and the plot of the novel will create itself. At the agency, we've read quite a few novels which are products of this line of faulty reasoning. In these rambling pieces, the writer gushes forth the story, giving no thought to where and when events should take place, or to whom they should happen. The plot is not structured or crafted for a specific affect or intent, but merely "vomited out," to use just about the cruelest but most candid term in editing.

Worse yet, some first-time writers, in a vain attempt to emulate their favorite action/adventure or mass market author, emphasize plot to the neglect of character. In successful fiction writing, the writer needs both. Neither plot nor character alone will create the dynamic fusion of person and event that propels a reader through a novel.

The Compelling Event

In most successful fiction, plot is structured. It is organized so well, so naturally that it appears that the writer gave no thought to organizing the story beforehand. As editors say, there are "no seams showing." The plot flows in a believable, almost inevitable way, like a river, and to make one change in that structure would ruin the flow of the plot.

Since a novel requires characters to react to events, make decisions and "grow," there must be events for the characters to react to and learn from. To paraphrase E.M. Forster in *Aspects of the Novel*, these events provide the "whys" and "hows" of the story. Taken as a whole, the events form the plot, or storyline, of the novel and give it breadth and depth. Because these events thrust the character into taking action, they are often called "compelling events," and the author must take care to position them in the novel so that they realistically flow from one to the other.

We can borrow a line from the Jewish Passover Seder and think of plot and conflict in this light: Why is this night different from all other nights?

In other words, at what point does the writer choose to peek in on the protagonist and why? What is happening in the protagonist's life that is about to change it (and him) forever? What new or unsolved problem must he confront? He wakes up in the morning as usual, brushes his teeth as usual – and then is slapped in the face with an unusual event that causes some sense of turmoil in his life. Has his wife left him? Does he hear of an accident involving his child, or is this particular day the anniversary of his child's death? (The latter event forms the basis for the plot of Eudora Welty's gripping short story, "Music from Spain.") Introducing something unusual, out of the ordinary or unsettling often sets up a conflict or dilemma, requiring the protagonist to react or make a decision.

Hooks

A hook is a piece of action that gets the attention of the reader in the beginning of the novel (initial hook) or a chapter (chapter hook).

The initial hook is usually the first compelling event in the plot, the incident which drives the protagonist to take action. To be a successful hook, the action must be related to the central conflict of the plot. (More on conflict later.) For example, in the beginning of *Lady Chatterly's Lover*, by D.H. Lawrence, the lady's husband is crippled during the war, leaving her feeling sexually unfulfilled. This sets the stage for the central action powering the novel: her love affair with the gardener.

How the protagonist responds to the compelling event of the initial hook establishes the foundation of his personality. Frequently, the protagonist shows bad judgment, recklessness or immaturity in making his first decision; this sets the stage for him to face the consequences of his actions.

A chapter hook is a compelling event or intriguing question which occurs at the end of a chapter. Its purpose is to create sufficient suspense to propel the reader into the next chapter. A chapter hook frequently takes the form of an action scene cut off abruptly and continued in the next chapter, or a leading question that the protagonist asks himself. ("Could it be that Lilly had no idea at all where they were headed?") Chapter hooks are powerful devices, especially effective in genre literature, where suspense typically drives the novel.

As with initial hooks, the action in chapter hooks should be related to the central conflict of the story, at least indirectly.

False Conflict

Writers often attempt to create hooks or other compelling events by writing sex or action scenes *simply for the sake of getting the reader's attention* and not for establishing conflict.

Ideally, the novel should start at or very close to the beginning of the conflict in the protagonist's life. Apparently not understanding this concept, one client began her first draft of a suspense/espionage novel with a sex scene between the female protagonist and her lover, who was never mentioned again in the entire manuscript. Since the reader had no idea who these people were, there was little reason to read about their intimate physical adventures. In any case, their act of sex was not creating conflict.

The writer thought she was establishing a "hook" to interest the reader; in reality, she was only delaying the start of the story. To establish a true initial hook, she would have had to establish the novel's central conflict and connect the action to the conflict.

Nowadays, it is almost *de rigueur* to include a graphic scene of sex or violence in a mainstream novel. However, such a scene may have absolutely nothing to do with the novel's theme, characters, or plot and may seem to the reader to be "tacked on" to an otherwise well-written and cohesive story. The popular theory is that the reader is titillated by such scenes and thus more likely to buy a book that contains them. While this may be true to some extent, a skilled writer will include explicit sex and violence only when they form compelling events integral to the development of a novel's plot, characters or setting.

Certainly the hair-raising, grotesque violence of Peter Blaty's *The Exorcist* is essential to the novel. The violence and obscenities serve to establish the presence of Satan, and for all intents function like another character. In the same way, graphic sex scenes may be intrinsic parts of novels about prostitutes, rape victims or rapists, gigolos, people with sex addictions, and the like. Romance novels and mainstream novels often use an intimate bedroom scene or two to establish the physical side of a love relationship...or the lack of love in fading relationships.

However, sex and violence should not substitute for central conflict or for character and plot development. For example, in *The Women's Room* by Laura French, a popular novel of the seventies, a graphic sex scene at the very end of the novel hits the reader like a blow to the stomach: It is totally unexpected, with no precedent in the rest of the text. While it perhaps symbolizes the female protagonist's new freedom from a failed marriage and conventional way of life, it is so mechanical and devoid of feeling (despite its depiction of "passion") that it gives the impression that the protagonist has lost some of her humanity, not regained it.

The Central Conflict

From the standpoint of writing technique, the purpose of the compelling event is to create a conflict in the protagonist's life. In other words, the writer often walks into his characters' lives "during times of stress." It is this sense of conflict or suspense that compels the reader to keep reading the story. If the conflict drives the suspense throughout the story, is crucial to the plot and is resolved in the climax, we call it the "central conflict" of the story. It may or may not be the compelling event, but the two will undoubtedly be related.

For example, Holden Caulfield in J.D. Salinger's *The Catcher in the Rye* leaves his private boarding school in the beginning of the novel. His adventures and subsequent emotional breakdown occur directly and indirectly as a result of his escape from the tedious but secure environment of the school into the chaos of the big city, a setting which mirrors his own troubled mind. The need to both confront and "run away" from his family problems and his general inability to do so form the central conflict in the novel...and are established right at the beginning.

No matter how many minor conflicts and events take place in the novel, the central conflict should always be present in the reader's mind. As Holden crashes his way out of one encounter into the next, we are always aware that he is desperately searching for the place where he belongs...and will never find it.

If a minor event takes place in every chapter, and there is no central conflict driving the plot forward, then the plot will appear episodic.

Episodic Structure

When many compelling events are piled one on top of each other, one following the next, we say that the structure is episodic. Action is taking place in episodes, or small sections that have their own conflict and resolution. For example, movies of the Indiana Jones ilk are episodic: The hero escapes a booby-trapped temple, then meets a pretty woman, then finds a treasure, then must escape from a snake-pit, then must capture the villains, then falls prey to the villains and must escape them. All these "episodes" are fairly complete in and of themselves, and form the plot merely because they are strung together like beads on a string. The ancient Greek sagas, like *The Iliad* and *The Odyssey*, are also episodic in format.

Episodic structure can be weak, but it can work for many kinds of genre writing that depend on active, adventurous protagonists. The key to making episodic structure work is to downplay the resolution of each episode and to attach minor conflicts to a central conflict. The protagonist escapes the villain's goons for the moment, but just ahead are even more terrors. In addition, the hero is pressured by the central conflict – rescuing a person, perhaps, or preventing a disaster. The central conflict overshadows the importance of the minor conflicts of the episodes, creating pressure which forces the character to act and react, and drives the story forward.

Fantasies and adventure tales are often successfully episodic. Characters in these types of fiction are often involved on a "quest" or journey, which may represent a larger journey of self-knowledge.

Certainly Frank Baum's beloved story, *The Wizard of Oz*, is episodic: Dorothy follows the Yellow Brick Road from one adventure to another, picking up new companions and avoiding dangers as she goes. But this classic children's tale works, precisely because of the complexity of the central theme which knits together all the various episodes and escapades. The theme works on two levels: 1) Dorothy is attempting to return home to Kansas, and must locate the Wizard in order to do so; each adventure brings her a little closer to her ultimate goal and helps build suspense. 2) Dorothy journeys from her bleak, humdrum existence on the farm to magical realms full of wonder. Are these adventures real, or is using one's imagination real enough? So, in an interesting juxtaposition of reality, Dorothy is both going back to Kansas and getting further away from it at the same time.

Episodic structure does not work, however, if the episodes are more or less complete in themselves, do not illustrate or enlarge a central theme or conflict, and do not serve to develop the central character. For example, a novice writer submitted a mass market romance in which the heroine flits from one lover to another and from one career to another, slowly amassing a fortune. There is no "plot," other than the flat progression from lover to lover and success to success. The protagonist is the very same person she was at the beginning of the novel, only wealthier, a weak resolution the reader can spot from the second chapter.

Drafting a careful outline before beginning to write will help you avoid an episodic structure or, alternatively, organize plot episodes around a central conflict in order to move the protagonist and plot toward an all-encompassing, satisfying resolution.

Rising Action

Conflict puts pressure on characters to develop. Under such pressure, the characters confront issues and make decisions, causing the action to accelerate and make the reader more and more anxious to discover "what happens next." This increased stress in the plot is called "rising action." The stakes are higher, and there is more for the character to win or lose than there was at the beginning of the novel. Ignoring conflict or failing to structure rising action in a plot often results in the "pyrotechnics" discussed earlier – unnecessary sex scenes, car chases, shootings, maimings, and so on: plot episodes which go nowhere and fail to advance the plot as a whole. Inattention to conflict and a lack of rising action can also produce a stagnant story that meanders into many tangents, seeking tension and suspense in vain.

Two Problems Regarding Conflict and Structure

Beginning writers often make one of two mistakes regarding the structure of their plots: Either they downplay conflict and end up with a character sketch or vignette rather than a novel or story, or they concentrate too heavily on plot and conflict, using characters merely as props to further the story. In the latter case, the plot – not a character – becomes the protagonist of the novel. One frequently sees an over-emphasis on plot in action-adventure movies such as *Under Siege* or *Robocop*.

If not corrected, these problems lead to the structural collapse of the novel. To inspect these problems in more detail, we'll examine two works sent to the agency. One we'll call *Island* and one we'll call *Conspiracy* (not the original titles).

In *Island*, a literary novel, we encounter a first-person protagonist who talks at length about his lifestyle, his acquaintances, the appearance of his acquaintances, and the places he frequents. While we get the semblance of something happening, nothing is really happening. Although the writer provides plenty of opportunity for a story to develop, the reader is soon caught up in details of cars, beach-houses, bars and floozies, to the exclusion of compelling events. Because there is no central conflict driving the plot forward, the novel begins sluggishly, then grinds to a halt, mired in descriptions and flashbacks which add little to the character of the protagonist and do nothing to advance the story. Unfortunately, as the story becomes static, so does the protagonist.

Conspiracy, an espionage novel, presents the opposite problem: Characters are sacrificed for action, conflict and storyline. In this novel, a terrorist group is intent upon destroying the United States using nuclear warfare, and a group of anti-terrorists must prevent the attack. If a strong protagonist and antagonist were involved in this scenario, then the reader could easily follow the story through the actions, reactions, thoughts and dialogue of the characters. Instead, the novel is packed with interchange-able characters who live just long enough to advance the story from one stage to the next.

A novel like this depends on conflict and suspense, and suspense is cre-ated by providing characters we care about and putting them in danger, not by moving chessmen around on an intricate board. Ultimately a reader will feel cheated by a conflict-heavy story such as *Conspiracy*, because it in-variably reduces complex human lives and actions to the level of a fifteen-minute cartoon show.

This is a good time to point out that writing genre novels, such as ro-mances, westerns, thrillers and mysteries, is not synonymous with shallow writing. Genre fiction is an extremely competitive market, and publishers will invest in only the best of the lot. Generally, there is no place in writing at all for novels with paper-thin characters or shallow, predictable plots.

If too much emphasis and not enough emphasis on conflict and plot are equally deadly, how should a writer proceed? How does a writer marry the two crucial elements of plot and character development?

There is no cookie-cutter approach to fiction, of course. Some novels will emphasize character development over plot, or vice versa. However, the careful writer will understand that character and plot often mesh together, and that one will impact the other, just as real people and the events in their lives are almost inseparable.

Helpful Outlines

To get some idea of how a plot should be structured and how a protago-nist figures in that plot, a beginning writer might consider writing a plot outline before actually attempting to write the novel. The outline will include the highlights of the plot and indicate how the plot is structured. The outline can take many forms, from the standard, indented outline format to the chapter-by-chapter outline, which mentions key events as they occur by chapter.

(Note: Now and then we come across a manuscript without chapters. We believe that it is a mistake for beginning writers to structure a novel without chapters, since chapters help break a story into manageable chunks that are easier for the reader to assimilate. Therefore we recommend that beginning writers outline and craft their plot in terms of chapters.)

Writing an outline to better grasp one's plot is analogous to writing a character sketch to better understand one's protagonist. Outlines are useful because they help a writer visualize what events take place in her novel and how the characters function in it. Of course, one should not assume the outline is cast in concrete. It is simply a tool to help the writer develop a better understanding of the work, and the writer can change it at any time, even halfway through the novel, or at the very end.

While writing the outline, it isn't necessary to have thought out every detail of the entire manuscript. If, for example, you want your protagonist to realize that her brother is a murderer, but you aren't sure how she finds this out, it is perfectly acceptable just to indicate that this key bit of information is still "under construction." Nine times out of ten, the answers to these kinds of details will work themselves out in the writing of the story by the time the writer must incorporate them.

Outlines pose a problem only if they become an end in themselves, rather than a tool for crafting the end product, the novel. Obviously, the writer makes the outline...and he can unmake it, too. He can change the outline any time and any way he likes, if he has reason to.

It may be helpful to fashion the outline *as you go*, writing only as much plot material as you need to get to a certain point in the novel. Once you have written the novel to that point and to your satisfaction, continue with your outline. Actually, at that juncture you may find you know the characters and plot so thoroughly you don't need the kind of guidance that an outline provides.

BEGINNING, MIDDLE AND END: A BASIC PLOT STRUCTURE

To give some idea of how a writer might develop character and plot to craft a novel from beginning to end, let's examine how novels generally proceed, with the help of a very basic outline. This outline indicates the barest bones of novelistic structure and is by no means intended to demonstrate that there is only one sound way to structure a novel. (Your outline will go into far more specific detail.) Each point or stage in the development of a novel presents separate challenges and requires specific approaches or strategies, which will be dealt with in the discussion of "conventions."

The Beginning

A. The writer might provide very brief descriptions of protagonist and setting. In other words, who is where? What is he or she doing and why?

The reader must get a sense of the character existing in a particular location early on. For instance, to use a fairly recent example, consider the historical/time-travel novel *Outlander* by Diana Gabaldon. Claire, an English nurse who has just experienced World War II, visits a village in the Highlands of Scotland with her husband. She meets some interesting folk and the reader becomes acquainted with the area. An important secondary character, her husband Frank, is introduced.

Point A may be dealt with very briefly, in a few pages. Avoiding vast detail will help prevent the reader from feeling that the novel is "going nowhere." In some cases, as with *Outlander*, which has a very complicated plot and many characters, it may take several chapters to establish the protagonist and setting. Nevertheless, sufficient suspense must be built up so that the reader feels "something" is about to happen and is intrigued enough to read on.

(At the agency, we receive many manuscripts which do not really begin until the reader is several chapters into the story. First-time writers will sometimes defend this slow start by saying, "Oh, the story doesn't really begin until page one hundred. The first hundred pages are background information." These writers are summarily told to drop the exposition and begin at the beginning. Few readers will wait so long to begin a story.)

B. Something happens. This is the hook or initial compelling event that gets things going, often setting up the central conflict that causes the character to act, reflect, change, and grow throughout the story. When editors and publishers urge a writer to "begin at the beginning," they mean that the writer should start the novel with a compelling event that creates a sense of conflict, which ultimately changes the course of the protagonist's life.

In the case of *Outlander*, the hook takes place when Claire, trapped inside some mysterious ruins, is catapulted back in time two centuries. She marries another man in that distant time, and her complacent life is shattered. Now she must question her own integrity and sanity, not to mention the very existence of her surroundings.

The "something" could also be the opportunity to sign up on a whaling vessel skippered by a strange, obsessive man *or* the news that the protagonist's parents have gotten a divorce *or* the sudden termination of one's job. In other words, something big takes place which forces the protagonist into a period of growth and transition in his life: He must make some sort of decision...or choose not to. Sometimes the protagonist is dragged, kicking and screaming, into this conflict. It takes him completely by surprise. Sometimes the conflict begins slowly, perhaps only with a rumor of marital strife or company layoffs, then grows steadily and becomes more menacing, until, in the later stages of the novel, it becomes the most important, all-consuming concern in the protagonist's life.

Remember, this initial compelling event often takes place quite early in the novel (and some genre fiction publishers demand that it do so). In many cases, the novel may begin with the compelling event, even before the reader knows anything about the protagonist.

C. The protagonist reacts to the initial event, making a decision for better or worse, or choosing to delay the decision. For example, Claire chooses to abet and follow a group of semi-barbarous Highlanders. (Actually, she has little choice.) As she becomes emotionally attached to the Highlander she is forced to marry, her decision-making process is hampered by feelings of love, and she becomes embroiled in life-threatening activities. This leads us to...

The Middle

In most cases, the plot in a conventional novel develops because of a central conflict which causes the action to rise during the course of the piece. That is, as the protagonist reacts to events and the consequences of his actions (often complicated by the actions of other characters), the plot becomes more complicated and tension is heightened. Conflicts – in the form of events, circumstances and secondary characters – exert more pressure on the protagonist, creating more suspense and causing the reader to wonder what will happen next.

A. The operative word in the middle of a novel is "more." The protagonist is confronted with more – more conflict, characters, more events, more decisions to be made, more intense feelings, more reactions and reflections on reactions and their consequences. Of course, there will be interludes in the rising action as characters converse and reflect and go about their everyday business, just as real people do.

B. Gradually, the pressure created by the central conflict, as well as minor conflicts, builds up, forcing the protagonist to make *more difficult* decisions. As a result, more and more lives or other important factors depend on the protagonist's actions. For example, Claire's central conflict is whether to stay with her 18th century husband or return to her 20th century mate. Even when she decides to keep her Highland hubby, she has difficulty protecting him and herself from the dangers of life without modern medicine or civil rights. Will she decide to try to prevent certain historical events from happening in order to protect her second husband and her friends...or will she allow them to face certain death in order to preserve the fabric of history? How will her decisions impact her life? Her morals? Her concepts of space and time, values and expectations, truth, love, change and permanence?

Consider this situation: An accountant with a neat, orderly life is visiting his parents, who are not getting on well together. When a heated quarrel breaks out between the two, the accountant tries to resolve the argument using logic and reason, only to find out that his father has a mistress. Just as he begins to restore order between his mom and dad, all hell breaks loose again as his father's mistress stops by the house. At this point, all sorts of possibilities for plot abound. The protagonist may choose to resist his father and the mistress and move in with his mother in order to help her through this ordeal. Or he may find the chaos of the situation so fascinating and taboo that he chooses to run off with the mistress himself, at her suggestion, thus throwing his life into further disorder. No matter what choice he makes, he will have to confront his own discomfort and uncertainty about permanence in his life and the untidy condition of mankind in general.

C. As events pile up, the writer must take care to prevent a linear, "episodic" feel to the story by emphasizing the central conflict. The purpose of all this pressure and complication, of course, is to lead us to the resolution of that central conflict or, as in *The Remains of the Day*, to avoid a resolution that seems inevitable. Now it is time to consider...

The End

The conflict has been well established, the characters are poised for a final act or set of actions, and suspense is tearing the reader apart: The time has come to sail the novel into its last harbor toward resolution or intentional lack of resolution.

A. Traditionally, fiction concludes when the conflict in the story is resolved. The protagonist dies...marries his beloved...wins the war...gets the job...fails and becomes a drunkard...realizes he can never break away from his narrow, safe life – whatever. Resolution is, classically, the release of tension built up over the course of the story. Minor conflicts may have separate resolutions. Also, many fine stories and novels end with unresolved conflict (*The Tin Drum, The Golden Notebooks*). Genre fiction, including romance, horror and science fiction, almost always ends with a satisfying resolution.

B. The climax is traditionally the scene in which the central conflict of the novel is resolved – or fails to resolve. It is the height or culmination of the rising action. (Small wonder that the word "climax" describes both this novelistic device and the height of human passion.) The climax in *Outlander*, for example, occurs when Claire cures her deathly ill husband by pretending to be his nemesis, thus inspiring his will to fight against his illness.

C. After the climax, action and tension nearly cease to exist, though the characters may tidy up odds and ends in the *denouement*, or descending action, following the climax, which often takes the form of an epilogue. In *Outlander*, the denouement depicts the Highlander's gradual recovery (including the performance of his conjugal duties) and a scene in which Claire reveals that she is pregnant. In *Moby Dick*, the climax occurs when the whale (in his first appearance, very near the end of the book) destroys Ahab's ship, perhaps indicating how the works and efforts of man are no more than toys in the face of raw nature. Ishmael's reduction to flotsam and his subsequent rescue form the brief denouement.

In summary, then, the plot of a conventional novel begins when something happens to cause conflict or put pressure on the protagonist. The protagonist's decisions following that event will increase tension on the character, or make the action rise, so that the reader feels an increasing sense of suspense and stress. The conventional climax and resolution represent a sudden release of the tension that has been building up, like a kettle full of steam, during the course of hundreds of pages.

Of course, not all novels are structured in this manner. Nevertheless, it pays for the beginning writer to understand how and why this very basic and successful plot structure works.

CHAPTER EIGHT

ELEMENT: SUBPLOTS AND SECONDARY CHARACTERS

S UBPLOTS AND SECONDARY characters are some of the tools
a writer uses to enhance characterization and plot. Just as a carpenter
must know how to use hammers, nails and levels, the writer must know how
to use subplots and characters.

Plot and protagonist are the main story and main character in fiction, but they are certainly not the only stories or the only characters.
While most short stories have only one plot and a few select characters,
a novel has the time and space to be luxuriant. Novels with a huge scope
covering many years and/or generations, such as Tolstoy's *War and
Peace* or Gabriel Garcia-Marquez's *One Hundred Years of Solitude*, will
contain many subplots in- volving secondary, tertiary and even less
important characters.

Tight Focus Versus Broad Focus

In general, the tighter the focus of a novel, the fewer the subplots and
characters required to advance the plot. For example, Hemingway's *The Old
Man and the Sea* has only two (unnamed) characters of any note, and the
only stories not related to the old man's capture of the "great fish" are revealed through his dreams. On the other hand, a very long novel or series
of related novels (such as *The Raj Quartet*, a series of four books by Paul
Scott) may have a very broad focus that involves a huge cast of characters,
all interacting on some level.

Some of these characters may seem quite removed in time or space, but
the skilled writer will bring these people and the events in their lives together.
The Raj Quartet, for example, begins with an act of *suttee*, or ritual suicide.
This is not explained until the end of the third book, as the imperialistic Raj,
the British colonial society imposed on India, begins to deteriorate. In the
final book, characters whose lives would never mingle under the Raj are
thrown together by the violent forces of revolution.

A Matter of Purpose

A beginning writer might do well to consider how her novel's subplots and minor characters serve her novel's main plot and protagonist. In other words, what is the purpose of subplots and secondary characters in any given novel?

In general, subplots lend depth and realism to the central plot, often offering a counterbalance or parallel. Many historical romances, for example, dwell on the developing romance between the heroine and the male protagonist, but also include a parallel romance, perhaps between the heroine's maid and the hero's closest friend. This secondary romance may be used to heighten or contrast the primary romance. For example, the maid's beloved may be fatally wounded in battle, and she must decide whether to abandon him or kill both him and herself. Obviously, the heroine cannot be in this position, yet this event will certainly have a great impact on her and her regard for the power of love.

Is the subplot helping to develop the plot? Perhaps some apparently minor event has extensive ramifications. For instance, in Michael Crichton's novel, *The Andromeda Strain*, a scientist hides the fact that she is suffering from epilepsy. This is important, since the disease causes her to ignore crucial evidence in the search for a deadly virus.

Of course, subplots may not be necessary. Fiction with a tight focus tends to move faster and be easier to follow than long, sprawling novels with scores of characters and many subplots.

Red Herrings

An unnecessary or misleading subplot is called a "red herring." Be careful to avoid subplots that do not advance character or plot. Sometimes the reader will become embroiled in a subplot, involving primary or secondary characters, only to find that the subplot is basically unnecessary, or that it only confuses the reader and ultimately leads to no resolution. It is as if the writer began to write another story, then abandoned it midstream and returned to the main plot. Many beginning writers fall prey to the temptation to tell too many characters' stories in a single novel. This is difficult to do well, since it is hard to maintain focus on numerous stories.

In one case, an enthusiastic young writer began to tell the story of a man who was abused as a child. In the middle of the story, the writer introduced a rafting trip which the protagonist organized. Suddenly the thrust of the story shifted away from the character's life of abuse to the adventure of the trip. This tangential story continued for several chapters, then suddenly ended and was never revived. In fact, the rafting adventure was never mentioned again throughout the entire novel. What was the purpose of the rafting story? There was no purpose. The writer was merely seduced into pursuing a blind alley, and when she realized it was not advancing the main story, she simply dropped it. This material could have been used to highlight, compare or contrast the man's past experiences, but instead it was simply wasted. The rafting story was a red herring, causing a delay in the *real* story and irritation for the reader.

In some genres, chiefly mystery and espionage, red herrings may actually help develop the plot. The protagonist of a murder mystery, for example, may follow a false lead for a while before realizing that it leads away from the solution of the mystery, not toward it. In this case, the reader is not confused, for he has no more information than the protagonist. The reader and the protagonist are both solving the case at the same time, and the protagonist will be just as disappointed as the reader when the scent gets cold.

Using Secondary Characters

Secondary characters, when not involved in subplots, are generally used to help develop the main characters and plot. Friends, spouses, lovers, servants, parents, siblings, employers and so on are all in a position to influence the protagonist, either to his benefit or his detriment. Secondary characters put pressure on the character – directly or indirectly, wittingly or unwittingly – to take a stand, make a decision or take action.

Consider a protagonist whose young daughter has been kidnapped. The abductor is, of course, unconcerned about the personality of the mother. Yet that woman is undoubtedly going to grow in persistence and strength of personality as a result of the kidnapper's action.

Antagonists are not the only secondary characters who influence the protagonist. A well-meaning friend, for example, may encourage the stricken mother to take every action possible to rescue her daughter. Her father, however, may be worried for the woman's safety and persuade her from getting personally involved in the investigation. The relationship between mother and daughter is also worth exploring. And what about the child's father?

In the end, however, it is the mother – the protagonist – who will react, respond, change, grow and develop as a result of the actions and beliefs of the secondary characters. This bears out a rule of thumb: While a complicated novel may have many secondary characters, or even several main characters, the novel ultimately will be only one or two people's story.

Some publishers use secondary characters as a sort of yardstick to measure the quality of writing. They *expect* protagonists to be gripping, often larger-than-life characters, but they like to see other characters who, if not fully developed, are at least well-drawn – colorful, perhaps even eccentric people whom the reader will not quickly forget. The works of Steinbeck, Hemingway, McCullers and Faulkner are full of such memorable secondary characters, as are the works of Stephen King, Victoria Holt, and most other successful genre fiction writers.

Minor Roles

Tertiary, or ancillary, characters usually have a much less dramatic part in a novel and far less influence on the protagonist than do secondary characters. Tertiary characters are the "bit players" who fill merely practical or logistical roles: the messenger who brings the bad news, the neighbor who discovers the body, the policeman who helps the protagonist extricate herself from a car crash, the housekeeper, the stablehand, the youngest child, the taxi-driver...and on and on. It is almost never a good idea to give these characters a point of view, that is, a personal perspective or observation on any aspect of the story, unless the viewpoint is expressed through dialogue and is essential to plot or character development. In many cases, it is not even wise to name these characters, unless they appear rather often.

A Secondary Character Flaw

It's not uncommon for a beginning writer to make a serious mistake and fall in love with secondary or even tertiary characters. This is not hard to understand, since secondary characters are often simpler, less *difficult* than the more realistic, more complicated protagonist, and are therefore easier to write about. (What's more, if they are well drawn, they are also colorful, eccentric and not easy to forget.) They tend to lack the deep reflections, problems, troubled backgrounds, and painful challenges that are the very factors that force a character to grow and change.

One beginning writer wrote a six-hundred-page historical novel, which we'll call *Pel's Kingdom*, scrupulously avoiding the title character, who ultimately unites several warring kingdoms. According to the novel's synopsis, Pel is the main character, and indeed he should be. However, the writer's main focus is on a spritely gang of less important characters – Pel's friends, a knight, a dwarf, a fair maiden, a youthful king, a tribal chieftain, an evil king, an evil counselor, an evil general...well, you get the idea. Almost everyone *except* the main character is vividly drawn and has several scenes to himself, in which he expresses his views on various aspects of various cultures and the upcoming confrontation between two warring factions.

Interestingly enough, the main topic of conversation among the lesser characters is Pel and his amazing potential as a leader. Pel himself is presented sporadically throughout *Kingdom*, actually appearing in about one third of the pages. Even then, more colorful secondary characters often "crowd him out" of his own story, interrupting it with their antics. Even a critical battle scene near the end of the novel is seen through the eyes of a minor character. In the last chapter, in which one of Pel's foes becomes his ally, Pel is a passive character: It is his erstwhile foe who makes the crucial decision to join forces with Pel. While the writer intended to craft several more books in this series, she was off to a poor start by letting her secondary characters bully and overshadow her main character.

Ghosts

Another problem with secondary characters is that they sometimes materialize as ghosts.

Consider this passage from a novice writer's manuscript:

"Professor Jackson?"

Jackson looked up from his desk and smiled. "Yes?"

"I want to know why you canceled the study group this afternoon. I have some questions, and so do my friends."

Jackson stroked his jaw. He didn't remember canceling the study session. Had his secretary done so, without his instructions?

What is wrong with this passage? The protagonist seems to be Professor Jackson, but who the heck is he talking to?

The second, unseen, unnamed character is a "ghost," a faceless voice that is never identified, or is identified long after his entrance. In this case, the ghost is probably a student, but the reader doesn't know this for sure until much later in the scene.

In order for us to visualize the scene and understand it, we *must* know who is talking to Jackson. This is only logical, since Jackson, the POV character, would be aware that someone is standing in front of him, addressing him. Jackson would either recognize the student or ask him his name, but Jackson would never *not* take some mental note of the person. If he could not see his visitor but only hear him, Jackson would certainly look around for the person, wonder about his identity and perhaps recognize his voice.

Ghosts tend to occur when the beginning writer has not developed a strong protagonist or an attached point of view, capable of relaying information and thoughts to the reader.

In general, strong secondary characters are an important supporting cast for a novel's protagonist. They act as his foils, antagonists, love interests and confidants, lending color, depth and interest to the plot. In the same way, subplots support the main plot and give the writing a richer texture. It is only when secondary plots and characters get out of control and begin to supplant the protagonist and the central conflict that a work of fiction is headed for major problems.

CHAPTER NINE

ELEMENT: SETTING — TIME AND PLACE

FICTION TELLS A story about someone, and that story takes place in one or more specific locales and at a certain time or times. Where and when you put your characters – their time and place – reveal a lot about those characters and are sometimes almost as important as the characters themselves.

Writers are frequently told to "Write what you know," meaning, write from personal experience only. If such were the case, we would have no writers of science fiction, historical novels, fantasy stories or other material which no one can experience directly. There is no reason that a beginning writer cannot exercise his imagination to craft a story in a remote time or place, or even a non-existent time or place. Of course, to do so, the writer will have to research the time, place and lifestyle of the era he chooses to write about in order to create a believable backdrop for his story. He must "know" it, not personally, but vicariously, through the power of his imagination.

Establishing the Dream

John Gardner wrote of the writer's need to establish the "fictional dream." By this he meant that the reader becomes so immersed in good fiction that she believes (while she is reading) that the events described in the fiction are actually happening to real people in a real place.

In order to accomplish the fictional dream, a writer must "set up" a time and place for the dream to happen. A battle scene, for example, should frighten and excite the reader; he can smell the smoke, taste the blood and hear the clang of swords and the whinnies of terrified horses. He knows the battle is taking place in, say, Concord, Massachusetts, and he knows that the protagonist has been leading a troop of Continental soldiers and has just been pinned by his fallen horse. The reader also knows that the battle belongs just where it should be in the time span of history and the story itself. Events have led up to this moment, or else it has been firmly established as a memory, or flashback, of a specific character.

SETTING: PLACE

When we think of setting, most of us probably think of place, but place is a pretty large concept. "Europe" is a place; so is Russia. So is Moscow. So is Red Square. So is the courtyard in front of the Russian White House. So is a bench on that courtyard. Consider too that "place" can refer to the positioning of a character, for example, which side of that bench he is occupying and how he is sitting. This is called positioning. For now, let's concentrate on the large picture of placement, as opposed to positioning.

A skilled writer will let the reader know very early on *specifically* where the story is taking place, both in broad and narrow terms. "Broad" might refer to a country, state or city, whereas "narrow" might refer to a specific location within that large place, such as a restaurant, a forest, or a house.

The writer will furnish the reader with enough details so that the reader feels as if he is in that place, smelling its smells and seeing its sights. On the other hand, the writer shouldn't clutter up the story with indiscriminate pieces of description relating to setting. If describing Red Square, for example, the writer might focus on a few key images: colorful onion domes, the freezing temperature, the scurrying people dressed in fur. It would be distracting and frustrating, at least when establishing setting, to launch into a long history of Red Square and its place in Russian history.

An excellent example of establishing setting in a few lines is the opening scene from the novel *Native Son* by Richard Wright. From the word go, the reader is involved in Bigger's world, a tiny ghetto apartment, as he and his family chase a rat around every corner of the room. Wright wastes no time letting his readers know exactly where they are and where the protagonist is, and he does it in active terms that grip the reader like a fist. Strong sensory images, such as the greasy smell of the room, the shouts of the terrified family, and a description of the dead rat, establish a strong setting the reader will not forget throughout the entire novel.

Research and Setting

As you might expect, establishing a sense of place, both narrow and broad, sometimes requires a certain amount of research. If you're writing about the Battle of Concord, for example, you'd better know what people wore and what weapons they used, as well as the physical setup of the battlefield. If you describe a grove of hickory trees, for instance, make sure that such trees grew in that region at that time.

Some research can be done in the library. Other settings will require actual visits to the place itself. Many narrow locations pose no problems. Most Americans have been to and could easily go to diners, skating rinks, stadiums, small towns, farms and the like. If you are writing about a specific setting, such as Yankee Stadium, or a more exotic setting, such as Yellow Stone Park, you might consider visiting the place or at least reading about it and viewing many pictures and videos about it. Broad places, such as foreign countries, will provide an even greater challenge for research, but it's important to describe the setting and create a fairly realistic backdrop for your characters if you hope to create a sense of reality in your fiction. Readers seem to have an uncanny ability to sense when a detail is out of place: a tiger in an African jungle, for example, or potatoes in ancient Ireland. This sense of appropriateness is as important in science fiction and fantasy as it is in period fiction, westerns or mass market novels.

If One Setting is Good, Then More Must Be Better

Television and cinema have apparently misled beginning writers into the belief that the more exotic locales the better, that interesting places can somehow substitute for developed characters and compelling stories. Film is a visual medium and can establish a change in scene in one shot. Fiction, however, requires the use of consistent, accurate details to develop the setting.

Abrupt changes to many locales tend to confuse the reader, and it is better to avoid zipping your characters off to an exciting new place *unless they have a good reason to go there.* In one manuscript evaluated at the agency, the locale keep switching from Paris to London to New York to Cairo...all without purpose or intent. The characters might as well have stayed in Philadelphia for all the good a change in setting did.

In some ways, madly changing locales is simply a variation on tossing unnecessary sex scenes, car chases and murders into your work. Exotic settings and glamorous details can never substitute for intriguing characters and sound plots.

SETTING: POSITIONING

Setting is more than a physical description of a place. As on the stage, setting also refers to the space that objects and characters occupy, that is, the "set." Beginning writers usually understand the importance of place but frequently overlook the importance of positioning a character in that place. Since the reader cannot see your characters, she must be able to visualize where they are at any given time. This tends to change constantly, since people tend to move about quite a bit, and establishing position is important to avoid confusing the reader.

To illustrate positioning, let's examine this passage from a manuscript edited at the agency:

> Johnny Taylor, wearing shorts and a loose T-shirt, stood beside his sister Wilma. The children watched with smiles on their faces as the skiff slowly pulled away from the dock and plowed into the river.

Where are the two kids? Did you realize they are on the boat? Unfortunately, the writer gives his readers no information in this paragraph to help us deduce that they are on the boat. Instead, he seems to indicate they are standing somewhere on shore, perhaps, watching the boat glide into the water. This confusion could be cleared up simply by rewriting the first line to read: "Johnny Taylor...stood on the deck beside his sister Wilma."

Now read this passage from the same manuscript:

> The screen showed the image of Luke Skywalker slashing his laser sword at a hulking Darth Vader. John Taylor glanced up at the screen, catching the action for just an instant. Science fiction movies were Senator Billings' favorite.
>
> John, the senator and his eldest son sat in the rear of the private theater, not watching the movie. The only reason they were in the theater was to get some private moments away from the guards who swarmed over the mansion.

How can the reader visualize just where these folks are? Obviously, the writer must first establish that his characters are in a theater before John can look at a screen or view what is on it. To repair the sense of setting and sequence in this passage, the writer might recast it in a more chronological order, something like this:

> John Taylor sat in the dark theater, Senator Billings on one side and the senator's eldest son on the other. As Billings conferred with his son, John glanced toward the screen and saw Luke Skywalker swing his laser sword at Darth Vadar. John quickly looked away. They were not there for entertainment, he reminded himself, though the senator could not resist running his favorite movie, with the sound off. They were there for privacy. The guards swarming over

the mansion would not think to look for John and his companions in the secluded theater.

Before writing a scene, try to visualize your characters in it, particularly your main character. Visualize where he is, why he's there, what he is doing, how and where he is located. Ask yourself what his state of mind is and how closely he is relating to other characters in the scene. This exercise will help you write the scene and position the characters so that the reader can clearly visualize every important detail.

Tableau Versus Scene

Setting is most likely to change after a space break or from chapter to chapter, or whenever a locale changes. Therefore, be certain to let the reader know where the protagonist is in relationship to other people and to objects in the setting. (Remember Johnny, the boy who was supposed to be on a boat but wasn't?)

This does *not* mean that you should set up a tableau. A tableau is simply a list of where characters are standing, sitting or lying, sometimes in relationship to each other. Sometimes such a description may be necessary, but often it is not. A tableau is static and gives the impression of a snapshot which has no purpose other than to relay logistical information. The following is a tableau:

> The four friends made themselves at home in the   forest clearing. Jim leaned against a tall snag; Lilly was sitting by the brook near the snag; Tom crouched a few feet away, setting up the tent, and Judith knelt about a yard away from him, poking a stick at a big brown beetle.

You can establish positioning and setting better by creating a scene than by writing a tableau. In a scene, the writer closely examines the conversation and actions of the characters present, paying special attention to the thoughts of the point of view (POV) character who *observes* the scene, trying to make sense of it. Dialogue almost always helps establish a scene, since it reveals the feelings of the non-POV characters, that is, the characters whose thoughts are not shared with the reader.

Here is the camping scenario above, rewritten in an attached point of view:

> Jim leaned against the tall pine snag, feeling the roughness of its

bark cut into his skin. He considered helping Tom set up the tent: His friend seemed to be having a pretty hard time of it, crouching in the dust, driving tent pegs into the sandy soil and swearing as he struck his fingers instead of the peg. "Need some help?"

Tom shook his head grimly. "Nope. I can do it myself." Jim shrugged. Sometimes Tom's fierce sense of independence got the best of him.

"What's this?" said Judith. Jim looked at her, kneeling in the dirt and pine needles a few feet from   the tent, poking a stick at a fat brown beetle. It was just like her, he thought, to do anything to avoid her husband's struggles with the tent.

"Scarab," drawled Jim.

"How about this?" It was Lilly. He hadn't noticed her sitting on the bank of the little stream that meandered through the clearing. She was holding a big crayfish that seemed on the verge of pinching her finger. It would serve her right.

Now the passage is not a tableau depicting merely the physical position of people, but a scene in which people are doing things, including communicating and reflecting. The reader knows just where these people are and has some idea of their personalities. One could go on to let Jim notice physical details of the setting – smells, types of plants, sounds of birds, etc. – to establish place more firmly.

On the other hand, a writer has to be careful to avoid chronicling the characters' every move. There's no reason, for example, to write something like the following: "Sasha walked down the street, turned a corner and continued down the block. At the end of the street he walked into a tavern, sat down at a bar and crossed his legs, picking up a napkin and idly twirling it in his hands." Such a blow-by-blow account of a character's movements could go on forever, adding nothing to plot or character development.

SETTING: TIME

Not all beginning writers realize that time is part of setting. Time refers not only to the period that the piece is set in (Ancient Rome, The War Between the States, Edwardian England, The Great Depression) but also to the way times passes in the story. Let's examine each of these entities separately.

PERIOD

Again, some research may be necessary to create a realistic picture of the period of a given setting. For example, writers should avoid anachronisms (unless these are an intentional part of the story). Even Shakespeare made the mistake of providing Ancient Romans with handkerchiefs. Also, be aware that some physical features of certain places did not exist in earlier times. Many of the beautiful heather-covered moors of the Scottish Highlands, for example, were covered with pine forests up until the late 18th century.

Even more important than the physical look of a period are the mores of the time, whether the setting is pre-historic Africa or San Francisco in the 1960s. At the agency, we have encountered a number of characters from historical periods who acted as if they stepped off the street in Pittsburgh just the other day. These include the 18th century farmer who was cheered when he struck a lady in the face in public...a young woman who gave birth to a child out of wedlock in the 19th century and was embraced and accepted by her community...and the Anglo-Saxon wife who was unfaithful to her husband, yet was accepted by him with dignity and understanding. In fact, all these people would have been highly censured by their society, ostracized or even put to death. Be certain to study the morals, ethics and values of the time you are writing about to avoid creating modern-day characters in period costumes.

Obscenities are always a little tricky to use in any age, but are more difficult in period pieces than in contemporary fiction. Nowadays, obscenities are much less shocking to most people than they would have been to, say, 19th century "respectable" people. (Of course, there are exceptions in every age. If your writing is set in a tavern in Elizabethan England, perhaps obscenities would be the order of the day.) Generally, beginning writers use obscenities as shorthand to indicate a certain kind of person or situation, or as shock elements to get the reader's attention. Unfortunately, the reader may pay attention to the obscenity – and nothing else on the page.

One writer submitted a novel set in 19th century Alabama that began with a scene in which a man stood in a town square, shouting obscenities. This man was tolerated and more or less ignored by the other characters in the novel. In the reality of this period, even making allowances for a fairly "rough and tumble" town in the deep South, the man would probably have been locked up for "indecent displays."

Switching Time Periods

If you thought that constantly moving characters about from one exotic locale to another was confusing, consider moving characters about willy-nilly from one time period to the next. Of course, some stories depend on time travel – *Outlander*, for one, as well as *Star Rover* by Jack London, and much science fiction, fantasy and young adult literature. Keep in mind, however, that sudden switches from, say, ancient Egypt to 1990 in America must be carefully set up in terms of scene and setting, and there must be some unifying factors which join both disparate times.

CHRONOLOGICAL ORDER

Every adult knows the concept of chronological time and chronological sequence. However, some beginning writers seem to forget these very important methods of organization or intentionally ignore them.

Generally, conventional novels are written in chronological order. An event happens at a certain time and is followed by events as they take place day to day, year to year. This allows the reader to easily follow the events in the plot as they unfold. Many writers employ flashbacks – or a character's recollection of events – to provide important facts that took place before the events of the novel began. In its simplest terms, a novel about the Civil War might begin with the attack on Fort Sumter, continue with the battles of Shiloh, Bull Run, Antietam, Gettysburg, Chattanooga and end with a scene at the courthouse at Appomattox. At any time, however, a main character may remember her childhood on the plantation or any other experience that took place earlier...if it's important to plot or character development. (More on flashbacks in our discussion of conventions.)

Writers who consciously try to be "different" or "innovative" sometimes invert the chronological order of events in their writings or structure events so that they follow no sort of chronology at all. When done well, this can produce a sort of dream-like quality, as in Doris Lessing's novel, *Briefing for a Descent into Hell.* When done without an understanding of the way chronological order functions in a novel, disjointed order can result in some very disorganized, hard-to-follow manuscripts.

Sequence

Closely allied to the idea of chronological order is the concept of sequence: Many events happen in a given order, with the clear, logical sequence of a man making a sandwich. First he takes all the food he needs from the refrigerator, then butters two slices of bread. He then adds meat, cheese, lettuce and so on to the buttered bread, puts the two halves together and eats the sandwich. Logical, simple and easy to understand.

But when sequence is awry, writing becomes illogical, and sense goes out the window. Consider this passage from a manuscript reviewed at the agency:

> Ted surveyed the park. It was a cold autumn day, and he was sad to realize he was probably the only soul in the park. He walked over to a flock of ducks in the deserted little man-made lagoon. The birds were biting and rushing each other, squabbling over bits of bread on the water's surface. Ted reached into his pocket for the last half of his sandwich and tossed it to the noisy ducks.

Because Ted is alone, the ducks cannot be fighting over bread until he throws it in the water. This passage illustrates that events out of chronological sequence also sound illogical.

Sometimes sequence is so confused that one cannot easily tell just what is happening when, as in this example:

> Elvira stood at one side of the winding street which led to the compound where the arriving dignitaries would be congregating to greet each other. It was minutes until the beginning of the international debates which were scheduled to begin later this evening, after a formal dinner.

So many potential events are expected, each before or after another with none dependent on each other, that the reader cannot keep track of them, even with a scorecard. The major purpose of writing is to communicate, but the above passage does just the opposite: It confuses and frustrates the reader without a reason.

Sometimes sequence is related to order, either natural or man-made. For instance, read this paragraph by a beginning writer.

> Roderick's apartment was in a large, old apartment building that housed a doctor, two accountants, and several musicians. A long staircase led up to the second floor, where he lived. The names of the occupants were marked on the doors with tarnished brass plaques. In the lobby stood two ancient India rubber trees and an assortment of dusty silk flowers.

This description suffers from an abnormal flow, contrary to the normal experiences of most people. On approaching a building, we first view the outside, not giving much thought to the inside or the occupants, even if we happen to live there. (The next time you approach your house, see whether you are thinking about its exterior or interior.) Then we would enter the lobby, proceed up stairs or an elevator, and probably down hallways to our apartment. In the example, however, we concentrate on the inside before we examine the outside, never really enter the building, go up a staircase and apparently down a hallway, then *end up* at the lobby at the bottom of the stairs, defying all logic.

This paragraph could be rewritten in a much stronger, more effective way:

> Roderick walked up to his apartment building, shuddering at the sight of the worn cement walls and peeling gray paint. *Looks like a prison*, he thought. He flung open the door and stepped into the lobby, musty with the smells of old potted plants, dusty silk flower arrangements and long-gone occupants. Climbing the long flight of stairs that led to his apartment, he slid his hand along the walnut bannister, the one touch of elegance in the entire building. On the second floor he made his way down a dark corridor, glimps- ing now and then the dull gleam of tarnished brass name plaques on the doors he passed. At last he came to his door: P. Roderick Simpson. He unlocked the door, turned the loose doorknob and stepped inside.

Now consider this passage:

> Red turned and sprinted down the steps, calling to his aunt as he ran, "I'll fetch the doc!" He rushed into the barn so fast he fright- ened Baby, his big roan mare. The horse rolled her eyes as he slipped the headstall over her ears and slung the saddle onto her back.
>
> "Sorry, girl," he whispered, tightening up the cinch. Each small task seemed to take an eternity, and his fingers moved like lumps of lead. "I know you're tired, but we gotta help Milly." He jumped into the saddle and urged Baby out of her stall, into the barn, then over the threshold. Once in the yard, he drummed his heels against the mare's flanks and rode her through the corral at a dead gallop. He didn't stop to open the gate but jumped right over it, the top pole brushing against the roan's ankles.

Many actions take place in this short section, and they all happen in a logical sequence. Red tells his aunt he'll get help (so we assume someone is ill or injured), runs to the barn, where he bridles and saddles his horse, mounts and leaves in great haste. It is important that the reader visualize what is happening in this passage, and it is important that he can visualize exactly where the protagonist is and exactly what he is doing. In this case, the motive for Red's haste is also clear: Someone needs a doctor's skills. The chronological and logical order of events piled up against each other like boxcars create a sense of urgency. Imagine what would happen if these events were not in strict chronological sequence.

Conditional Time

The conditional time ("Each Wednesday he would ride into town," or "Every spring we used to go to Glacier National Park") is a technique which can be used to establish a character's everyday life. For example, "Normally, Sarah would spend her Saturday mornings at the Teatime Cafe, eating a leisurely breakfast while talking to her friend Kelly. But this Saturday was different: Alan was in town."

There is nothing inherently wrong with the use of conditional time, and it is useful to a degree. But it can certainly be misused, especially when novice writers try to substitute it for the ordinary past tense. While stories in the past tense progress naturally in a chronological order, conditional time involves keeping time static. There is no progression in time in the conditional state.

Writing in conditional time seems to set characters' actions in cement. Once you establish how a character gets through his day, you have set up a continuum that is hard to break, and to introduce a compelling event, the writer must break the "normal" way his protagonist does things. In addition, the conditional time encourages long narrative sections and discourages scenes. Consider this example by a young writer:

Every day David would rise at 7:00 sharp, take a shower and get ready for work. He would take his lunch with him in a paper bag and stop at the corner convenience store for a soda pop and chocolate bar. Then he would drive to the factory and spend the morning applying enamel to window frames. Sometimes he would talk to the other people on the line, but mostly he would work in silence. At lunchtime he would wolf down his food and spend the rest of the time watching soaps in the employee lounge.

The passage goes on to describe what David would do in the afternoon and evening, all in the same plodding timeframe. How much more natural this situation would sound if the writer simply set up scenes showing David at work on a normal Monday, for example, right before the occurrence of the compelling event (which in this case is the breakup with his girlfriend).

Most editors discourage writing fiction in conditional time, except for the odd passage now and then which contrasts normality with unusual events, such as the first paragraph of this section.

CHAPTER TEN

ELEMENT: THEME, VOICE AND TONE

THEME

THEME IS WHAT you say in your writing, not in the words, but behind the words. Themes are ideas which, in the best writing, are never overtly explained, but implied. Consider some themes from great literature:

— Man's impotence against nature and his arrogance at thinking his needs and obsessions matter in the scheme of the cosmos (*Moby Dick*)
— The destructive side of passion (sexual and emotional) and how flaws, inadequacies and limitations define our capabilities and relationships (*The Sun Also Rises*)
— The perilously thin line between reality and madness, and the chaos and cruelty that result when madness is postulated as reality (*The Tin Drum*)
— The nobility, depravity and resilience of the human spirit when faced with a series of disasters (*The Grapes of Wrath*)
— How easy it is to strip away the thin veneer of civilization which hides mankind's inherently savage nature (*Lord of the Flies, The Heart of Darkness, A Clockwork Orange*)

All of these famous novels are more than just a combination of fascinating characters and intriguing plotlines. They all reflect some universal truths which give the reader a deeper insight into the ways of the world and the tragedies and triumphs of the human condition.

Theme, as it is often understood, is the main idea of a novel, story or poem. However, this is a very confining definition. Theme is not something that is "tacked on" to a piece of fiction; it is an integral part of the work, without which the entire construct – no matter how great the plotting, setting or character development – would fall apart.

A theme develops as a story and protagonist develop, and the job of the writer is to lead the reader to uncover the theme as the protagonist's story progresses. If handled well, a theme (or sometimes several themes) ties together many if not all events and characters in the story and gives them a rich emotional and intellectual meaning.

Great literature reflects profound truths in brilliant, profound ways, yet one need not write great literature in order to thread a strong, insightful theme throughout one's novel or story. Ideas and themes which frequently arise in genre fiction include:

—The differences between love, lust, passion and affection, and how each can lead to ruin or validation (Romance, Literary)

—The conflict between good and evil, as elements inside one individual, or represented by kingdoms, races, species or supernatural beings (Fantasy/Adventure, Horror)

—The war between the sexes and the inherent differences which lead to that war (Romance)

—How appearances can be deceiving and how truth itself can be slippery and obscure (Just about any genre)

—The resourcefulness of the human mind, especially when pushed to the limit (Espionage, Western, Mystery)

—The disastrous consequences of tinkering with natural laws and the environment (Techno-thrillers, Science Fiction)

Establishing Theme

There are more themes possible in fiction than can be listed here, and virtually all are potentially moving and illuminating. Once a beginning writer has created some notion of her plot and characters, she may ponder what sort of theme her novel reveals, that is, what insights does it give regarding human nature, and how does it reveal those insights. It may even be a good idea to write down the theme you intend to use and consult it from time to time, just to keep it prominent in your mind. However, one should always remember the following: Plot and character should not be manipulated to demonstrate theme. Theme should flow naturally from the events of the plot and the development of the protagonist.

The key to developing a strong theme is to develop strong characters, for they are the people whose lives illustrate universal truths. As characters struggle against obstacles, the characters learn more about themselves, others and life in general. The reader, vicariously sharing the characters' struggles, will grasp the deeper meaning in your story, for he has *lived through* the same triumphant or tragic experiences as your characters.

Lectures and Rhetoric

Creating a theme in your writing is not the same as lecturing to the reader. When you alert the reader to the significance of events or a character's reaction to events, you are not creating theme but merely intruding in your own writing. For example, avoid obvious attempts at creating themes, such as "Bennet clasped the staff, a symbol of the struggle he would have to undertake to free his country."

Instead, let the character's actions speak for themselves. Let characters act in ways that demonstrate their personalities or reveal their thoughts and growing awareness of the human condition. A rewrite of the sample sentence above might read: "Bennet clasped the worn staff, smooth with the oil from his father's hands. Tears began to form in his eyes as he thought of his father, lying dead on the battlefield at Arles. *I will avenge you, Papa,* he thought, *and France as well.*"

In *The Old Man and the Sea*, Hemingway never *tells* the reader that the old man is searching for meaning and a sense of worth in his life as he struggles against the vast forces of nature; the old man is simply searching for a big fish in the open sea. It is the *reader* who is able to draw the deeper conclusion throughout the story, based on the old man's actions and his reactions to events in the novella.

By the same token, beginning writers should avoid *dogma* or rhetoric, unless creating a dogmatic, rhetorical character. Including a personal lecture on the evils of censorship is not creating a theme. (It is simply authorial intrusion, which will be discussed in detail in a later section.) To successfully deal with the theme of the corrupting nature of censorship, a writer might develop a protagonist who fights against censorship, perhaps a dedicated journalist, author or teacher.

One first-time writer, whose stated purpose for writing her novel was to alert readers to "the immorality of child abuse" and the "lack of ethics among the psychiatric community," seemed to forget she was writing a novel. The theme, not any of the characters, was the protagonist of the piece. Instead of scenes, the writer presented long discussions about the child welfare system and its many failings. Characters became mere symbols, and passionate rhetoric replaced natural, considered dialogue.

TONE, VOICE AND STYLE

"What the hell do you mean by 'tone' and 'voice'?"

That's what a novice writer once asked his editor. The editor replied that the writer had just answered his own question, for he had asked it in a way that "set the tone" for an entire combative discussion about the editor's credentials and her knowledge of writing. The writer didn't trust her, and she could tell this simply from the way he phrased his question and his "tone of voice."

The words "tone" and "voice" are often used to indicate the same thing in writing, and indeed they are but flip sides to the same coin. Both refer to the emotional feel of the narrative or dialogue, and, in a very basic sense, to the "sound" of an author's writing.

What a Voice!

Voice is used almost exclusively to indicate the state of mind of a first person narrator <u>or</u> that of a third person character when thinking or speaking. (Note that the term "voice" is also used to describe passive and active sentence construction.) One recognizes instantly, for example, the urgent, distraught voice of an Edgar Allan Poe narrator. In his long, intricate sentences, feverish musings and breathless revelations of disaster, the narrator presents the voice of one just waiting to commit a murder, fall into a pit, or be buried alive. Vladimir Nabokov crafts a singular voice for his first person narrator, Humbert Humbert, in *Lolita*. An intellectual pedophile devastated by his uncontrollable desires, Humbert has the voice of a man who understands his immorality and drive toward self-destruction, but is not about to apologize for either. The result is both intriguing and chilling.

In the third person, the voice of the POV character helps explain her mental state, whether we are in her thoughts or listening to her direct speech. Word choice, sentence length and structure cue the reader regarding the character's frame of mind.

For example, imagine a protagonist struggling with the decision to leave her husband. Is she a battered wife who has lost so much of her self-esteem that she can barely conceive of herself apart from her brutal husband...or is she an independent career woman who has had to fight to get herself to the point where she can call herself successful? Each woman has a very different mental outlook. Though each may experience the same event, each will provide a very different account, using a different voice.

Consider this paragraph from a novel in which a young Englishwoman, Emily, contemplates a hunting hound belonging to her friend.

Emily watched Jenny fling her arms around Ruffian's neck. Save for his large, intelligent eyes, the dog was quite plain, not at all like the hunting stock Emily was used to. His legs were short, his coat shaggy and matted, the pads of his paws cracked and dry. He had been rolling in some unmentionable substance and stank like a barnyard. Why, her husband would not have let such an animal spend one night in his kennel!

In this passage, Emily's revulsion for the dog is quite clear, though she does not come out and say she is repulsed. It is the "voice" of her inner thoughts, reflected in such words as "save for," "quite plain," "short legs," "shaggy, matted coat," "cracked, dry pads," "stank," that gives away her feelings. In her last remark, she relies on her husband's imagined opinion to suggest her own.

Setting the Right Tone

If the above example were not so closely attached to the POV character, one might call it tone. Tone is similar to voice, in that it reveals the emotional content of a manuscript. However, while voice describes the state of mind of a character, tone refers to the emotional content of a more distant third person narrative, or even the author himself. Indeed, tone is most obvious in pieces written in the omniscient third person.

Tone is readily observable in the many forms of satire. Jonathan Swift, in *A Modest Proposal*, mockingly suggests the English solve the problem of excess Irish population by eating Irish babies. Swift cannot hide his tone of loathing for the British domination of the Irish, although he appears to be offering heartfelt advice.

Tone can also convey how the writer feels about his characters or subject matter. John Steinbeck, in *The Grapes of Wrath*, lets his admiration of the hard-working, stoic farmers of the Oklahoma dustbowl shine through in the tone of his prose. His positive feelings are especially evident in this excerpt from his first description of Tom Joad:

His cheek bones were high and wide, and strong deep lines cut down his cheeks, in curves beside his mouth. His upper lip was long, and since his teeth protruded, the lips stretched to cover them, for this man kept his lips closed. His hands were hard, with broad fingers and nails as thick and ridged as little clam shells. The space between thumb and forefingers and the hams of his hands were shiny with callus.

On the other hand, Charles Dickens shows his contempt for the cruel

French aristocracy of the 18th century in the icy, sarcastic tone used throughout *A Tale of Two Cities*. This particular passage describes the death of a heartless marquis:

> ...There was one stone face too many, up at the chateau. The Gorgon had surveyed the building again in the night, and had added the one stone face wanting; the stone face for which it had waited through about two hundred years. It lay back on the pillow of the Monsieur the Marquis. It was like a fine mask, suddenly startled, made angry, and petrified. Driven home into the heart of the stone figure attached to it was a knife.

Tone can also be used to convey the theme of a work of fiction. For example, Joseph Conrad in *Heart of Darkness* uses a consistently bleak, threatening tone to establish his theme, which concerns the brutality that lies hidden in the heart of mankind. In the following description of a landscape, Conrad uses a dark tone to suggest the viciousness and savagery in the heart of man, symbolized by the wilderness:

> (His gesture) seemed to beckon with a dishonoring flourish before the sunlit face of the land, a treacherous appeal to the lurking death, to the hidden evil, to the profound darkness of its heart.

A word of warning about tone: It is inherent in a description. It is a subtle matter of choosing words and phraseology to convey feelings, such as admiration or disgust or terror, and is not to be confused with authorial intrusion. When an author intrudes in a manuscript, he baldly tells his readers his opinions and observations, and this is rarely a good strategy.

STYLE

Note that style, perhaps the most elusive aspect of fiction writing, has been omitted from both the list of elements *and* the list of conventions. Style is neither an element of writing nor a convention. It is more akin to a personal signature or a mode of dress.

We speak of style in many terms: minimalist (using as few descriptions as possible); effusive or expansive (using copious, florid descriptions); realistic (attempting a feel of gritty realism in description and dialogue); naive (not an insult, but a reference to a style reminiscent of the way a young, inexperienced person might write); and on and on, including almost as many styles of writing as there are writers.

Writers are not born with a style. They develop an individual style as they write, based in part on what they read and what they have experienced in life, and the more they write, the more distinct their style becomes. As William Styron once remarked, "Style comes only after long, hard practice and writing."

For example, Ernest Hemingway and John Steinbeck are often accredited with developing what has been called the "American" style of writing – crisp, unadorned prose, yet elegant and lyrical in its lean, bluntly honest way. It is perhaps the antithesis of the "European" style, exemplified by the English writers Somerset Maugham and E. M. Forster – rife with descriptions and reflections, slow in pace, nearly ponderous at times, wide in scope, rich in meaning. Henry James, an American, also wrote in this rich, expansive style.

Many beginning writers, when told to avoid a certain easy-to-misuse technique – shifting points of view, perhaps, or non-chronological progression – are often quick to defend their writing on the grounds of style. They heatedly contend that "Hemingway did it; why can't I?" or "I've read a lot of Michael Crichton, and I want to write just like him."

Our standard response to such statements is this: "When you are on the level of Hemingway or Michael Crichton, you may write whatever way you wish. You will be free to experiment, because, like Hemingway, you will have mastered the art of writing powerful fiction or, like Crichton, you will have huge popular appeal and a very loyal following. Until then, you will simply have to learn the craft of writing, just as every successful writer has done before you."

This does not mean, however, that a beginning writer should ignore the works of the literary masters or successful popular writers. If a writer runs up against a problem while writing (say, she is not sure how to establish an exotic setting without going into great detail), it is very helpful to consult other writers' works to see how they handled a similar situation.

The bottom line in fiction is not whether the writing is "good" or "bad," but "Does it work?" In other words, do all the elements of the story function powerfully and successfully, aided by effective use or manipulation of writing conventions? If the writing "works," then it's a good bet the writer's style has emerged throughout. By studying literary elements and conventions, a writer increases her chances of making her fiction work.

CHAPTER
ELEVEN

CONVENTIONS: COMMON FICTION WRITING TECHNIQUES TO USE...AND TO AVOID

THERE IS NOTHING really "conventional" about novelistic conventions. In fact, most of the conventions discussed here are attempts to eliminate trite, derivative or over-used approaches to fiction. It is simply a fact that certain writing techniques are very helpful in the development of specific elements of the novel or short story, and many writers have put these techniques to good use.

As you study effective writing conventions, consider the importance of readability. The writing techniques recommended here can be used to make your writing more accessible to the reader and ultimately more engrossing.

In this book, we'll examine these important literary conventions and how they can be used to enhance the elements of the novel and fiction writing in general.

1. Point of view (POV)
2. Gingerbread (frames, flashbacks, prologues and epilogues)
3. Plotting techniques (pressure and suspense, drama vs. melodrama, parallel structure)
4. Scene and narrative (showing vs. telling)
5. Transitions
6. Imagery (physical imagery, the resonating image)

TECHNIQUES FROM HELL

Before studying each convention or technique in detail, it may be helpful to take a look at some common writing devices that may best be left alone, techniques that are difficult to use successfully or cause more harm than good.

There are ever so many reasons why your writing may not work, and we have covered a few already (non-chronological time, sequence problems, prominence of secondary characters, and so on). However, nothing sinks a good story faster than these seven writing gremlins.

1. Cinematic/scenic point of view
2. Deus ex machina
3. Authorial (or author) intrusion
4. Abrupt shifting (point of view, tense, stories, protagonists, tone, settings)
5. Cliches
6. Predictable or "pat" structures
7. Present tense

1. CINEMATIC POINT OF VIEW

The Cinematic Mindset

To understand the cinematic approach to writing (and to ultimately avoid it), it's necessary to understand that writing is writing and movie-making is movie-making, and never the twain shall meet, not even in a screenplay. (Screenplays, of course, are not intended for publication, unlike most other writing. See Chapter Twenty for more information on screenplay writing.) This seems obvious, but perhaps not to everyone.

Thanks to television and America's obsession with the movies, we have, for good or bad, become a nation of watchers. We have become accustomed to observing visuals on a small or large screen, absorbing one interpretation of any given story, usually the director's. Images appear before us at a distance, and unless the acting, directing, special effects and photography are unusually skillful, we sense a certain distance from the events on the screen, almost as if we are watching the screen through a camera lens.

Writing, especially fiction, does not work this way. The most effective fiction tends to be intimate and involving, leaving itself open to hundreds of interpretations and envisionings. Feelings, thoughts, memories, fears and dreams are communicated through words directly on the page, not through the expressions of actors or other visuals.

Yes, writing and movie-making are distinct fields, and the techniques of one medium don't readily translate to the other. That having been said, why do so many novice writers try to craft a novel or short story with the same skills they would use to view a movie? It is truly astounding how many manuscripts come into the agency each week, reeking of celluloid.

Point of View

Point of view (POV), which will be covered in the next section, is the perspective in which a story is told. Normally, someone observes the events in a story and relays this information to the reader. This observer could be a third person protagonist, a first person narrator, a third person omniscient observer or a *scenic observer*. In the scenic point of view, events are described to the reader as if an unseen reporter is recording the external action and dialogue. Mental processes, such as thoughts or memories, are rarely recorded. Because of its vast distance and lack of emotion, the scenic POV is rarely used successfully in long fiction.

The cinematic point of view is the term we apply to an extreme form of the scenic POV. In a manner of speaking, the cinematic POV is as close as one can get to an *absence* of POV, practically devoid of interpretation. In the cinematic POV, narrative proceeds as if the reader is observing actors, props and actions on a movie set through the lens of a camera. While appropriate for screenplays, the cinematic POV is disastrous for novels, since it reduces character and plot to two-dimensional terms and discourages the reader from thinking too much about either.

The Third Dimension

As discussed earlier, one of the most important tasks of the fiction writer is to create believable, realistic characters who react to events in the plot, changing and growing as the story progresses. By exploring in some depth the characters' thoughts, his motivations for behaving a certain way and his reactions to events, the writer creates an illusion of a third dimension, allowing the character to experience deeper and deeper insights into his own behavior and that of others.

In the cinematic POV, characters are reduced to cardboard figures acting out the action in the plot. The reader is rarely privy to these shallow characters' thoughts, except perhaps what can be gleaned through dialogue. Consider the following:

> Miranda and her mother entered the dress shop and began looking at skirts, blouses and jewelry. Miranda chose a short-sleeved floral print blouse, while her mother bought a blue sundress with red piping around the neck. "That's a pretty color on you," Miranda told her mother.

Because the characters rarely reflect, remember, mull things over or ask themselves questions, all action takes place on the exterior, not in the interior of the character's minds. Therefore the characters seem unrealistic and hopelessly flat. The story does not seem to function as a natural outgrowth of human behavior. Instead, the plot is manhandled to produce a predetermined result, much like a half-hour TV show.

That is why so many manuscripts written in this POV feature "type" characters or caricatures often seen in movies, such as the cocky young man, the crusty old sailor, or the temperamental artiste. These characters need no development because they spring from the writer's head, fully-formed. Because these characters are never developed, they never "come alive" or seem real. The reader has little reason to continue reading, for she knows these characters will not change or grow realistically.

Too Much Distance

The cinematic point of view is also problematic because of its extreme distance. Writers using this POV employ camera techniques – such as zooming in on the details of a person's face or drawing back a great distance from characters and action – to tell their story or set a scene. Unfortunately, this technique actually *removes* the reader from the characters and the action, preventing the high level of personal interest that makes a reader curious about the fate of the characters.

Novels have no visual aids, yet cinematic authors write as if their readers can observe the novel's action unfolding on a screen. Descriptions are often terse, vague or nonexistent. Characters are catapulted from one scene to the next without transition, as if the scene is fading out or the writer is cutting to another scene. Thus the cinematic POV and scenic POV actually *encourage* the writer to write in a very superficial, disjointed manner. For this reason, the beginning writer should avoid these POVs at all costs. They will consistently trip him up and prevent him from developing his characters.

(To be totally fair to the scenic POV, we confess that two of our favorite short stories, Hemingway's "The Killers" and Flannery O'Connor's "A Good Man is Hard to Find", are both partially written in the scenic point of view. This just goes to show what a master can do.)

Writing in first person, in attached third person or even in a true omniscient narration will bring the reader closer to the characters, thus preventing the distant cinematic feel and resultant lack of development.

2. DEUS EX MACHINA

Deus ex machina is a Latin term meaning, "god from a machine." It refers to ancient Greek theater, in which an actor dressed as Zeus or another divinity was lowered onto the stage by means of a crane, as if descending from the heavens. The "god" would then slay the villain, right all wrongs, and generally see that everything ended happily.

Some modern examples of this contrived technique include the cavalry riding to the rescue of the pioneers just in the nick of time; the heroic officer arriving out of nowhere to save the heroine from the clutches of the evil baron; the hunter who shows up just in time to shoot the wolf that is about to leap on the hero (*a la* Little Red Riding Hood); the cop who magically appears to arrest the homicidal maniac threatening the protagonist; the friend who bursts into the dinner party and spirits away the heroine before she can make a fool of herself, and so on and so on, *ad nauseam*.

Deus ex machina may be all well and good in Classical drama, but it is a contrivance, that is, an obvious, unsubtle manipulation of characters and events to attain a predetermined end. Contrivance does not usually work well in modern fiction. Why not? Because good fiction writing depends on creating the *fictional dream*, the sense that the reader has stepped into another reality. Hence the need for realism, at least in terms of how events take place in real life, whether the setting is Mars, PA or the planet Mars. When readers encounter a savior in a novel who appears abruptly without introduction or foreshadowing, they are likely to just say, "No! I don't believe this," and set the book down.

To expect the cavalry to pull the hero out of a jam at the last minute is not very realistic or believable. There is some precedent for this in young adult novels, but even a sophisticated 10-year-old will recoil from obvious contrivances and strained devices.

To the Rescue

This does not mean that your protagonists cannot be rescued from dangerous or embarrassing situations. Generally speaking, however, your protagonist should probably try to rescue himself. It will show the reader how the character reacts in a crisis and demonstrate how resourceful he is (or is not). How glad we are, for example, when quick-thinking Ishmael in *Moby Dick* saves himself by clinging to Queequeg's coffin.

Alternatively, you can set up a *deus*, not from a machine, but an established ally or sidekick whom the reader knows is on the way to bring help. This friend's arrival at the scene of the hero's struggle should not come as a surprise to the reader but as a natural consequence of events in the plot. For example, the ship which picks up Ishmael is the "Bachelor," searching for her "missing orphans," a fact which was established much earlier in the novel.

One of the most moving and dramatic examples of such a rescue in American literature occurs in Harper Lee's *To Kill a Mockingbird*. Near the end of the novel, Scout is saved from an attacker by Boo Radley, the village's mystery man. Throughout the novel, Lee wisely gives hints about Boo's personality: Is he mad? Is he retarded? Is he a murderer? Is he dangerous? Or is he just misunderstood and very shy? Scout thinks of him often and imagines she glimpses him in his house now and then. Boo also leaves small gifts for Scout and her brother in a hollow tree.

By the time the climax rolls around, the reader is dying to meet this enigmatic, possibly threatening person, and is quietly thrilled to see him come to Scout's rescue and dispatch the villain. The reader is pleased, after waiting so long, to see Boo act in a heroic, loving way, vindicating his existence. Therefore Boo does not appear out of nowhere like a *deus ex machina*; we've been waiting for him all along.

3. AUTHOR, OR AUTHORIAL, INTRUSION

Beginning writers often "intrude" in their fiction, commenting on the action, the characters, the theme, the setting, and so on. Note this passage from an inexperienced writer, especially the last sentence:

> Alice, who had been sheltered all her life, did not know what to do. She had gone to her mother's room that morning, as she did every morning, with a tray of toast, eggs and tea. But this morning her mother did not waken when Alice announced her presence. Alice set the tray down and shook her mother's shoulder gently, but the older woman seemed stiff and lifeless. Then Alice noticed that her mother's face and hands were the color of fresh lilacs. Alice gasped and ran from the room, screaming. This is not unusual behavior for people who have been deprived of dealing with life's hardships.

Excuse me?

The writer does a nice job of setting up Alice's predicament, then inexplicably "walks into" Alice's story and comments on it. The last sentence is not Alice's opinion, nor is it even the opinion of some omniscient narrator who is telling us Alice's story. It is the voice of the *author*, intruding in his own work of fiction, where he has no right to be. It is up to the reader to decide whether or not Alice is acting appropriately or not, based on her background; it's certainly not the writer's job to *explain* the behavior of his characters.

Imagine reading a novel in the third person. You come to a scene describing a character's difficulty finding an English speaker in France. Suddenly you read a line that is not attached to the speech of a character: "I myself found this to be true in a recent trip to Paris," or "The behavior of the rude waiter was very similar to that of a shop attendant I met one summer in Orleans."

Such an intrusion seems absurd, yet one does encounter it now and then in the works of beginning writers. While this sort of private aside might work in nonfiction, it is intrusive, disruptive and obnoxious in fiction, where, once again, the writer is trying to establish the fictional dream, the alternative reality of his characters, plot and setting. These particular intrusions would sound almost as ridiculous in the third person as in the first, unless they are closely attached to the POV character.

Sometimes a writer uses authorial comments to "explain" situations that he thinks the reader might not understand. This is almost always an unfortunate idea, since it yet again disrupts the fictional dream and reminds the reader that she is participating in a construct, not an alternative world. Consider this example:

> "Go on up to the top of that crag and get a bearing," said the guide. Brad shook his head. He was deathly afraid of heights. "Sorry, I can't." Brad's fear of heights was no doubt caused by an incident in his youth, when he had fallen out of an apple tree on his grandfather's farm and broken his leg.

The writer is in such a hurry to explain Brad's phobia that she rushes right into the pages of her own story, as if she could somehow speak for Brad. In this version of the same passage, Brad gets to explain himself, with much better results:

> "Go on up to the top of that crag and get a bearing," said the guide. Brad shook his head. He was getting dizzy just thinking about climbing the tall rocks. A sensation of falling washed over him, and he remembered the horrible day on his grandfather's farm, years ago, when he had reached for an apple high in the branches of a tree, missed and lost his balance. He had fallen, fallen, fallen. The wind had rushed up around him, and the ground had leaped up to smack him on the side, breaking his left leg. "Sorry, I can't," he mumbled.

Occasionally one finds a published author intruding in his fiction with little tidbits of explanatory information. Richard Adams, for example, in his otherwise skillful novel about the secret lives of rabbits, *Watership Down*, writes at one point that the rabbit hero, Hazel, gazes all around himself on a hill, looking for danger, because "rabbits cannot back up." It's nice to know this about rabbit physiology, but the reader still wonders who is saying this.

4. ABRUPT SHIFTING

Anyone who has ever driven a stick-shift vehicle – especially an older model – will be familiar with the awkward hesitation that occurs when the driver shifts from first to second gear, or downshifts from second to first. The transmission disengages for an instant or two, as if the car is making up its mind on how to proceed.

Writing is no different from driving in this regard, although shifting gears in fiction takes many forms. One could shift tense; shift from active voice to passive; shift from one tone to another, or from one setting to another. Whenever the writer makes any of these shifts, a brief awkwardness is likely to occur.

Of course, it is necessary to switch setting when the scene of action changes, and this can be done smoothly through the use of careful transitions or even space breaks. However, it is rarely if ever necessary to shift tense or to switch from active to passive voice. Rapid changes in tense or voice construction serve only to interrupt the flow of the novel and distract the reader.

Shifting POV

Similarly, many beginning writers change POV abruptly from character to character, sometimes on the same page, sometimes in the same paragraph or even the same sentence. This is politely called "multiple POV," but if POV is changed often and suddenly, the work will seem to be written in "muddle POV," as in the following extreme case.

Bertram looked at Lucy, repressing the desire to strike her, while she glared at him in indignation, feeling as if he had already hit her. She turned at the approach of Florence, the maid, who sensed the electric presence of anger and became frightened. Something was not right between her two employers; she was sure of it.

In the ridiculous passage above, we first find out how Bertram feels, then how Lucy feels, then how Florence feels. A paragraph down we may be introduced to the thoughts of the gardener who witnessed this scene, or the governess who was told about it. Soon the reader is suffering from POV overload; with so many perspectives on an issue, it is hard to maintain any balance or stability. The reader begins to feel as if she does not know any of the characters very well. It is also difficult for the writer to set the action of the story moving forward again in the midst of so many reactions.

As we've already discussed, a novel does not require ensemble acting. The focus is on the protagonist, the main character, the person whom the story is about, the person who is most influenced by events and other characters, and changes or develops throughout the novel because of them. Therefore the writer who abruptly and constantly shifts POV would seem to be defeating himself, since he is not giving his protagonist a chance to develop.

5. CLICHES

"Dead as a doornail."
"He couldn't see the forest for the trees."
"Her bosom heaved and her blood ran cold."

We're all familiar with cliches, those overused images and phrases which convey information so quickly and handily that people use them without thinking. Cliches are a sort of verbal shorthand, which is fine for everyday speech and informal writing. But in fiction writing, where creativity and originality are highly valued, cliches, by and of themselves, have no place, except in dialogue.

What does that phrase mean, "cliches by and of themselves?" Perhaps there is another way to look at cliches which will give the fiction writer a chance to use them, if only indirectly.

Telling the Truth

Cliches are used so often and so wantonly because they fill a very important role in language: They tell the truth succinctly. If someone says he is "as fit as a fiddle," there is no mistaking his opinion of his health: He believes he is in excellent physical condition. If the same person informs his children that "money doesn't grow on trees," we know immediately that the kids must be little wastrels. The challenge for the writer is to take the cliche and "stand it on its head," as a wise professor once said – to present the trite, the weary and the overdone in a new light, revealing new depths of truth or understanding.

For example, a skeptic might examine his "fit" friend and conclude he was as fit as a fiddle, all right – a fiddle that had just been run over by a ten-ton truck. A contrary child, enduring his father's speech on the relationship between money and trees, might recall how he once found a ten-dollar bill in the shrubbery.

On a deeper level, writers can also examine literary cliches in a new light: stock characters such as the prostitute with a heart of gold, or stock storylines, such as The Quest. It is always helpful to the writer to play the game of "what if," pulling at the meanings of cliches and stretching them beyond their obvious truths. What if, for example, that prostitute suffered incest as a child? What if she has always been searching for the "father" she never really had, and sex is the only way she knows to communicate emotionally with men?

What if, say, two fantasy characters set out on a quest in a land crawling with all the fantasy cliches: dragons, griffins, evil sorcerers, enchanted swords, gloomy castles and so on. However, they find out that the actual quest – the quest for personal growth and the meaning of honor – lies within themselves, their background and their behavior, that the dragons they seek to slay are really their most personal fears.

The beginning writer should avoid cliches, unless he can mine them for additional meaning. The one exception to this suggestion, as noted earlier, lies in dialogue.

Characters' Use of Cliches

While the writer is morally committed to the reader to try to use words and ideas creatively, his characters have no such limitations. In fact, you might create a character who speaks in nothing but cliches, or mixes up cliches. ("It was so quiet you could hear a mouse drop," said Jeff.) What sort of character would speak in cliches or bits of cliches? Is he afraid to express himself in more original terms? Is he so distracted or dull-witted that he cannot be more original in his speech?

Of course, perfectly normal characters will use cliches now and then, just as real people do. In some genres, however, this tendency is taken to extremes. Hard-boiled detective fiction, for example, is infamous for containing protagonists who spontaneously cry out such tired phrases as, "It hit me like a ton of bricks," or "Haven't eaten yet? How'd ya like a knuckle sandwich?"

There is nothing new under the sun, and cliches reflect this fact. Still, rather than using cliches, the beginning writer should think about creating fresh images and intriguing ways to say what has been said a million times before.

6. PREDICTABLE OR "PAT" STRUCTURES

In the preceding selection, I mentioned formulaic or cliched storylines, specifically, The Quest. There are several others: The Fish out of Water (*Outlander*), The Reformation of the Outlaw – or Rake or Harlot or Egoist, etc. (*Jane Eyre*), Man's Struggles Against Nature (many Jack London stories), Coming of Age/End of Innocence (*The Catcher in the Rye*), Facing and Avenging an Act of Evil (*Ivanhoe* by Sir Walter Scott), Overcoming Adversity (Steinbeck's *The Grapes of Wrath*), and Coping with or Challenging Authority (*The Handmaid's Tale*) by Margaret Atwood). This is by no means a complete list. Most of the novels written today (and in the past) use some variation of these standard plots. While there is almost no such thing as an "original" plot line today, there are certainly plenty of creative ways to approach hackneyed storylines and breath new life into them.

To promote a feeling, even a semblance, of creativity and originality, the beginning writer is strongly advised to avoid predictability in his writing, unless the protagonist himself is haunted by his own predictable lifestyle.

Happy Ending

Does this mean that one cannot write a happy ending in which the boy gets the girl or the hero slays the villain? Of course not! However, the reader should not be thinking, "I know just what's going to happen" as she finishes each page.

Just as one must examine the truth behind cliched phrases or ideas and "stand them on their heads," one must also work toward crafting a plot that the reader cannot write for herself. Perhaps it is so full of twists and turns that the reader cannot anticipate what will happen next, or perhaps the structure is predictable only up to a point. For example, the male protagonist rescues the female protagonist's child from an island castle (just as the reader thought he would) only to end up stranded on a beach, surrounded by enemy soldiers.

Rattling the Bars

The same professor who recommended that writers invert cliches also urged them to "rattle the bars of their stories." This wonderful analogy suggests the image of an aged lion in a zoo, overfed, placid and thoroughly dispirited. But what happens when you take a stick and strike its cage? It springs to dramatic life, roaring and snarling, showing some of the danger and daring that captivity has masked.

How does a writer increase the drama, spirit and power of a story that might seem dull, predictable and sluggish? The novice writer should always be aware of the importance of the element of surprise and use it to counter predictability and "obvious" plotting. A powerful example is the short story, "Good Country People," by the great American writer, Flannery O'Connor. In this story, mentioned earlier, the reader guesses that the female protagonist will either be seduced by the traveling salesman or refuse his advances. Surprise! It's neither. The salesman is only after the girl's wooden leg, which he carries away as a sort of trophy. What started out as a simple story of seduction and "coming of age" transcended a jaded plotline and became a story of deception and an examination of people's true intentions.

Predictability in plotting often takes place because the writer is simply not alert enough to prevent it. Just by being aware that it's often a good idea to "keep the reader guessing," the writer can prevent his work from reading as if it has been written before.

7. PRESENT TENSE

The present tense has one primary reason: to suffuse writing with the sense of urgency, to give the impression the story is happening "as we speak." This in turn creates added tension and suspense, if done well.

Many fine short stories have been written in the present tense; however, it is much harder to sustain the present tense throughout longer fiction. This is simply because of the nature of immediacy. A reader readily accepts the fact that the short story he is reading is happening "right now." He is much less likely to accept that premise for 500, 400, even 200 pages that cover a fairly long period of time.

In addition, flashbacks are very difficult to craft in the present tense. If written in the past tense, they sound contrived and out of place; if written in the present, they sound unbelievable, since they concern past events.

Inconsistent Tenses

The problems of writing in the present tense are borne out by the fact that, of all the many present-tense manuscripts we have reviewed in the agency, not one has used present tense consistently. They slip into the past tense from time to time, sometimes re-emerging in present tense, sometimes staying in past. The result is, without exception, confusing and disjointed.

Why is this so? Probably because the past tense is part of the art of the storyteller, and to some extent, a fiction writer is a storyteller. All fairy tales are told in past tense, as are almost all anecdotes. It seems natural to write a story in the past tense, about events that have occurred (so therefore the writer "knows" about them). The present tense, however, creates the illusion that events are happening as the writer is tapping out the story on the keyboard. This might strike the reader as a contrivance or obvious convention, and make it that much harder for him to suspend disbelief and buy into the fictional dream.

While the agency by no means condemns use of the present tense for fiction writers, we caution the beginning writer to avoid writing novel-length manuscripts in the present tense. Its use is simply too tricky and demanding to pull off successfully.

Note that our caution against present tense applies to long fiction, not short stories or nonfiction. This book, for instance, is written in the present tense because its purpose is to disseminate information, not to create an alternate realm of reality.

CHAPTER TWELVE

CONVENTION: POINT OF VIEW (POV)

POINT OF VIEW is without a doubt one of the most perplexing and bewildering concepts for beginning writers. Approximately 95 out of 100 writers who contact the agency have no idea what POV is, and many never feel comfortable with the idea. We have even spoken with many teachers and professors of English, Communications and Writing who are totally unfamiliar with the term "point of view" as it applies to literature.

Editors, on the other hand, often think of POV as a very straightforward concept and have difficulty understanding why it throws so many writers into a panic. (One agency client referred to his editor as the "point of view police" for insisting on maintaining a consistent POV.)

POV means what its name says: point of view, or a specific perspective or angle of observation. Since a novel is basically a story, then someone must be observing and reacting to the characters and action in the story. This observing character is the POV character and is often the main character.

An event, in life or fiction, takes on different meanings to the different people involved in the event. Each person will have different feelings, and therefore a different perspective. This is the basic idea behind the concept of POV.

Kid, Mom and Doc

For example, imagine a scene in which a mother is watching a doctor give her four-year-old son a shot. All three people – mother, child and doctor – will have vastly different perspectives on the event. The child is terrified; to him, the doctor seems like a monster and his mother is an accomplice. Perhaps the mother is concerned for the child's health and happy that he is getting treatment, yet moved by his fear. To the doctor, the shot is simply an accepted part of patient care. She doesn't want to frighten the child, yet the boy's screams and contortions frustrate the physician because they make her job harder.

In some ways, we all see things from different people's points of view every day. We hear about the overburdened employee who threatens his demanding boss, and can understand both the employee's and employer's point of view, that is, their sides of the story. We feel sorry for the innocent motorist who, through no fault of her own, hits a careless pedestrian, but we also understand the grief, anger and confusion of the victim's family. That is because we can view events from many different angles, and each view produces a different interpretation.

In fiction, the writer takes advantage of this concept by telling the story from a specific character's – or characters' – point of view. POV is often used to develop a character, but also can be used to enhance setting, and broaden or condense the range of the novel. In fact, POV is often so closely connected to the plot and protagonist that they become inseparable. Even if you were to decide to tell a story *without* a POV, you would end up with a POV anyway, namely scenic or cinematic, the most distancing and least effective forms.

Penny for Your Thoughts

Beginning writers always seem very eager to describe their main characters. These writers give detailed physical descriptions of people, usually in a scenic or omniscient POV, very near the beginning of their novels, almost as if they are afraid the characters will not exist unless the reader is familiar with their appearance. But in the grand scheme of things, physical descriptions tell us very little about anyone. Using point of view, we can show a lot more about a character than how she looks.

An effective point of view is an essential part of good writing because it allows the writer to examine the inner workings of his character's mind.

Feelings and Fears

As you read the following discussions of the different types of POV, notice how they can be used to explore characters' feelings, thoughts, dreams, fears, aspirations, reactions and reflections. These are the aspects of your characters which will appeal most to your readers, for they will raise many interesting questions:

— What motivates your characters? Is it money, fame, sex, power, revenge...or love, family, justice and loyalty? Are your characters' actions rising naturally from their motivations?
— How do your characters react to events? Are they impetuous and

flighty, or deliberate, considered and careful? Do they have high expectations of themselves and others, or do they just try to get by with what they've got?

— Are your characters' feelings and reactions appropriate to events? How would they feel and react if their best friend died? If a stranger died, and they found his body? If they discovered they had won a million dollars? If they were asked to deliver an important document to a foreign power? In short, how would they act if they were under maximum stress?

— Are your characters reflective? Do they frequently remember events or images from their childhood? Do certain topics or people make them feel nostalgic...or angry, sad or fearful?

— How do they express strong emotions, such as anger? Do they beat their fists on a table or slug the person standing next to them?

— Are they curious, forever seeking an answer to any question that should arise?

Of course, thinking should not predominate the plot of a novel. However, as you write, be aware that your protagonist probably has an opinion about everything that happens in the plot. The less your protagonist thinks, feels and reacts, the more your writing will read as if it is written in the scenic or cinematic point of view – cold, distant, and emotionless.

THREE BASIC POINTS OF VIEW

There are many kinds of POV, but we will examine only those that are used most frequently by beginning writers: first person, third person attached, and third person omniscient. (Two problematic POVs, cinematic and shifting, have been discussed earlier.) We recommend the first two POVs, but feel that beginning writers, in most cases, should avoid omniscient, cinematic and shifting POVs.

I. FIRST PERSON, OR "I"

In this POV, the protagonist narrates the story directly. ("Call me Ishmael.") The first person narrative has many precedents in literature, not only *Moby Dick*, but also many of Edgar Allan Poe's stories, *Gulliver's Travels*, F. Scott Fitzgerald's *The Great Gatsby*, and many, many more. Beginning writers frequently choose the first person, since it almost always focuses POV and neatly reduces it to one definite narrator.

FIRST PERSON BENEFITS

1. *Creating Intimacy and Immediacy*

Literary novels are often written in the first person, perhaps because of the immediacy and sense of intimacy it creates. Of all the POVs, first person is the one that is most "in your face," the most accessible and the most personal.

First person is the POV of choice for detective novels and related fiction which depends on creating suspense and solving mysteries. Why? Because the first person POV greatly reduces the distance between the reader and the protagonist. The reader feels as if he is conversing with the narrator, that he is actually part of the story, the "you" whom the narrator is addressing. It is easy to get caught up in the action and suspense of such an immediate story.

First person narrators are also an essential ingredient of the "fictional reminiscence," a sort of pseudo-memoir in which a fictional narrator relates incidents in her past, especially her youth. *To Kill a Mockingbird* by Harper Lee is a famous example of a fictional reminiscence. Of course, non-fictional "true stories" and real memoirs are often best told in the first person, too.

2. *Ease of Developing a Protagonist*

A first person narrator is easier to develop than a third person character, since people, even fictional people, love to talk about themselves. The narrator is not only telling a story about himself but is also revealing himself through his reflections, ideas, word choice, casual comments, and memories of childhood and other stages in his life. Of course, this is not an excuse to let the first person narrator ramble on at length about her birth, childhood, schooldays, love affairs, etc., *unless* these have a direct relation to the development of the plot or the protagonist's role in it.

For a brilliant example of a first person narrative which reveals the personality of the narrator, read the beginning paragraph of *Lolita*, by Vladimir Nabokov.

3. *Unreliable Narrator*

The first person POV also allows the writer to try a very arresting but rather difficult technique called the unreliable narrative. If a story is in the first person, the reader gets no opinions save those of the narrator, or other people's opinions filtered through the narrator's sensibilities. But who is to say that the narrator is reporting the truth? Perhaps he is a criminal trying to convince the reader of his innocence...or perhaps he is insane. Often the reader must figure out the narrator's condition and come to his own conclusions.

This challenging technique is hard to sustain in long fiction but can work well in a short story. Edgar Allan Poe used the unreliable narrator in many of his stories, and "Haircut" by Ring Lardner is a famous example of the technique. Of course, if one creates an unreliable narrator without being aware of it, that will create more problems than it solves.

FIRST PERSON DRAWBACKS

1. *Multiple POVs*

Some novels have more than one first person narrator, but most novices wisely avoid this difficult technique. It is simply too hard to establish a new narrator. More commonly, confused writers begin in the first person and *switch* midstream to the third person, which usually confuses the reader to no end. Beginning writers should avoid having more than one first person narrator and switching from first to third person (or vice versa) like the plague.

2. *First Person Pompous*

First person narrators have a tendency to take over manuscripts. Since they are the only POV characters, other characters and their dialogue are sometimes ignored by the narrator. The first person narrator is always "on stage," speaking in his own voice, giving his own opinions. The difficulty of crafting the first person narrator's "speech" is summed up by this quote from an editor at the agency: "Every word of the narration has to be appropriate to the narrator's voice." In this respect, the first person narration is similar to poetry, since every word is crucial.

Because of the pressure on the writer to create a strong, distinct voice for his narrator, first-time writers sometimes go overboard, creating a narrative voice which is more bombastic than strong, more haughty than distinctive. These "first person pompous" narrators usually employ an immense vocabulary (for no good reason) and seem terminally wrapped up in their own affairs. This intellectual self-absorption sometimes produces an unintentionally gothic voice, dripping with portent and inappropriate gravity, as in this example:

It is the midnight hour as I sit down to write, to pour out my heart about incidents and their dire consequences which I can neither comprehend nor totally desire to.

This is the opening sentence in a novella about a contemporary man cheating on his wife – serious stuff, perhaps, but not "dire." In the 19th century, Poe or Mary Shelley might have been able to pull off such a narrator, and indeed their stories did concern gothic, frightening experiences. No, the inexperienced writer simply leaped off the deep end, trying to craft a suitably concerned voice for his repentant narrator.

To avoid first person pompous, try to keep your narrator's language simple and natural, in keeping with his background and education. Remember that even a well-educated narrator would probably concentrate on communicating his story, not on trying to impress his audience. Let him express his personality through his thoughts, memories, reactions and anecdotes, as well as his word choice.

3. *Inner Monologues*

Because first person narrators have the show to themselves, so to speak, it is very easy for the inexperienced writer to lose control of them. When the narrator is allowed to become too introspective, he may go into an *inner monologue*, that is, a long, rambling account of some personal reflection, opinion or memory. Proust's diatribe about eating a madeline cake and experiencing a flood of memories is perhaps the most famous of these monologues.

Generally speaking, the beginning writer would do well to avoid long inner monologues. It is too easy to lose sight of the plot when the narrator is having a lengthy discussion with himself, and pacing problems frequently develop. First person narration seems to work best when it makes ample use of dialogue and the narrator's interaction with other characters.

4. *Lack of Distance*

Lack of distance or objectivity between the reader and the first-person narrator is one of this form's strong points, but it can also cause problems. Just how do you describe the narrator or learn other people's thoughts and opinions when you are locked very intimately in one person's viewpoint? This can be handled through dialogue to some degree, and the narrator may guess at another character's thoughts, but the reader is more or less stuck inside that narrator's mental processes. If the narrator suffers a trauma, such as a punch to the face or the loss of a loved one, the reader suffers right along with him, at the same level of suffering. There is no distance between what the narrator is feeling and what the reader is experiencing, and this can sometimes cause a sense of lack of control or disorganization in the writing.

Take this example:

> The searing metal touched my leg. I screamed in agony. Tears filled my eyes and I could not see anything. It was the worst pain I had ever felt, worse than the pain of childbirth, worse than the pain I had felt when I had broken my arm in a fall from a swing as a child. I couldn't imagine a worse pain, and I certainly never wanted to feel it again in my life.

All well and good, but what is happening to the narrator while she is getting in touch with her pain? What if someone is attacking her with a white-hot poker? This is not a good time to reminisce, and the reader will not show much patience with such deeply introspective writing. A little distance from the narrator here would allow the reader to see, perhaps, that the narrator is struggling out of a train wreck or being tortured in a concentration camp.

5. Death of the First Person Narrator

If someone is "writing" his story, how is it that he can die at the end of his story? If he did, he would not be able to write it, would he? Such a gap in logic poses a problem for the writer who wants to "kill off" his first person narrator. In the main, this approach strains credulity so much that it simply won't work.

One beginning writer created a first-person narrator who is shot at the end of the manuscript and perceives himself being unconscious. Somehow he knows he is taken to a hospital and pronounced "dead on arrival." Unless it is clear from the start that the narrator is addressing the reader from the spiritual realm, such self-awareness of death strikes the reader as patently false, contrived and unbelievable.

Another writer told most of her story in flashback (as a memory) from one woman's POV in the first person, then *killed off* this narrator and let the novel choke out its last few chapters in another character's first person perspective. This is not only highly confusing writing, it is structurally weak and disjointed.

II. THIRD PERSON POV

There are many varieties of third person POV – attached, omniscient, cinematic/scenic, and shifting. All third person POVs are presented from someone other than an "I" narrator. The observer could be a man, a woman, a child, an animal, an unspecified narrator, or even a group (as in William Faulkner's short story, "A Rose for Emily"). Third person POVs allow for statements such as: "She entered the room, feeling as if she had just stepped off a cliff," (attached); "Eustace had no idea that Jonathan had known about the murder all along," (omniscient); "David hated Spike with all his heart and wanted to see him dead. Spike didn't much care for David either, and thought he was a few bricks shy of a load," (shifting); or "They walked down the beach together, and Bill bent down to pick up a shell. Mary looked out at the ocean, and after a few minutes walked away from Bill, into the waves" (cinematic).

The third person point of view allows for greater distance between character and reader than the first person POV. However, some types of third person POV provide greater distance than others. The cinematic POV offers the most distance: Scenes are presented from a sort of "camera eye," rarely going into the thoughts of the characters. The omniscient POV and shifting POV offer a little less distance, since the writer can enter characters' minds at will and reveal any thought or memory. The third person attached POV, as its name indicates, provides the most attachment to – and least distance from – a character.

Let's take a look at these POVs separately, since they are much more different from each other than one might imagine.

A. THIRD PERSON ATTACHED, OR CENTRAL INTELLIGENCE

This POV was made popular by the great early 20th-century novelist Henry James, and his novel, *A Turn of the Screw*, is an excellent example of the technique. Third person attached POV is perhaps the easiest to use for beginning writers, as well as the most helpful. It allows a happy medium between being too close to the protagonist (as in first person POV) or too distant (as in omniscient POV).

In the attached POV, the reader gets no information save what the POV character (usually the protagonist) can provide, hence the name "central intelligence." The reader knows nothing the protagonist does not see, hear, smell, taste or feel, remember or deduce, intuit or guess at. Most of the story will probably be in the protagonist's POV, but some chapters may be in other major characters' attached POVs.

In some cases, some intimate scenes may work best if POV switches back and forth rapidly between two POV characters, but this is difficult to pull off. Generally, the fewer attached viewpoints you use, the more direct and easy to understand the writing will be. In any case, it is usually a good idea to *firmly establish the POV of the protagonist in the beginning*, perhaps for at least 50 to 100 pages, before introducing another point of view. This initial adherence to the protagonist's viewpoint will help establish the main character's personality clearly in the reader's mind before moving on to another perspective.

BENEFITS OF THE ATTACHED POV

1. *Ease of Character Development*

The agency strongly recommends the attached POV to our new clients because it forces the writer to develop a protagonist. Since the protagonist is doing all or most of the observing, thinking, acting and concluding in the story, he is bound to reveal a lot about himself along the way. Also, he is bound to comment on why he makes decisions and how those decisions affect him, as well as how his life might have been easier (or harder) if he had made different decisions. This point is made abundantly clear in well-written romance novels or westerns, where third person attached POV protagonists are very common.

The third person attached POV also allows the protagonist to be *wrong*, unlike, say, an omniscient narrator. The POV character can completely misjudge an event or another character, thus driving the progress of the plot as the protagonist pursues false leads or attributes false qualities to other people. For example, a protagonist may mistakenly view someone as cruel, selfish or uncaring at first, until she gets to know him better and realize that he is actually just insecure or misdirected.

2. *Ease of Plot Development*

Third person attached POV also helps the writer develop her storyline. Because POV is attached to the protagonist, the reader is getting rather limited information about the protagonist's world, just as in the first person POV. There will be many gaps in the protagonist's knowledge of what is happening about him, and he will in most cases struggle to fill those gaps and find out the answers to questions as they arise.

Does it sound as if we are discussing a mystery? In a way we are, for most good novels have an aspect of mystery about them. In most conventional fiction, the protagonist is faced with a conflict which he must strive to resolve, a question he must attempt to answer, or a situation he must prolong, change or rectify. In other words, circumstances in a novel are constantly changing; actions are taking place, begetting other actions, and the protagonist must dismiss or deal with them all.

The attached POV is ideal for this task, providing just enough distance so that other characters and POVs may be introduced, yet maintaining a strong observer who can freely comment and reflect on events as they occur, making decisions – rightly or wrongly – and following leads to their conclusions.

Take, for example, Henry James's *A Turn of the Screw*, mentioned earlier. The governess (the POV character) observes a great deal: apparent ghost-like figures, changes in the behavior of the children she cares for, conversations by others about events and people in the past, as well as her own tumultuous feelings, drives, repressions and impressions. Under James's mastery, the governess, like a sleuth, experiences and puts together all the haunting parts of this tense but tragic psychodrama.

In the same way, even an inexperienced writer can use the third person attached POV to wend his way through a plot outline, using the discoveries, reactions and responses of his main character as a guide to the action in the novel.

3. *Emotional Depth*

Like the first person POV, the attached third person POV allows the reader to access the protagonist's innermost thoughts, fears and dreams...with a bonus: We also access the feelings of other major characters from time to time, as necessary, usually in separate chapters.

In addition, while we are close enough to the protagonist to understand his feelings, we are *not* so close that we easily become mired in them. It is easier to avoid inner monologues, since we are far more aware of other characters interacting with the protagonist. Dialogues are also easier to write in the attached POV, since they simply occur in a natural time frame. We are freed of the notion that the protagonist is "recalling" a conversation word for word, as a first person narrator might.

4. *Avoiding the Problems of Other POVs*

One editor said he preferred that beginning writers use the third person attached POV, not for what it offered, but for what it avoided. Stuffy inner monologues, extremes of distance (too close or too far), problems with voice, author intrusion, shifting tenses and POVs, lack of description and sensual imagery, exclusion of feelings and reactions, journalistic prose – these usually pose no serious threat in the third person attached, if done properly.

Of course, that last caveat is a large one, and it often takes some practice to craft an attached POV so that it achieves just the right amount of distance, or objectivity. The range of distance varies from being very closely attached to the mental process of the POV character (as in the first person) to nearly the distance of an omniscient narrator. A skilled writer will experiment with the amount of distance available within the third person attached POV, and vary that distance within the novel as circumstances dictate.

DRAWBACKS OF THE ATTACHED POV

1. *Mock Inner Monologues*

The famous writer John Gardner was unimpressed with the value of the third person attached POV and advised writers not to use it at all. He pointed out that the "central intelligence" nature of this POV created a POV character that was ridiculously introverted and obsessively attached to his own observations. Nothing happens, claimed Gardner, unless the attached character watches it happening and reports on it. His spoof of the attached POV is very amusing and worth reading.

Gardner does have a good point: The attached POV can be *too* closely attached to a POV character. When this happens, we get an almost claustrophobic sense of entrapment within the character's psyche, much like a first person inner monologue. In this case, the reader is likely to be inundated with the character's thoughts, often expressed directly, just as if the attached POV character were a first person narrator:

> *What am I doing?* Doris said to herself. *If I tell Robert about the secret micro-chip, he's bound to tell Caspar, and then we'll both be in trouble.* She watched Robert's face intently, searching for some clue to his weakness, but found nothing. *Why did I ever get mixed up in this whole affair?* Doris scolded herself. *If I'd listened to my sister, I would have been on a beach in Hawaii right now, catching some rays and enjoying life. Why did I ever take up computer programming?*

Why, indeed? And why take up the third person attached POV if the first person is more effective? Note that the above passage would sound much less awkward if rewritten so that all the direct thoughts were expressed indirectly. ("What was she doing? If she told Robert about the secret microchip, he would be bound to tell Caspar, and then both she and Robert would be in trouble.")

A certain amount of self-searching is probably necessary in the attached POV. The trick is not to overdo it.

2. *When the Material Demands a Broader or Narrower Scope*

Not all types of fiction work best in a third person attached POV. Some fiction seems to cry out for an omniscient narrator who can organize a host of characters and details. This includes works that rely strongly on a story-telling approach, such as Karen Blixen's short stories; novels of huge scope, such as Tolstoy's *War and Peace* or *Anna Karenina*; and most stories with a base in fantasy or myth, such as J.R. Tolkien's *Lord of the Rings* trilogy. Some very personal stories, such as *The Catcher in the Rye* or Philip Roth's *Portnoy's Complaint*, demand the very intimate narration of the first person. So do fictional reminiscences, some satires, and many detective mysteries.

3. *Describing the Attached Character*

Imagine a beginning writer starting a novel in a POV attached to a female protagonist. At some point the writer is confronted with the need to tell the reader what that woman looks like. (She's not going to suddenly describe herself to someone, is she? Probably not.) Therefore, the panicked writer shifts into the omniscient or cinematic point of view and simply *spews out* a description of the protagonist. The effect: a POV that comes out of nowhere and hits the reader over the head with desperate information. The reader reels in disbelief. Up until this moment, he had bought into the "fictional dream" of the novel, but the sudden shift in POVs has ripped him out of it. He is now observing the character whom he thought was observing the action.

So...how *do* you describe the protagonist in third person attached POV? There are several ways, short of letting the character examine herself in a mirror, a tired cliche which many publishers dismiss on sight.

— Let another character describe the protagonist in dialogue. ("Gee, Mama, you look beautiful today.")
— Let the protagonist have some reason to describe herself.

She just couldn't get it together that morning. Her brown curls seethed around her head like a storm, although she had tried to comb them out with a stiff brush. Her skin felt smooth and taut, but she could not apply any blusher: The bruise on the top of her cheekbone hurt too much. At last she gave up all together, reasoning that if she didn't look elegant, at least she looked real.

(Note that this character is probably looking in a mirror, but that fact is never stated.)

— In a separate chapter, let another POV character describe and react to the protagonist.

4. *Keeping Secrets*

Characters in a third person attached POV cannot keep secrets from the reader...although first-person narrators can. Read the following passage:

I put the sample slide in the microscope and gasped. Now I knew just how Davis had killed Renee. All the evidence I needed was staring me in the face. I carefully placed the slide in a box, put the box in my sample case and hurried out of the lab.

Keeping secrets from the reader is a well-established convention of first-person mystery novels. It is done to heighten suspense, and usually takes place right before the climactic scene, in which the "secret" – a piece of evidence, a motive, a hiding place or a *modus operandi* – is uncovered. Since a character is telling the story directly to the reader, it makes sense that the narrator might choose to conceal information from the reader and reveal it at a more critical time.

This is the basic premise behind the "unreliable narrator," too: The first person narrator never has to show all his cards, and he can therefore keep readers guessing about his motives and truthfulness. In the case of the mystery, the narrator is only withholding a piece of information for greater narrative impact.

However, this technique doesn't work in the third person attached, in which the reader is privy to the thoughts of the protagonist. Read the microscope scene again, this time in the third person attached POV, to see how awkward it sounds.

Johnson put the sample slide in the microscope, his hands trembling. What would the sample reveal? Was this finally the key he needed to solve the crime...or just another blind alley? He peered through the lens and gasped. Now he knew just how Davis had killed Renee. All the evidence he needed was staring him in the face. He carefully placed the slide in a box, put the box in his sample case and hurried out of the lab.

This passage displays a cinematic approach to writing, an approach which relies on visual information instead of characterization. The reader expects the POV character to "tell us everything" – his thoughts, feelings, suspicions, and so on, as he does in the first four sentences. It doesn't make sense to believe that Johnson would say he had the evidence and then not reveal what the evidence is or why it is so important. The reader should be a party to those thoughts, but isn't, which is confusing and frustrating. The writer – not the character – keeps the reader at arm's length.

Keeping secrets is actually a form of author intrusion, a contrivance to preserve suspense. While it may work for the right first person narrator, it makes third person attached writing seem illogical, hokey and contrived. The writer would be far better off building suspense by allowing the POV character to uncover the truth bit by bit, letting the reader try to solve the case at the same time. When the protagonist has amassed his clues, he can put them together, using his own amazing resourcefulness, to achieve a solution.

B. OMNISCIENT POINT OF VIEW

Once upon a time (in the 18th and 19th centuries) most novels were written in the third person omniscient viewpoint. These novels were narrated by a God-like voice able to understand every character's thoughts, interpret all actions, presage all events and in general control and shape the entire story. This voice, though never actually attached to a character, nevertheless appeared to function as a character, with a distinct personality and personal opinions. Henry Fielding, Jane Austen, Charles Dickens, Nathaniel Hawthorne, Leo Tolstoy, and Karen Blixen all relied on third-person omniscient narrators.

Although the omniscient narrator is never seen or named, he is a character in the story, and the writer is as responsible for creating that narrator's voice as she is for creating her other characters.

Many novice writers don't realize this. They believe that if they simply vomit out the story, slipping in and out of characters' points of view as they please, making comparisons willy-nilly and tossing in personal opinions as the spirit moves them, they will somehow end up with a novel in the omniscient point of view. How misguided they are! In order to write in an omniscient viewpoint, one must first craft an omniscient narrator.

BENEFITS OF THE THIRD PERSON OMNISCIENT POV

1. *A Container for a Long, Complex, Rambling Story*

As mentioned earlier, certain novels seem to require, or at least accommodate, an omniscient narrative. Fantasies, tale-like novels, and historical novels or family sagas of enormous scope often benefit from a well-developed omniscient narrative voice which is broad enough and versatile enough to hold together a complex plot and many characters. Because the omniscient narrator knows all and sees all – past, present and future – the writer has abundant opportunity to foreshadow events, comment on characters' wisdom or foolhardiness, and even offer "personal" opinions, anecdotes or even moral sermons, preferably when they are pertinent to the story at hand.

2. *A Sense of Enchantment*

When done well, the omniscient narration is powerful, sometimes even magical, recalling ancient sagas such as *Beowulf* and *Gilgamesh*, or fairytales, such as the stories of Hans Christian Andersen and the Brothers Grimm.

Modern novels, such as Gabriel Garcia-Marquez's *One Hundred Years of Solitude*, sometimes take advantage of the supernatural element inherent in the omniscient voice to create a sense of enchantment and other-worldliness. Because the narrator is free to flit from one time, place or mindset to another, the omniscient POV can function as a kind of time machine, carrying the reader back to days long ago or epochs in the future...or even into different realities, where women can rise into the air, lifted by their laundry. It is a good POV in which to describe larger-than-life characters and events from fantasy, legends and popular history, since it is not limited in scope in any way, unlike central intelligence.

3. *Added Distance*

The third person omniscient POV offers more distance between reader and material than any other literary POV *except* cinematic (which provides too much distance). More distance means that the reader is less intimately involved with the thinking processes of the protagonist. Omniscient POV usually delves less deeply into any one character's thoughts, though it frequently reveals the thoughts of many characters, even minor ones. Therefore there is much less of a tendency for the reader to become bogged down in inner monologues, the bane of the first person and a potential drawback of the third person attached.

DRAWBACKS OF THE THIRD PERSON OMNISCIENT POV

1. *Biting Off Too Much*

Of all the POVs, the omniscient requires the most structure and control, probably because it has the most information to structure. The writer of the omniscient novel is not just responsible for representing the thoughts and actions of one central character – but many, some of whom are in direct contention with the protagonist and have antithetical opinions and goals. Juggling so many viewpoints, events, responses, and thoughts can be a challenge even to the most skilled writer, let alone a novice.

Too often the beginning writer is overwhelmed with the job of riding herd on so many personalities and perspectives, and simply loses touch with the characters and the plot altogether. At this point, the writer frequently begins spewing out the story, without regard to any omniscient voice he may have been trying to create. He feels the desperate urge to hand the reader a sack of expository information and get the story over with as quickly as possible. It is as if the writer is in a field, picking up straws; eventually he will have too many to hold in his hands.

A related point of view – the limited omniscient perspective – can solve some of the problems mentioned above. In limited omniscience, the third person omniscient narrator delves solely into the consciousness of the protagonist; other characters' thoughts are never revealed. This POV, similar to an attached POV, allows for the creation of a distinct narrative voice that is far more manageable than the traditional omniscient narrator.

2. *It's Not Easy Being God-like*

Of all those who write in an omniscient voice, fantasy writers have the easiest time of it. Armed with a knowledge of historic, heroic tales and legends, they can craft a narrative voice which sounds as if it is attached to a storyteller such as an ancient bard of yore. This voice, almost a standard fixture in fantasy writing, is wise and warm, all-knowing, solicitous and ethical – one part grandparent, one part newspaper reporter and one part seer or sage. Tolkien uses such a narrator; so do science-fiction/fantasy writers Ray Bradbury and Isaac Asimov.

If you're not writing fantasy, you simply must create your own narrator out of thin air, and this isn't easy. Who is God-like? Who can see past, present and future, then tell us about all three as easily as any of us reads the daily news? Given you can create such an all-powerful narrator, what would motivate him to care about the trials and tribulations of your main characters? A writer must, on some level, think over all these questions about her omniscient narrator *before* she creates him and before she enlists him to tell her tale. If she doesn't, the story will not have the essential voice it needs to carry the reader through the many details and convoluted paths of the narration.

3. *Distance*

The sense of distance in the omniscient POV that prevents the writer from creating inner monologues is the very same distance that can cause problems. How distant is too distant? The reader must relate to the protagonist and other major characters on some level. He must sympathize with them (or dislike them), but he must not be indifferent to them.

The very fact that an omniscient narrator is poking about in the minds of the characters often creates such a sense of distance in the readers that they can't become too closely involved with any one character. After all, in an omniscient narration, it is the narrator telling us that, for example, an old man likes the color green because it is the color of a beloved childhood toy. Technically, the old gent cannot offer his opinion directly, for he is not an observer; he is being observed. Thus some of the emotional impact of thoughts, dreams, fears and memories is blunted because it comes to us from an indirect, often impersonal source.

4. *All Things Must Pass*

In many literary circles, the omniscient POV is considered passe, obsolete, dated: a dinosaur from the Jurassic era in the development of fiction.

We at the agency don't condemn the omniscient narrative on sight, but we do know, by having read many unsuccessful attempts at omniscient narrations, that it's a hard concept to execute well. Back in the 18th and 19th centuries, when omniscience was in vogue, writers were feeling their way around in the novel. This large, cumbersome literary form was new (hence its name), and it made sense for writers to draw from past omniscient tradi-tions of sagas, myths, tales and campfire stories to find a way to structure large, potentially unwieldy works such as *Tom Jones* and *Pride and Prejudice*.

Today's writer, however, has more choices and need not feel shackled to the story-telling customs that appealed to audiences of ages past.

5. *A Matter of Pace*

A long, sprawling omniscient tale told from many perspectives, usually encompassing a long period of time, offers many opportunities for a slow pace.

"I have a leisurely writing style," one beginning writer told us. "I don't model my work on these modern writers who are in such a hurry to tell their story." She meant to say that her novel moved at a slow pace and that she expected her readers to put up with a lot of exposition and extraneous in-formation, so common in omniscient novels.

Alas, the day of the snail-paced, laborious, Walter Scott-style omniscient novel is just about over. Those of us who grew up wrapped around a book will recall with a poignant sigh those long hours spent plowing through huge works such as Scott's *Castle Adamant* or Lew Wallace's *Ben-Hur*. It was a labor of love just to get through such dense material. However, audiences used to sound bites, two-hour movies and half-hour TV shows will find it hard to endure pages of exposition about, say, the quarrying of the stone used to build a certain fortress...or the way a lake slowly transforms into a swamp. James Michener has developed a huge following based on exactly this prem-ise, but few of us are such master storytellers.

Because of all these factors, the third person omniscient POV is one of the hardest to use successfully. Therefore, in general, most new writers would be best served by studying the attached third person POV and writing their first novel in that perspective. (Fantasy, science fiction and some historical novels might prove exceptions.) Third person attached is far simpler and less demanding to write, easier to read, and often easier to market.

CHAPTER
THIRTEEN

CONVENTION: GINGERBREAD — FRAMES, FLASHBACKS, PROLOGUES AND EPILOGUES

IF YOU'VE EVER seen a Victorian house, you've probably noticed the "gingerbread" on the fascia, windows and porch: ornate carved wooden ornaments, usually white, like the fanciful icing on ginger cookies. While not an integral part of the house, these additions add character and grace to its design.

Literary gingerbread also consists of non-essential items carefully added to a novel to enhance its design and make it "easy on the eyes." But, unlike the ornaments on the house, literary gingerbread is part of the structure of the larger work.

Not all houses need gingerbread, and certainly not all novels require frames, flashbacks, prologues, epilogues and similar devices. Sometimes, however, these tools can be very helpful in constructing a sound narrative structure. To better understand how these devices work, let's take a look at each. (We'll consider prologues and epilogues as a unit.)

THE FRAME

The word "frame" connotes a picture frame, and to some degree this is an apt description of the literary term. The frame is a story which leads into another story and surfaces at the end of the second story to bring the novel to a close. Usually the two parts of the frame are much shorter than the story in the middle. Sometimes the story will be front-framed only, that is, it will have only the introductory part of the frame, not the conclusion, like *A Turn of the Screw*.

Unlike a picture frame, the literary frame is an integral part of the work. Writers use frames for many reasons: to establish a narrator, provide a comparison or offer background information for the "main" story.

One of the most famous examples of the "framed" novel in English literature is Joseph Conrad's *Heart of Darkness*, in which several men discuss an issue, and one of them tells a story to illustrate it. These men "return" at the end to discuss the interior story. This technique is useful for establishing an omniscient narrative voice and introducing a larger-than-life character such as Kurtz.

Now and then one finds a work in which the frame *is* the story. Eudora Welty's short story, "The Petrified Man," in which women in a beauty parlor discuss the fate of a sideshow swindler who pretends to be petrified, is a good example. The real "petrified man," however, is the son of one of the women, who is ignored, humiliated and ultimately beaten by his mother.

FLASHBACKS

The flashback is basically a character's memories, recollections, and reminiscences, recalled at strategic points within a story. It is a useful device for giving the reader critical background information and insights from the character's childhood, or other experiences that have occurred before the "time" the novel "takes place." These events could have occurred in the distant past or the recent past.

Recalling the past is a normal part of life. People remember the past to help them understand the present and often simply for the joy of reliving a happy experience. In fiction, flashbacks can be used for several more specific purposes, including:

— To contrast the present with the past. To illustrate, imagine a scene from a story in which a young man is in prison, undergoing the tremendous rigors of a prisoner's life. In order to preserve his sanity and give himself a reason for living, he recalls his idyllic boyhood years on a farm in Iowa, riding horses and swimming in the river. These beautiful memories are in harsh contrast to his present life, and give him as much distress over innocence lost as they give him comfort.

— To reveal important details which drive the plot. These flashbacks are most apparent in mystery novels, where a detective, for example, might recall the first time he met a certain person, a suspect in a murder. Some inconsequential fact – the person is left-handed, or is allergic to peanuts – gains importance in retrospect if it implicates or acquits the suspect. These details are often remembered in leisure.

— To give important personal insights on a character and increase pressure. For example, say the main character is called on to drive a truck but panics when he sits down to drive. If, through a previous flashback, the reader knows that the character has been involved in a serious trucking accident, the reader will understand the motivation behind the character's fear of driving and his panic when he enters the car. This knowledge enhances the tension in the situation.

— To allow a character to search his past so he may come to grips with a conflict. For example, a protagonist may frequently flash back to his abusive childhood in order to better understand his brother's suicide.

— To maintain or explain a "relationship" with a deceased friend or relative. In Gabaldon's *Outlander*, for instance, Claire often thinks of her late anthropologist uncle, who raised her as a child. Her memories of him provide her with the strength to overcome difficult situations and understand other cultures.

Common Problems with Flashbacks

Skilled writers use flashbacks to add dimension to characters and plot, allowing characters to develop and "stretching" the time period in which the story takes place. This adds scope, depth and breadth to the novel.

In general, however, flashbacks are memories, not stories. They are events which have already happened, and whatever tension they create is not immediate. Not realizing this, beginning writers often end up in trouble when they depend on flashbacks to tell their stories or establish exposition. Common kinds of flashback problems include:

— Awkward structure or progression. Rust Hills, in *Writing in General and the Short Story in Particular*, tells of one "terrible novel" in which the writer goes into a flashback every time his protagonist takes a step up a flight of stairs. Thus the story is delivered in fits and starts, very distant from the "present" action. Such strained contrivance almost never works in fiction, and only serves to make the reader highly aware of the novel as a construct.

— Weak beginnings. Novice writers frequently begin a novel with a flashback, after briefly establishing the main character. This premature use of the flashback is usually done for one of two reasons: 1) to start the story in the past and work toward the present, or 2) to present exposition. Neither reason is usually justifiable. The flash- is totally inappropriate for the beginning of a novel, since it imparts a feeling of distance in time and a sense of languid reflection. A skilled writer might be able to pull off this kind of feat, but we encourage beginning writers to avoid it. It only muddies the writing waters and delays the development of the plot.

A story should begin at its beginning, usually with a compelling act that will drive the progress of the entire novel. This will create a sense of immediacy, intimacy and urgency. If the story begins with an episode in the protagonist's childhood, then begin with that episode, as if it were occurring in the present action of the story (not present tense, mind you). Chances are, however, that the story actually begins much later.

—Inappropriate background information. Exposition, told directly, in narrative, or indirectly, in a flashback, has little purpose in a novel. A writer beginning her novel with a flashback may feel she is presenting exposition in a clever, more accessible form, but she is really only making the character appear more distant and somehow detached from his own story. How much more effective it would be to present the character with a compelling event and allow him to react to it. His reactions will tell us much more about his personality than any accounts of his childhood in North Dakota and his college days at Notre Dame. Once again, it is a matter of beginning where the story begins, not where the protagonist begins. Of course, any vital information from the past can be worked into the novel in terms of later flashbacks, where appropriate, or in dialogue. (Note that an initial flashback construction is not the same as a frame construction, which usually involves characters other than the protagonist of the central story.)

— Too many regressions and digressions. Flashbacks may be the spice of fictional lives, but they are not the meat. We often see manuscripts flooded with flashbacks, as if the writer is so unsure of her story that she feels compelled to search backward in her protagonist's life to find something worth writing about.

While there is no numerical limit on flashbacks in novels, more is definitely not better. The inexperienced writer should pause after every flashback and ask herself whether or not her plot and characters demand such a device. What is she achieving through the flashback, and what does she hope to achieve?

— The double flashback, or flashback within a flashback. Flashbacks should be used with caution, since they "recreate" a time before the present action of the story takes place. They therefore pose the reader with the opportunity for confusing time and place within the novel.

If written skillfully, one flashback at a time is easy enough to follow. But what if, in the middle of a flashback, the character recalls something that happened in an even earlier time? The result can cause serious disorientation for the reader.

In one example by a beginning writer, a character named Sebastian, an artist, is reflecting on his life. He remembers an event that happened to him while he was a 20-year-old student in an art academy: He met a famous artist who later became his wife. In the flashback, while Sebastian is talking to the artist, Sebastian recollects his first serious art class as a child of ten. Now we have a flashback within a flashback. If something takes place – for example, Sebastian is in an accident and breaks a finger – the reader might wonder in which time frame the event is occurring: the present, the first flashback or the second.

To confound matters even further, this inexperienced writer included a *third* flashback (triple flashback) in which Sebastian, as a ten-year-old, recalls the first drawing he made, at the age of four. Even if the writer is *meticulous* about his transitions into these stacked flashbacks, the risk is just too high that the reader will not be able to follow the character through the times that these events are taking place. She will also have difficulty figuring out "which Sebastian" she should be imagining at any given point – the older man, the young man, the schoolboy or the pre-schooler.

All these flashbacks can be used, if they are important. The key is not to string them together without a solid reference point. Each flashback should be presented as an individual memory of Sebastian, looking back on the past from his present situation. Or the writer can tell Sebastian's story chronologically, starting when he is four, hitting on all three events in his life. Sebastian as an older man can still flash back on past events to gain further insight from them.

Therefore, we strongly recommend that the first-time writer stick to one flashback at a time, and use it only where it logically belongs to reveal character or further the plot.

The Flash Forward: Foreseeing the Future

Premonitions, predictions and some dream sequences are all examples of "flash forwards," in which future events (as opposed to past events) are foreshadowed and/or examined. Flash forwards are staple conventions of several genres, primarily horror, romance, young adult and fantasy. The flash forward is a forecast or warning of things to come, and almost always comes to pass within the reality of the story. A child's dream about mud monsters (which eventually appear out of a polluted swamp); an Elizabethan lady's premonition that she will be abducted by a handsome but dangerous bandit (which of course comes true, but perhaps with a twist of some sort); and a wizard's prediction that only the future king of England can draw the sword from the stone (sound familiar?) are all examples of flash forwards.

The flash forward can be effective or ridiculous, depending on how skill-fully it is used. If done well, it will create tension and suspense, but if done poorly it will come across as a contrivance that takes the place of a well-structured plot. (Flash forwards should not be confused with omniscient remarks such as, "Little did she know that the house was already sold," or "If only Phil had realized that gila monsters are poisonous." If not firmly anchored in the voice of an omniscient observer, these comments represent authorial intrusion and should be avoided.)

R.L. Stine, well-known writer of horror stories for young adults, suc-cessfully uses dreams to foreshadow frightening events. Part of the strength of such dreams is that they create a feeling of suspense, posing the question of how the protagonist will triumph over the inevitable visitation of horror.

Dream Sequences

Some dream sequences are flash forwards, but not all. Dreams can also be used to let the protagonist mourn for a time or person long gone, as in *The Old Man and the Sea*, or to create a feeling of general distortion, threat-ening circumstances and perhaps even flirtation with insanity, as in Poe's story, "The Premature Burial." The dream or series of dreams can also be used to help the protagonist explore his darkest fears and secrets.

One problem beginning writers seem to have with dream sequences is the inability to create the sense of distortion and uneasiness that are part and parcel of dreams. This is partially due to descriptive details: Dreams meld the real with the unreal, and so must the writer of dreams. For example, a character having a dream about brushing his teeth may feel uneasy for some unknown reason as he puts toothpaste on his toothbrush and scrubs away at his teeth. At some point he may begin to feel a roughness on his tongue or hear strange noises. Eventually he may realize that the brush is not a brush at all, but a small snake. His reaction to this event may be just as peculiar as the event itself, and he may find himself putting the snake into the toothbrush holder as if nothing is amiss. A dream sequence is one of the few places in fiction in which character's reactions may be totally inappropriate...and yet totally acceptable.

There is some question among writers about whether the dream is a contrivance or a legitimate device for accessing a protagonist's innermost thoughts. Our guideline about dreams is the same as it is for any other technique: If it works, keep it. The more the sequence resembles a real dream (complete with the character's reactions of fear or confusion upon wakening), the greater its chances of working. A dream sequence may be appropriate for one story or protagonist, and not for another. Certainly they should be considered a "special effect," used sparingly, and only for specific reasons. For instance, dreams are especially useful for indicating a character's fears, apprehensions, tensions and emotions he may strive to keep to himself during waking hours.

One place a dream definitely does *not* belong is at the beginning of a novel. This is a cliche and is usually also used as a contrivance for dredging up exposition, which also has no place in the beginning of a story.

PROLOGUES AND EPILOGUES

Like the frame, the prologue/epilogue combination acts as bookends for a central story, giving it a definite beginning and a definite end. Also like the frame, the prologue/epilogue is separate from the rest of the story, yet cannot stand by itself. A prologue is not a full-fledged story, but a scene or part of a scene which reveals information crucial to understanding the story. Its sister, the epilogue, is basically a denouement, depicting the fate of the main characters, sometimes taking place far in the future.

Prologues and epilogues are fairly recent conventions in novels, having come to fiction via the techniques of nonfiction. In nonfiction, it is often necessary to give some background on a story in the beginning (the prologue) and, in the end, to wrap up any loose threads, even if to do so is simply a matter of admitting ignorance about what happened (the epilogue). In fiction, the prologue and epilogue are usually found in historical novels, science fiction or fantasy, where exotic backgrounds or cultures or complicated events require some explanation or depiction.

One resourceful writer wanted to match her female protagonist with a married man whose family (unbeknownst to him) had been tragically murdered. The writer knew it was important to show the reader that the man was actually available, even though he didn't realize it. Therefore, she created a prologue which showed the murders and introduced the antagonist. Her epilogue was a typical denouement, "wrapping up" some stray threads left over from the central conflicts.

Of course, prologue and epilogue may be much more closely bound by content or form. For example, imagine a central story about a young man's experiences in college. A prologue to this story may show his struggles during the SAT and applications or visits to colleges, while the epilogue may show his reactions during and after graduation.

Obviously, not all novels require a prologue and epilogue, and a beginning writer should carefully evaluate his story to determine the best structure for it. As so many new writers believe, creating a prologue does not mean simply writing the heading "prologue" above the first chapter. The action of the prologue usually takes place before the action of the central story but is somehow crucial to the story.

At the agency, we frequently review manuscripts which misuse the prologue. Sometimes writers actually repeat the prologue during the course of the novel, or create a prologue about an event which is peripheral or unimportant to the central plot or character. These errors should be avoided when crafting your novel.

Does some incident prior to the central story play an important role in the story? Do specific actions take place before and after the central story? If so, consider the use of a prologue/epilogue to "set up" and "set down" the story.

FRILLS

Frills are similar to gingerbread, but are usually not integral to a story. They are additions which add flavor, variety and interest to the fabric of a novel. Journal entries, letters, or verse are all examples of frills.

Just like gingerbread, frills should not be used very frequently and should only be used if there is a good reason to use them. For example, if your protagonist is a poet or a poetry lover, you might very appropriately include some verses in the novel. Perhaps the character reveals her deepest emotions only in verse. If the story is set in the 18th or 19th century, when journal writing was all the rage, some pages from a diary might give added insight to a character, as would letters. A novel composed solely of letters is called an "epistolary novel." Like Alice Walker's *The Color Purple*, these novels can be very effective, but are usually difficult to structure.

CHAPTER FOURTEEN

CONVENTION: PLOTTING TECHNIQUES

MUCH HAS BEEN said here already about how to plot a novel or short story, and much that you read in this chapter may seem repetitive. However, achieving an effective plot is such an important part of the writer's craft that we at the agency believe it cannot be overemphasized. In this chapter, we'll explore some of the specific techniques for structuring a plot that works.

SUSPENSE, PRESSURE AND TENSION: THE STRESS FACTORS

You might think that these terms apply only to mysteries, espionage novels, police dramas and the like. Actually, nearly every successful, conventional novel has an element of suspense and creates a significant feeling of tension as it progresses.

Suspense may be defined as the reader's sensation that something – usually something unpleasant, dangerous or disturbing – is about to happen. This sensation may be aroused by subtle observations (a suspicious glance) or by direct threats of violence.

Tension is often used to mean suspense, and the words are somewhat interchangeable. However, there is an important distinction. Suspense is caused by the reader's perception of danger; tension is the character's reaction to his own perception of danger. The reader may feel the character's tension, and this builds suspense.

Pressure is the force the writer uses to get a character to react or respond to a potentially threatening situation. If a group of people are driving two vehicles toward a distant destination in a desert and one vehicle breaks down, the change in the situation puts greater pressure on the people in the party to survive. This in turn builds suspense.

That All-important Protagonist

Too often, writers lose sight of their protagonist's development and concentrate on building suspense, solving a mystery, or contriving a resolution. In most cases, they will have a stronger, more compelling novel if they emphasize the protagonist and how a central conflict increases his insights and changes his outlook on life.

Conflict may come from external or internal sources. External conflicts come from direct threats or dangers in society or nature, such as stalkers with guns or elephant stampedes. An internal conflict arises from feelings of guilt, jealousy, fear, anger and other uncomfortable emotions that demand a character's attention.

The following is an example of external conflict.

Let's say that a man embezzles money from his firm, perhaps with misguided but noble intentions. (We'll say that he needs the money for his mother's heart operation.) Immediately the writer has created a scenario for suspense. The reader knows the character has set events into motion because of his theft. Tension is created too, since the character is going to be paranoid, afraid of every noise. He may brush off as coincidence the fact that he sees the same woman twice on a hotel elevator in one day, but when he sees her four times the next day and six times the next, he will become increasingly suspicious. His own guilt is driving his suspicions. Perhaps the woman is harmless. Perhaps she is a detective, or perhaps a hired killer.

By introducing the mysterious woman, the writer exerts pressure on the character to *do something* – call a friend, leave the hotel where he has decided to hide out, go to the police and confess, confront the woman...whatever. In turn the reader wonders what the characters will do, creating even more suspense. Because he is curious to know how the character will react, the reader will keep turning the pages to find out what happens.

So far the writer has the reader's curiosity. But he is wisely discontent to leave the matter where it is, so he *increases* the pressure to increase tension and suspense *and* make the situation more difficult on the suffering protagonist. The embezzler returns to his room from dinner to find a note on his nightstand: LORRAINE THREE FIVE. Lorraine is his mother's name, and she has had three heart operations in the past five years. The embezzler is now puzzled and disturbed, as well as nervous: Is the note a threat? A warning? A mean-spirited joke? Is the note from the woman, or someone else? What should he do now? Call his mom? Or wait to see what happens, lest he upset her needlessly or even make her an accessory in his crime? This man is used to taking calculated risks; otherwise he would not have stolen the money. But now he must take risks in a game which he does not control, providing him a chance to change for the better...or the worse.

If the conflict is internal, the suspense will be far more subtle. For example, a woman whose father has Alzheimer's Disease may be faced with a guilt-producing decision: Should she keep Papa at home, though he is growing increasingly hostile, or ship him off to a nursing home, where he may be unhappy, resentful or even neglected? Once she makes her decision (let's say she keeps him at home), his further deterioration and her increasing weariness, perhaps coupled with complications in her marriage or children's lives, force her to reconsider her decision.

Suspense and Plotting

Do you notice how suspense, tension and pressure move the story along in both scenarios above? The action *rises*, that is, suspense and tension increase as the stories develop. The effect is cumulative, not episodic, because stress is growing, and there is no resolution in sight. Of course, the characters are important, but the reader knows that they will develop depending on how they confront the increasing tension and conflict in their lives.

Of course, not all novels will rely as heavily on suspense and tension as these samples, but keep in mind that stress factors – suspense, tension and pressure – can cause action to rise and characters to react, respond, grow and change.

As a writer, it's your responsibility to keep the reader wondering what will happen next. One beginning writer attempted to tell the tale of a small-town police chief who gets involved in solving the murder of one young woman and falls in love with another. Unfortunately, the characters distance themselves greatly from the victim, to such an extent that the reader almost forgets from time to time that a murder has been committed. To correct this situation, the writer should consider increasing pressure on the protagonist by making the victim *important* to him, even though he has never met her before. The easiest way to do this would be to make the victim the best friend of his love interest, thus giving the chief a vested interest in the murder. This change would connect the death with the chief's present sit- uation and add tension, urgency and a dimension of personal debt to his investigation.

Time Limits, or Limited Time Offers (LTOs)

In advertising parlance, an LTO is an offer one must respond to by a certain date. After the date, the offer is void...or at least a little harder to negotiate. The LTO is a favorite ad ploy to create pressure on the potential buyer to snap up a service or piece of merchandise while it is available at "bargain prices."

In fiction writing, a time limit builds suspense while putting tremendous pressure on the character to act. Of course, time limits are especially useful in murder mysteries, horror and espionage novels, and law stories, where suspense is crucial to plot and character development. The central question becomes this: Can the protagonist succeed before his "time is up?" For example, can the detective find the murderer *before* an innocent person is convicted of the crime? Can the special agent locate and disarm the neutron bomb before it blows up Washington D.C.? Can the besieged housewife hold off the deranged killer until the blizzard lifts and the police can come to help her?

These "LTOs" may or may not involve a specific time or date; however, they are all dependent on specific, time-limited circumstances. The trial will end, the time bomb scheduled to explode will explode or be defused, the blizzard will abate. The protagonist has an hourglass full of sand, and his time is up when all the sand is out. The closer he is to the last grain of sand in the hourglass, the greater the suspense and tension in the plot.

Let's take a look at Stephen King's horror novel, *The Shining*, in which King puts an interesting spin on the LTO. Here the burden of the time limit is on the antagonist: the haunted hotel. If it does not force the zombie, Jack, to adjust the pressure of the building's boilers in time, the whole evil place will blow sky-high. Which is just what happens.

Of course LTOs increase suspense in literary works as well. Jack London's "To Build a Fire", set in the frozen north, has a natural, extremely basic time limit: Can the man find his camp or otherwise keep himself warm before he dies of hypothermia?

DRAMA VERSUS MELODRAMA

What is Drama?

The word drama comes to us from the theater and still has very strong connotations of the stage. Drama refers not only to a serious play, but also to the riveting manner in which that play unfolds, and the arousal of emotions in the audience as they react to the actors on the stage.

In written fiction, suspense, tension and pressure all work together to heighten the reader's emotions and create a sense of drama. Drama is the result of gripping, intriguing action or insight, or the resolution of a troubling, difficult, believable conflict. In order to be believable and to make an impact, the drama must involve the feelings – or sentiments – of the characters in the fiction.

Think of your favorite moment of drama from literature. Is it Lord Jim's death scene, in which he finally redeems himself for an act of cowardice? The climactic scene where Rosasharn suckles the starving migrant worker in *The Grapes of Wrath*? The scene from Faulkner's *As I Lay Dying*, in which eight-year-old Vardaman, bereaved over his mother's death, drills holes in her coffin "so she can breathe"? Or the graphic description of the murder of Piggy, the shy, endearing boy in *The Lord of the Flies*?

These dramatic scenes involve strong emotions: revulsion, spiritual release, compassion, irony, grief and love. But these scenes are *successfully* dramatic because of three reasons: 1) The emotions are attached to believable characters, characters the reader cares about, 2) each makes use of an extremely strong visual image, and 3) the scenes appear to occur as natural outgrowths of the characters and the story; they do not seem contrived or "phony."

One might add a fourth reason, namely the brilliant quality of the writing in these examples, but few of us can hope to approach that level of art. Any writer can, however, understand the first three reasons and make use of them when she writes to give a sense of drama to her work.

Punch

Neither a fruit beverage nor an English puppet, the writer's "punch" is more closely related to a right hook. Editors often speak of punch when they are referring to a sense of drama in the language of a story (or a lack thereof). Punch in this case means strong, bold words that grab the reader's attention while conveying all the meaning of a longer, boring string of words.

For example, one novice wrote that his character "rubbed his injured leg gently but vigorously to make it feel better." To add punch to his language, he could have written: "He massaged his injured leg." The same meaning is conveyed in less time, with less reader effort, with a more dramatic effect.

Or consider this sample:

Dick drew back and delivered a massive wallop right on Will's jaw.

versus:

Dick punched him.

What is Melodrama?

Melodrama bears the same relationship to drama that the Three Stooges bear to comedy: It works for the moment, and the moment is all that matters. The melodramatic scene of the beautiful young woman dying of cancer, accompanied by a weeping child, makes us reach for our hankies, but moments later we are reaching for the Milk Duds. Our emotions have been stirred, but only on the surface. A melodramatic scene is the emotional equivalent of Larry gouging Curly's eyes: It's funny, but we are a little ashamed for having laughed at it.

The reason we are a little ashamed of melodrama is because we realize it does not ring true, yet we have nevertheless responded to it with heartfelt emotions.

We've all seen melodrama more times than we like to admit: Cheap movies and exploitive novels are replete with melodrama. Both drama and melodrama attempt to appeal to our sentiments, or emotions, but drama, like fine wine, takes time to create realistic displays of emotions. Melodrama takes shortcuts to emotions. The result is that we remember truly dramatic scenes in novels, but we forget the mawkish excess emotions, or sentimentality, of melodrama.

Sentimental Icons

Melodrama is a matter of delivering the most emotional bang for the buck. Therefore, it stresses the "strong emotional image" at the expense of the other aspects of drama, such as well-developed plots and characters. To get the most emotional impact with the least effort, melodrama depends on the use of *icons*, that is, cultural symbols that represent or trigger strong emotions, to instantly pull on people's heartstrings.

Melodramatic icons include: the death of a child, young person or beloved pet, to elicit grief or anger; graphic violence and gore to elicit disgust and horror; symbolic representations of innocence (a child) and evil (often represented by a sinister person dressed in black) to elicit a sense of danger and dread; American Indians, to elicit pride in the innate nobility of mankind (at least since the 1960s); and nuns, to elicit a feeling of respect or sanctity. In order to create instant outrage in the reader, therefore, the writer need only create a very shallow scene in which a nun is raped or an Native American is humiliated or tortured. Or should the native be raped and the nun tortured? The images are easily reversed, since the characters and the events are never fully developed. Such a tactic could backfire on the writer, however, especially if the reader feels the writer is patronizing her or trying to take advantage of her emotions, rather than honestly eliciting them.

Of course there are many more sentimental icons. All bear a strong resemblance to another kind of canned image we have discussed before, the stock character. Like stock characters, sentimental icons are used by writers who are not interested in developing characters, creating suspense, or adding depth to their writing: They want to hit the emotions hard, with as little effort as possible.

Victorian writing is full of crass melodrama and sickening sentimentality. Even great writers such as Dickens were not above using crippled children (*A Christmas Carol*) to wring instant emotions from their audience.

Seeking Drama in Everyday Life

More often than not, drama is found – not in the unusual or outlandish – but in the courage of living from one day to the next. While melodrama often seems highly contrived and unrealistic, drama springs from real life and truth. There is more real drama to be found in the act of a person driving past an abandoned shoe from an accident victim (*Lolita*) than in thousands of sick children, suffering nuns and bleeding limbs. This is not to say that suffering and violence are not suitable subjects for novels, but they must be explored with depth, compassion, and understanding.

A successful writer often gradually prepares his readers for dramatic scenes to prevent the scenes from appearing shallow, distant, false, garish...and melodramatic. For example, Conrad spent over 100,000 words leading up to Lord Jim's death, the long-awaited act of repentance and absolution that brings the story to a climax.

PARALLEL STRUCTURES

We have briefly discussed parallelism in fiction earlier, in terms of the romance novel, which often contrasts a minor romance between minor characters with the major romance between protagonists. Parallel structure is simply the positioning of two like incidents or situations for purposes of contrast or comparison.

One famous use of parallelism occurs in Nathaniel Hawthorne's novel, *The Scarlet Letter*. At the beginning of the book, Hester is publicly humiliated on a scaffold, in view of the entire village. In the middle, Hester and Arthur, her lover, stand on a scaffold to watch a comet, a symbol of their adultery, pass through the heavens. At the conclusion, Arthur confesses to his sin, once again, on the scaffold, in full public view. Also, he is physically and symbolically elevated, because he is confessing the truth and seeking repentance. The novel is structured around these three similar scenes, and the reader is likely to compare and contrast each one.

Parallel scenes often form the beginning and end of a novel or story. For example, a novel may begin with, say, a scene in which a young man leaves his family home, only to return in the end to find his family, their situation and even the house completely changed. This use of parallelism often provides a sense of closure to a piece of fiction.

Certainly this device can be powerful and viable, although it is not used very often in modern fiction. The beginning writer should be aware of it, keeping in mind that parallel structure can easily become a contrivance if used sloppily or without good reason.

Strong plotting is vital to any novel. Although a novel may well be a man, what happens to that man shapes his personality and his destiny. At its bare bones, plot may be seen as a device which reveals the development of the protagonist. Too often we receive manuscripts in which the plot is the protagonist, and characters merely foils for the action. Such an imbalance between plot and characters almost never works in written fiction.

While plot should not be emphasized over characters, neither should it be neglected. The key is to unite plot and protagonist, so that the two are inseparable. The plotting conventions are the "magic tricks" that will help you accomplish just that.

CHAPTER FIFTEEN

CONVENTION: SHOWING AND TELLING — SCENE AND NARRATIVE

A FICTION WRITER IS a storyteller, but much more than that. A storyteller in the ancient oral tradition of the Greek, African and Celtic bards concentrates on the *narrative* of her story. She tells the listener what happened, usually using the omniscient viewpoint so common in fairy tales and legends. The emphasis on storytelling is on the circumstances leading up to a conflict, and the action involved in resolving that conflict. Most folktales, such as the Anansi stories from Africa or "The Seven Sorrows of Deirdre" from Ireland concentrate on exposition, conflict, and resolution. The protagonist is usually a one-dimensional hero or heroine like Wily Ulysses, Scheming Anansi, Brave Cuchulain, and Beautiful Deirdre.

In most successful modern fiction, however, writers show more of the story than they tell. They trust the reader (who, unlike the audience of, say, a television show, can reread whatever he does not immediately understand) to pick up clues about the personality of the protagonist, the nature of the conflict, the direction of the plot, and the overall theme of the novel. The skillful writer implies much about those important points but rarely makes them obvious or tells them out-right to the reader.

The fiction writer uses two different means to write a novel or short story: narrative and scene. Narrative, as discussed above and below, *tells* the reader what is happening in a story, while scenes *show* what is happening. If a writer hopes to be successful, it is important for him to understand both narrative and scene *and* when to use each.

I'm Telling You...The Narrative

Fictional narrative is narrated prose, that is, the POV character tells the reader what is happening in the story, whether it is a change in place or time, or a description of a person or object. However, narrative can also be used to set a scene. In addition, the specific action in a scene – a fight, a chase, a stroll in a park, a sexual liaison or a sporting event – is usually narrated

Such action does not make use of extended dialogue and is sometimes called a "narrative scene."

Narrative can take place in any point of view, as these narrative descriptions of two people approaching a spruce forest indicate.

— (In the first person POV, from the first person narrator:) Ahead of me I saw a forest of white spruce, stunted by the high altitude. I breathed in the tangy scent of the scrawny trees, glowing in the half-light of dawn, and followed Melissa down the trail.

— (In the omniscient POV, from the omniscient narrator:) Steven and Melissa noticed the forest at the same time, the little spruce trees rising from nowhere as they rounded the bend in the trail. The scent of turpentine reminded Steven of his youth in Oregon; the glow of dawn through the branches made Melissa think of the long nights she had spent with her ailing grandfather.

— (In the third person attached, from the POV of the main character:) Steven rounded the bend and gasped at the sight of the spruce forest directly ahead of him, silver in the light of early dawn. It was just where Melissa had said it would be, he thought. He stared at the stunted trees marking the edge of the timberline. Their spicy fragrance reminded him of the scent of Melissa's shampoo. What kinds of secrets could these ancient trees possibly conceal? he wondered.

Traveling Music

Narration is particularly useful as a transitional device to get a character from one place to another...or from one time to another. For example, if Martha is graduating from college in the early spring and looking forward to the late summer, when her job begins, narrative can move her from spring to summer quickly and effectively, to wit:

The dark greens and browns of summer replaced the bright colors of spring. A stifling Fourth of July burst and passed, bringing Martha that much closer to August and the new job. Three days before she was to start, she laid all her skirts, blouses and jackets on her bedroom floor and selected the best of the lot, a gray tweed suit and white chiffon shirt. The outfit was too warm for the season, but it would have to do.

Problems with Narrative

"Show, don't tell! Show, don't tell!"

One writer's eighth-grade English teacher apparently bombarded her with this message in creative writing classes. "But I'm glad she did," says the writer. "If she didn't, I would always be holding my readers at a distance, and they would never get to know the characters in my stories."

Too often, beginning writers use narrative to force exposition on the reader and "spew out" the story. It is so easy and simple just to tell the reader what sort of person the protagonist is, or what his childhood was like, what he looks like, or why he is afraid of thunderstorms. But too much narrative exposition is almost never a good idea. The reader wants to deduce such information for himself. He wants to "see" the characters interacting with each other and revealing their personalities through their speech, movements and thoughts, just as real people do.

In addition, long narrative in an omniscient or cinematic point of view can create a flat or static feel, especially if it takes the form of description not attached to a central character. A lengthy omniscient description of a setting, for example, will soon grow tedious to most readers, unless they sense there is an important underlying reason for all that narrative.

Long narratives tend to undercut conflict and lessen the effects of suspense, tension and pressure. Remember, while narrative is useful, it is the duty of the writer to create the impression that the plot is moving forward, and it is best moved forward in scenes. The same is true in plays and movies, where narrative by a character, on or off stage, provides "traveling music" to establish changes in place, time or circumstance.

Care must be taken when writing narrative to match the language with the narrator. Formal, stiff writing will create a definite narrative tone which may or may not be appropriate to the story. Such writing will also give the reader a feeling of added distance. Narrative is generally not the place to try out one's expansive vocabulary, since most successful writing is based on simple, unpretentious language.

Let Me Show You...The Scene

Just as the idea of drama was nurtured in the ancient theaters, the concept of *scenes* also comes from the stage. In a play, a new scene usually takes place when time or location changes, when different actors are on stage, or other significant changes take place.

In fiction, a scene is most often an extended interaction between two or more characters. It can be a narrative scene, but will often include dialogue as well as narrated action. A scene can also feature only one character, usually the protagonist, involved in some physical activity, in which case there is no dialogue. This kind of scene will be highly personal and introspective.

Here is the description of the spruce forest at timberline, rewritten as a scene between Steven and Melissa:

> Steven led the mule around the bend and saw a grove of stunted spruce in the distance. "Is that the forest you talked about?" he asked Melissa.
>
> She nodded, breathing in deeply. "Yes. Smells like Christmas, doesn't it?"
>
> "You must feel pretty sad about your grandfather."
>
> "I do," she said, with half a smile. "But I'm glad I came back. At least we can get him home now."
>
> He twisted his walking stick round and round in his hand, suddenly uncomfortable in her presence. "Then you're pretty sure you'll find his body here?"
>
> "I don't know," she murmured. "We'll just have to see, won't we? Don't the trees look nice in the sunrise? Grandpa would have liked that."
>
> "Come on," he urged her, tugging the halter of the pack mule. Maybe if he acted as if he knew what he was doing he could make his uneasiness go away. "We'd better get started."

Now the passage has an entirely different feel and meaning to it. Instead of just setting a scene or providing description, the writing advances the story. Melissa and Steven are at the spruce forest for a reason: to recover the body of Melissa's grandfather. We know a little bit about each character: that Melissa is strong-willed, and Steven is uneasy about the entire mission but unwilling to show his discomfort.

When should the writer use scenes instead of narrative? The scene is used to help construct the fictional dream. The closer the reader is to a fictional "reality," the more he will believe it and live it vicariously. Narrative, on the other hand, tends to produce a greater feeling of distance.

As a rule of thumb, when pressure is being exerted on one character by another, the action should be shown in a scene. The reader does not want to be told that the protagonist is in danger; she wants to see, hear, and smell the danger, as well as the protagonist's reaction to it. It is not enough, for example, to tell the reader that the antagonist released a pack of dogs on the heroine but she managed to escape. The reader wants to hear the antagonist's taunts and the protagonist's pleas or show of defiance. The reader wants to see just how the dogs look and how they attack, how the protagonist responds and just how she gets away or fools the dogs.

If two or more characters are conversing about something which is important to plot or character development in the story, show the conversation in scene. If the protagonist is nervous, show his anxiety in his voice, his speech patterns and gestures. It should not be necessary to *tell* the reader the character is nervous if you imply his feelings well enough.

If action accompanies this conversation, the narrative action will become part of the scene. In one well-thought-out student espionage novel, for example, a terrorist tries to coerce a woman agent into telling him the location of an army installation – while dangling her over the side of a bridge! The scene, attached to the female protagonist, includes many of her thoughts, much dialogue between the two, and plenty of action, as the woman struggles for her life.

TRANSITIONS

Once the writer has crafted several effective scenes in the order he wishes them to occur, the question arises as to what to do with them. In other words, how does the writer move gracefully from one scene to the other? How does he bring the reader with him when he makes that move? This movement from paragraph to paragraph, scene to scene, or chapter to chapter is called a "transition," and is one of the most annoying and least obvious techniques a beginning writer must learn.

Transitions often seem like a nuisance to a new writer because she fails to see the reason for them. After all, she has written an outline and is following it, so the scenes and chapters seem to flow well from one to another, at least to her. But the reader does not have the benefit of an outline, synopsis or any other road map for interpreting the action in the novel. All he has is what is on the page.

Cut to the Chase

"Cutting" to a scene, that is, shifting immediately to a new scene without a logical transition, is a common cinematic technique. In a movie, visuals on the screen help the observer move from one scene to another.

However, writing fiction is not a cinematic task. Writers have no visuals to help them move their readers from one section of the novel (scene or chapter) to the next. If written scenes "cut" dramatically from one place or time to another, without a chance for the reader to "catch his breath" or a clue to help him understand why the change has been made, the reader will be confused at best and angry at worst. If the reader does not comprehend where or when the action is taking place in a new scene (or who is present in it) within a sentence or two, the resultant confusion will shake him out of the fictional dream and his idle mind will cast about for other, more rational amusements – a nice movie, perhaps.

Love Thy Reader

When crafting transitions, it's a good idea to remember the reader. After all, without him, the writer would have no reason to write transitions...or anything else. Think of the reader as a student learning a difficult mathematical equation from you, the professor. The equation is composed of many parts, and if the student does not understand just one of these parts, he will not understand how to structure the entire equation; furthermore, it will not make the least bit of sense to him.

In the same way, writing must flow relatively smoothly from incident to incident, time to time, place to place, person to person. If the reader cannot follow the storyline, the conflict or other important aspects of the writing, he has no good reason to continue reading.

Types of Transitions

The following are some of the many ways a writer can affect a smooth transition from one scene to the next.

1. *The Use of Narrative*

As discussed earlier, narrative descriptions of the passage of time can move a reader from Christmas to spring, or from the protagonist's barbecue party to his son's football game. This technique probably should not be used too often in a novel or story, since it could become predictable.

Narrative descriptions of places may also be used to establish a new scene with a new setting. Such transitions are often found at the beginning of chapters.

2. *A Word or Two*

Transitional words such as "later," "meanwhile," "nevertheless" are the easiest form of transition, but they are not very effective. They may help a writer move from one paragraph to another, but are probably too weak to form a good transition from scene to scene or chapter to chapter. Phrases such as, "Meanwhile, back at the ranch," or "Hours later, in a bar in uptown Manhattan," are a little stronger and occasionally will serve to move a story from scene to scene. Again, these should not be used too often or they will look like contrivances. Care must be taken when using these phrases to make them appear attached to a first person narrator or POV character; otherwise, they will sound scenic, the words of a distant reporter.

3. *The Transitional Sentence*

The transitional sentence is by far the most effective way to create a solid transition between scenes or within scenes. Of course, this approach involves some effort and may even necessitate a transitional paragraph or transitional scene.

The transitional sentence moves the reader from one time, place or circumstance to another. To get an idea of how this works, read the following paragraphs, first without a transitional sentence (A), then with a transitional sentence (B).

(A)   Pete sat down at Alan's regular table to wait for him. After a few minutes, a waitress came up and gave him a hard look, as if she were thinking of asking him to leave. Instead, she said, "'Morning! What'll you have? The blueberry pancakes are really good today."

"That tip you gave me on the locksmith paid off," said Alan, by way of greeting. "He said he had installed a new lock in the Rutger's home just a week ago."

(B)   Pete sat down at Alan's regular table to wait for him. After a few minutes, a waitress came up and gave him a hard look, as if she were thinking of asking him to leave. Instead, she said, "'Morning! What'll you have? The blueberry pancakes are really good today."

Alan arrived just as the waitress was leaving, threw himself into the chair opposite Pete and slammed his Stetson down on the table with a triumphant crash. "That tip you gave me on the locksmith paid off," he said. "The fellow said he had installed a new lock in the Rutger's home just a week ago."

In the first version, Alan's arrival comes abruptly and awkwardly. He simply appears on the scene, and the waitress disappears. In version B, the transitional sentence paves the way for Alan's arrival, gets rid of the waitress and gives the reader an idea of how Alan feels. In a more complex situation, an entire paragraph might have been needed to achieve a smooth, believable transition.

Let's take this scenario a bit further. Assume Alan has left and Pete is sitting alone at the table again. In the next scene, Pete is driving down a country road on his way to visit a robbery suspect. Again, note versions (A), without a transition, and (B), with a transition.

(A)   Pete ate his pancakes slowly, thinking about Raoul. Why would the young construction worker want to get mixed up with a lowlife like Harper? Did Harper have something on Raoul, some information which could get the kid in trouble?

He drove through the town toward Raoul's house, picking his way through the narrow streets filled with tourists and hawkers selling carnival souvenirs. At last he reached the young man's apartment house and parked on the street. He didn't want to call attention to himself; it might not be safe for him or for Raoul.

(B)   Pete ate his pancakes slowly, thinking about Raoul. Why would the young construction worker want to get mixed up with a lowlife like Harper? Did Harper have something on Raoul, some information which could get the kid in trouble?

He finished the last forkful and lay his knife and fork neatly across his plate. There was nothing for it: He would have to go to Raoul's apartment and ask him if he were involved with the break-in at the Rutgers, although Alan would probably be upset.

Acting quickly before he could change his mind, Pete paid his bill, jogged to his car and threw himself inside. He started the engine and had backed onto the street by the time he got his first twinge of worry: Maybe he was wrong. Maybe Harper's thugs were watching and waiting for him. Nah, he decided, pulling into the boulevard. He had to take the chance.

> He drove through the town toward Raoul's house, picking
> his way through the narrow streets....

In example (B), two entire paragraphs have been added to provide some explanation for Pete's decision to drive to Raoul's apartment. Without those paragraphs (A), the reader has no clue why Pete is driving to visit Raoul, and the sense of the scene begins to break down. If the gulf in time, place or circumstance between one scene and the next were very wide, an entire transitional scene might be required to help the reader follow the action and the character's thought processes.

When moving from chapter to chapter, special care must be taken not to lose the reader. The end of one chapter might conclude with a question or a piece of business which is left "up in the air," to be answered in the succeeding chapter (a chapter hook). If done with subtlety, this will help create a feeling of suspense and form a natural bridge to a new chapter.

Make certain that the reader understands *who is where doing what* very early on in the new chapter. Although some writers begin chapters with dialogue to establish a scene, this is difficult to do and may actually distract the writer from crafting a transition to the chapter. It might be more effective to describe the setting in the POV character's perspective.

A WEIGHTY MATTER

Unlike people, not all scenes are created equal. Some have more importance – or weight – than others. Some are going to be crucial scenes, which reveal or resolve major conflicts or develop the protagonist, while some are important for structural reasons. Other scenes will be peripherally important, while those of the least importance should probably be cast in narration.

Beginning writers often run into problems deciding what to show and what not to show. They frequently include unnecessary material that does not further plot, character or setting; this should be condensed or omitted. On the other hand, they sometimes fail to include important scenes or develop critical information in depth.

For example, we recently evaluated a manuscript entitled *After the Quake,* in which the central character is supposedly affected by his experiences during a huge earthquake in Los Angeles. However, the writer never elaborates on the character's experiences, nor does he reflect on them in any detail other than to "often think back on the quake" or "recall those horrible minutes back in June."

If the earthquake is important to the character, then the writer should give us some scenes in which the reader can observe the quake's effects on the protagonist. Does he crumple up in a ball whenever a subway train goes by? Does he start at loud noises? Does he remember specific horrors – buildings falling on people, children trapped in fires, bridges collapsing? Most important of all, how do these memories affect his everyday life and attitude toward life? If the quake is not important, then any reference to it should simply be removed from the manuscript, since it adds no tension, suspense or insight into the character.

It's not always easy to determine which scenes or information should be emphasized, expanded, condensed or deleted entirely. Making an outline of the plot will help a writer visualize the importance of each scene and where it fits into minor and central conflicts. Sometimes the writer will have to read the entire manuscript aloud in order to get an idea of misplaced weight – scenes which are missing; which are included but belong elsewhere; which do not belong at all; which should be trimmed back or filled out.

PACING

We have mentioned pacing earlier, in the discussion on the omniscient point of view. Pacing simply refers to how fast or slowly the story is proceeding. In execution, the pace of the writing equals the rate at which events occur in the story, and the emphasis placed on each.

Generally speaking, the quicker the pace, the more likely the reader is going to wish to continue reading. Of course, a plot which introduces too many events too quickly is likely to frustrate or confuse a reader. It is a challenge to a writer to vary the pace of the novel so that it is unpredictable, thus whetting the curiosity of the reader. The pace might range from neurotically dizzying to lugubrious, depending on the subject matter, intent and style.

Many excellent lyrical or introspective novels have been written with a consistently slow, leisurely, even ponderous pace. In those cases, it is usually the sheer power and insightfulness of the writing that causes the reader to keep reading. Since few beginning writers have the skill or experience to write with the brilliance of Somerset Maugham, Henry James, James Joyce, Thomas Wolfe or other writers who favor a consistently languid pace, the agency encourages our clients to pay special attention to pacing to avoid losing the reader's attention.

When to Increase Pace

Some scenes will have to move faster than others. For instance, an action scene full of physical movement, such as a chase through a forest, should move much faster than a more physically static scene in which two characters are sitting before a fire at night, calmly discussing the state of their friend's marriage.

In the first – the chase scene – many minor events will pile up on each other quickly. The protagonist will sight the person he wants to capture, shout out to her and move toward her. She will back off, then turn and run away into the woods, causing him to break into a run after her, dodging trees and roots, perhaps stumbling or even falling. In any case, one minor event or incident follows another until the protagonist captures his quarry or she escapes.

In the second scene – the chat by the fire – the "action" is of a different kind, cerebral instead of physical. Movements, such as gestures, or actions, such as getting up or pouring a drink, complement the characters' dialogue and the protagonist's thoughts. The pace will probably be slower than that of the action scene.

How to Increase Pace

Consider the scene above. While physical action is limited, the pace may still be increased. The writer does this by heightening tension and suspense. The greater the tension on the characters and the stronger the feeling of suspense for the reader, the faster the scene will appear to move.

To increase suspense and quicken the pace of the fireside scene, the writer can up the ante by increasing pressure on one character. The husband and wife in the scene are discussing their friend's failing marriage, but what if one of them is romantically involved with the friend or his wife? What if, for example, the husband is trying to hide his affair from his own wife? Regardless of the point of view, tension will be increased for both characters, and the reader will be increasingly curious to discover "what happens next." It is the speed of this movement from one point to the next that defines the pace of the scene, although pace may vary from slow to fast within a given scene.

Besides using physical action and increasing suspense, a writer can pick up the pace of his fiction by increasing the intensity of emotions in his characters. Intense feelings of sexual passion, anger, hate, love or jealousy will make the story appear to be "moving faster," since the reader's own feelings will be stirred. The love scenes from any competent contemporary romance provide plenty of illustrations on how writers accelerate pace by accelerating pulses. As the lovely young protagonist and the handsome hero become more and more intimate and passionate, the reader becomes more deeply drawn into their relationship. The rapid pace caused by these intense feelings usually won't last more than a chapter, since such intensity of emotion does not last long in real life.

How to Slow Down the Pace

The use of flashbacks, introspection and narrative descriptions all tend to retard the pace of fiction. This is because all these techniques *distance* the reader from the action at hand. In a flashback, for example, the writer holds up an imaginary "pause" sign to indicate to the reader that the protagonist is going to think of something not directly related to the present action.

Slowing down the pace is a legitimate way to vary the pace of the novel, especially following fast-paced action or scenes of intense emotion. Slow-paced moments of reflection and introspection add depth to the characters and help the reader understand them more fully.

One can also slow down the pace by creating calm, restful scenes – two friends reminiscing at a restaurant about old times, or a father and son quietly discussing the son's newfound interest in the opposite sex. These will be low-key scenes. Though important insights may be revealed, they will take place in a subtle, gentle, thought-provoking manner.

In addition, a deliberately slow pace can be used to build suspense. For example, imagine that a grandfather has just told his granddaughter, Amy, that he is going to tell her a story that reveals a family secret. But Grandpa takes his time doing so, choosing just the right tobacco, slowly tamping it in his pipe, selecting a match, lighting it, and finally lighting his pipe. The character himself is building Amy's suspense by his delay, causing her (and the reader) to champ at the bit with impatience.

Whether picking up the pace or slowing it down, the careful writer will be certain to vary pace enough to hold the reader's interest. Of course, some genre novels, such as thrillers and action/adventures, will have a very fast, driving pace which rarely slows down. Other, more reflective stories, such as reminiscences or introspective, literary pieces, will move at a slower pace, since they concern interior, not exterior, action.

Pace and Weight

Pacing can be slowed down to the detriment of the novel if the writer includes too much excess material. For example, one beginning writer created a potentially tense, dramatic scene in which the protagonist unwittingly invites a murderer into her house. The pace should have been swift as suspense increased and the protagonist figured out her predicament. Instead, the writer became hopelessly bogged down in interior decorating details such as the style and period of furniture and the color scheme of the rooms. The scene turned into an unnecessary tour of the protagonist's house, and pace deteriorated to a crawl. Worse yet, the killer simply exited the house without incident, undercutting the importance of the entire scene.

Narrative and scene are two of the most important and versatile techniques a writer can develop. Knowing when to use which is virtually an art in itself. In a nutshell, a writer must decide what to paint with broad strokes (narrative) and what to render in great detail with a fine brush (scene). His decision to use scene instead of narrative will be based on how important the material is to the development of plot and character, whether it is suited to dramatic portrayal, and whether or not dialogue, a key ingredient of many scenes, will enhance the writing.

As a rule, when in serious doubt about using narrative or scene, choose the scene. Scenes are usually more exciting to read, though frequently harder to write.

CHAPTER
SIXTEEN

CONVENTION: DIALOGUE, THE KEY TO THE SCENE

SOME BEGINNING WRITERS tell us, in a sheepish voice, that they "don't like to write dialogue" or are "having a hard time with the dialogue."

There is no doubt that constructing effective dialogue that appears natural and realistic is one of the hardest skills for a fiction writer to master. Effective dialogue is also an essential part of scene-building and an important technique for developing characters. Writers often create scenes containing dialogue to establish realism, conflict and characters' personalities. How characters speak and act during a conversation provides the reader with great insight into their feelings, philosophies and basic natures.

Most novice writers are concerned with making their dialogue sound "natural" or "realistic," and with good reason. If dialogue sounds stilted, wooden or out of place, the reader will awake from the fictional dream. The characters mouthing the dialogue will no longer seem real, and the entire dialogue, perhaps even the entire novel, will look artificial – an obvious construct, not an alternative reality.

For example, rustic characters without a formal education are not likely to use extensive vocabularies or allude to classical poetry. By and large, English professors will speak in a very different manner from, say, dock workers, and vice versa. If the dock worker in your novel is speaking like a typical English professor, then you'd best have an excellent reason for why he does so.

In Search of "Real Speech"

Fictional dialogue has a different purpose than the speech we hear every day. People talk to each other as much out of courtesy and social expectations as out of a need to give or receive information or discuss important subjects. Fictional dialogue, however, *always* has a reason. Some of the reasons to use dialogue include:

— to reveal the personalities of the characters through their speech

— to reveal a plot complication or other important information. For example, in *Outlander*, the fact that Claire's second husband is a virgin (while she is not) is revealed in a private conversation just before their marriage.

— to show the protagonist's reactions to important events and revelations. Although Shakespeare's play *MacBeth* is virtually nothing *but* dialogue, the scene in which MacDuff discovers the deaths of his wife and children is brilliant in its depth of emotional reaction.

— to render confrontations, reconciliations, confessions and other tense communications in a forceful, realistic way

— to physically describe POV characters

Since fictional dialogue carries so much importance, it does not sound much like everyday speech although, paradoxically, it must appear to sound like everyday speech.

When beginners first write "realistic" dialogue, it usually reads something like this:

"Hi, Bob," said Alex. "Nice shirt."
"Oh, thanks, Alex" replied Bob. "Got it at a sale."
"Any more left, Bob?"
"Dunno, Alex. Maybe. You want one like it?"

The first thing the writer must ask himself is, "What's the purpose of this dialogue?" If it has a specific reason for being, then it belongs in the novel. If it is merely marking time, as if the writer became desperate because the manuscript had too little dialogue, then it is extraneous and should be omitted. The passage above probably adds nothing to the larger context.

Worse yet, the passage doesn't sound realistic at all; it sounds stiff, stilted and decidedly unnatural. This is partly because the speakers really have nothing important to say to each other. It is also stiff and stilted because the speakers are trying to compress too much information into too few words. Anyone trying to give the impression of everyday speech should note that people usually speak in complete sentences, except when under stress, bored or answering questions. Also, it is much harder to read fragments, in narrative or dialogue, than it is to read complete sentences. Notice how choppy the sample conversation sounds.

Finally, people rarely call each other by name when addressing each other, unless they are in a large group and are addressing a particular person. Note how ludicrous the excessive name-saying sounds in the example.

Crafting "Real" Dialogue

New writers striving for a brisk, active feel to their dialogue often try to mimic the "snappy dialogue" of the thirties and forties, made popular by Ernest Hemingway and adopted by mystery writers such as Dashiel Hammet and Ray Chandler.

"Did you see him?" asked the chief.
"Yes. Once, on the stairs."
"And he was wearing...?"
"A red shirt and black pants."
"Sure?"
"Positive."

The trouble with this sort of dialogue is that it is often not attributed to specific speakers, and the reader therefore has trouble following just who is saying what. This is not always a problem when two people are conversing, but when three or more are speaking, confusion reigns. Also, the emphasis is on fragments, which here indicate stressful questioning, but are also harder to read.

Ernest Hemingway, accused of writing "inspired baby-talk," was a master of lean but effective dialogue. When Jake Barnes in *The Sun Also Rises* whispers to his girlfriend at her first bullfight, "You'll be fine. Just don't look at the horses," we understand the barbarity of the sport with a precision that a flood of dialogue could never achieve. We don't even need to be told what happens to the horses; we can guess and let our imaginations fill in the blanks.

Beats, Scripts and Attribution

In general, dialogue that appears realistic is presented in a larger context than simply the spoken word. When people speak, they do not cease to think and move. They continue to act, to think and to process information through the senses. As a main character is speaking, for example, he may pick up an object, say a spoon, and move it around in his hands. The person he is addressing may light a pipe, tap his foot, run his hand through his hair, or make some other gesture which indicates his feelings. Such bits of stage business are sometimes called "beats." Like the beats in music, they give a sense of order and organization; they also provide the illusion of reality.

When writing dialogue, try to attribute it to a particular character; that is, identify your speakers. Unless he has a good reason, a careful conventional writer will avoid writing a "script," which consists of a page or more of unattributed dialogue. The reader must know who is speaking, as well as what the protagonist is thinking, what he guesses other speakers are thinking, and what each character is doing as he or she is speaking.

The best way to attribute dialogue is through the use of a small, humble word: said. "I'll be going now," he said; "I love you," Meredith said, "and I need you." The preferred use of the verb "said" is "John said," as opposed to "said John." Too much use of the latter can give your writing a somewhat formal sound.

Occasional use of strong "speaking verbs" – snarled, grumbled, muttered, mumbled, spat, barked, whispered – can add color to your writing, but you should be careful not to overuse them. Like ice cream, they provide pleasant variety, but not sustenance. Don't attempt to use dramatic speaking verbs as a short-cut to express a character's feelings or create a sense of conflict or tension.

One can attribute dialogue without the use of a word like "said" or "asked" or "shouted" by simply positioning a quote adjacent to a sentence in which a character performs an action. For example:

"Where is the money?" Hogan stuck his hands in his pockets and glanced around the empty street.

Attached Dialogue and Natural Speech

Read the following dialogue between two military officers and a private and ask yourself if it gives the impression of natural speech. Is it easy to follow?

"Did you hit him?" asked Major Reynolds.
"Yes, sir," said the guard.
"More than once?"
"Yes, sir. Four times."
"Four times?"
"Yes, four times."
"Christ almighty! Why?"
"He wouldn't leave, sir."
"And did he leave after you hit him?" asked   Captain Baker.
"No, sir. He was sitting down, holding his head."

"What did you do?"

"I left, sir."

"Left?"

"Yes, sir. I went to call headquarters."

"Did you call an ambulance?"

"No, sir." The guard coughed nervously.

"Dismissed. I'll send for you if I need you."

The guard left quickly.

"Damn you, Reynolds," said Baker. "You let him go."

"For now."

Notice that, once Baker enters the conversation, it is impossible to tell just who is speaking. Part of the problem with this dialogue is that it reads as if it were lifted from a screenplay. It is the audio portion without the video portion. Since it is not attached to any character's POV, we're not sure about the importance of the scene or the feelings of the characters. Here is the same scene, rewritten from the POV of Major Reynolds. Note how much more crucial information can be included in a developed, attached, attributed dialogue.

"Did you hit him?" Major Reynolds leaned back in his chair and lit his pipe. "Well?"

"Yes, sir," the guard said. Reynolds noticed that the young man had broken out in a sweat and that his hands were clenched at his sides.

"More than once?" Of course it was more than once, Reynolds thought to himself. The poor man had a broken wrist and thirteen stitches in his forehead.

"Four times, sir."

"Four times! Christ almighty!" exclaimed Captain Baker, slapping his hand against the table.

"Easy, Doc," Reynolds said, exhaling a stream of smoke. The doctor had a temper on him. Who knew what he might do if he got worked up? "Now, Polaski," Reynolds continued, keeping his voice low and soft, "that's a lot of blows. What did you use? Your baton?"

"Yes, sir." Polaski stared straight ahead, his eyes wide.

"Just why did you hit this guy?" Reynolds asked.

"Because the kid's a scum-sucking son of a bitch," Baker said.

"That's enough, Doc. Go ahead, Polaski. What happened? Did he threaten you?"

"No, sir, but he wouldn't leave." Polaski's legs were trembling now. Reynolds remembered the first time he had hit someone with a baton. He had trembled too, and thrown up by the side of the road. But he had not struck a civilian. "Well, you hit him once, right? Did he go to leave then?"

"No, sir," Polaski said. The guard's voice shook as hard as his legs. "He didn't leave after I hit him once, and so I hit him again but he didn't leave, so I hit him again. Then again."

"Did he leave?"

"No, sir."

"Speak up, Polaski. I can't hear you very well." Reynolds took a puff on his pipe, but it had gone out. It was just as well, he thought: He didn't feel like smoking anymore.

"No, sir." The young man's voice was louder but higher. "He just sat in the road, holding his head."

"Didn't you call an ambulance, dummy?" snarled Baker.

"No, sir, but I did call headquarters. I didn't know what to do."

Reynolds sighed, nodding at the terror-stricken soldier. The sight of blood had probably driven the kid away from the wounded man. Polaski had struck like a tiger and run like a rabbit. "Dismissed, Polaski. I'll call you back if I need you."

Polaski saluted with a shaking hand. One moment he was in front of Reynolds, and the next he was gone. He did not leave so much as he disappeared, thought Reynolds.

"Damn you, Reynolds! That bastard almost killed a civilian," cried Baker, "and you just let him off."

Reynolds smiled sadly. "Not true, doctor. I let him go. For now. You and I have to talk."

Because of the attached POV, this scene is now much more developed. We understand a little about all three characters, and also understand what happened to whom and why Reynolds and Baker are so upset. We get a little insight into Reynolds' past and some feel for what kind of a person he is — an understanding, compassionate but honest person. The tension of the "snappy dialogue" is maintained, but the reader knows who is speaking and has a clear picture of what people are feeling, as revealed through their actions as well as their words. It seems more realistic than the first version, because the dialogue is not divorced from the characters and their bodies. The writer has given the reader visual clues that were missing in the initial version.

Heavy-handed Dialogue

Dialogue is an excellent, subtle way to get background information across to the reader. However, the reason for the dialogue must not be that the writer wants to give the reader information. If the writer is obviously using dialogue as a contrivance to pummel the reader with exposition, then we call the resultant dialogue "heavy-handed." Heavy-handed dialogue is an occupational hazard for those who write mysteries, espionage, science fiction and period novels, in which there may be many details which the writer feels obligated to explain. As we'll see, though, he may not have to.

Imagine a scene in which two lovers are in bed, plotting the murder of the woman's spouse.

"Mary, your husband's got a heart condition, doesn't he?" Michael asked.

"Yes, Regis was in the hospital for three weeks last year after a heart attack. He had bypass surgery, and has to be real careful about his diet and exercise now. Why?"

"Well," continued Michael, "I was just thinking...ever since you won 100,000 bucks in the lottery last June, we don't really need all the money Regis makes as president of Alexander Hamilton National Bank, do we? We could go away, leave the country...maybe go to Thailand, where your cousin has that crocodile farm."

"But what about Regis?" Mary said. "You know how jealous he is. Remember when he got drunk at the Christmas party and swung that broken bottle at you just because you were holding my hand?"

"Yeah. That's why I think we'll have to...dispatch him."

This dialogue is merely for the convenience of the reader, since Michael and Mary already know all this information and would not, in all probability, repeat it to each other. The dialogue reveals little about Mary and Michael's personalities, but much exposition about the problematic husband – his health, his job, his financial status, his temper, jealousy and problem drinking – all of which could be much more successfully and forcefully rendered in scene.

Heavy-handed dialogue is frequently a problem for beginning writers, who want to reveal all the details of the story as quickly as possible. It is much more effective to build the story slowly, revealing pieces of the conflict in scene, in more realistic dialogue.

After the writer of the passage above rethought his strategy, he decided to rewrite the scene to reveal only Regis' health problems, and to do it in a way that does not pound the reader over the head with the information or the situation.

> Afterwards, Michael lit a cigarette and lay back in bed. He put his arm around Mary, and she cuddled up to him. "So, how's Hubby these days?"
>
> Mary laughed. "As if you care, right? Ever since his bypass surgery he can't...you know...do anything. The doctor said he'd be able to, but so far, no go."
>
> "You've got me for that," Michael murmured, nuzzling her neck.
>
> She laughed again. "You're a riot," she said, smiling. "Sometimes I wish, well, that it was just you and me."
>
> "Me too, baby." He squeezed her hand, then took another drag on his cigarette, thinking about Regis. An idea, a very dangerous but appealing idea, was slowly forming in his mind. "Regis is very sick, isn't he?"
>
> "I guess so." Mary paused, glancing sideways at Michael. "Why do you say that? You don't care about him."
>
> "I mean, he takes a lot of medicine, doesn't he?" Michael remembered the bulging medicine cabinet in Regis's bathroom.
>
> "Oh, man! Does he ever! Dozens of pills and tablets and things." She fiddled with the coverlet, smoothing out non-existent wrinkles.
>
> Michael finished his cigarette and lit another. "It would probably be real easy for him to take too much medicine. Hell, he might take some and get disoriented, and then you might give him some extra, by accident. Or he might forget how many pills he should take. Or he might take some pills together that shouldn't be taken together. It happens all the time. Don't you think that might happen?"
>
> Mary looked up from the coverlet. "I'm not sure I want to hear what I think you're saying," she said.

Skillful dialogue helps craft the scene, showing us insights into characters and situations. The background details are far less important than character and conflict development, and those details will come forward somewhere in the plotline, if they are important.

Indirect Dialogue

Indirect dialogue, or indirect discourse, is an extremely useful tool for the writer, since it allows him to indicate the high points of a dialogue without recording a lengthy conversation word for word. In effect, the writer can *narrate* a conversation or parts of it, revealing the results of a direct dialogue. This is especially useful for handling a long conversation which has little results, or for alerting the reader to the truly important parts of a conversation.

Read the following passages and note which one seems most effective and direct.

(Direct discourse) — Evelyn finished the rest of her drink and sank back in the beach chair. She gazed out at the ocean, then turned to Maggie, smiling. "It's a beautiful day."

Maggie nodded eagerly. More than anything else, she wanted to impress her successful sister. "Oh, yes! It's much nicer than yesterday, with all that rain."

"No rain today," said Evelyn. "The weather report said sunshine all day today and tomorrow, with a high of eighty-five."

"If it's that warm, we can swim in the ocean instead of the pool."

"No, we can't," said Evelyn, rolling her empty glass between her hands. "I'm leaving this afternoon."

(Indirect discourse) — Evelyn finished the rest of her drink and sank back in the beach chair. Maggie, eager to impress her successful sister, started talking about the weather, which was supposed to stay nice for the next few days. Evelyn listened, nodding politely now and then. Once, when Maggie paused for breath, Evelyn leaned forward and looked into her eyes. "I'm leaving this afternoon," Evelyn said.

Unless a dialogue is truly revealing, necessary or interesting, try writing it in indirect discourse. Narrate sections of a longer conversation that seems to go on forever without making much impact. By the same token, individual remarks can be handled indirectly, if they seem lackluster or out of place, or if you wish to indicate speech but don't want to emphasize it. "'Don't forget to wipe your feet on the welcome mat, Doug,' said Anne," might become, "Anne pointed to the welcome mat and ordered Doug to wipe his feet."

Direct and Indirect Thoughts

Akin to the concept of expressing dialogue in writing is the idea of expressing thoughts in writing, in the third person. (In the first person, *ipso facto*, all the character's thoughts are expressed directly.)

Like dialogue, a third person character's thoughts may be expressed directly or indirectly. Thoughts should never be set in quotation marks, as these are used exclusively for indicating dialogue (or sometimes for emphasizing a word or phrase, especially one used earlier in dialogue). Instead, direct quotes must be written *in italic*. If your printer cannot print in italic, simply indicate it by underlining the direct quote.

A brief direct thought is a very striking and effective way to express a character's strong emotions or his questions and directions to himself. For example:

> *What a fool I am!* David thought.
> *I never should have let her go,* Harry mused.
> *What am I going to do now? I've never played tennis in my life!* Susan thought.
> *I'm going to march right in there and ask him about that job,* Alice told herself.

However, long stretches of italicized direct thoughts are tedious to read and often turn into those horrible mock inner dialogues ridiculed by John Gardner. They also frequently cause the writer to change tense for a paragraph or so, which can be confusing. But one of the reasons you choose to write in the third person is to explore your characters' thoughts. So...what can a writer do to plumb a character's mind?

The best technique to express long, complex or profound thoughts is the use of indirect thoughts. This is related to indirect discourse and written almost exactly the same way. For example, the direct thought *I'm going to march right in there and ask him about that job* might become: "Alice considered marching right into Bob's office and asking him about the job *or* Alice thought she might just march right into Bob's office and ask him about the job."

When the thought is brief, either direct or indirect expression may be appropriate. But when the thought is long....

Consider this passage, written here as a direct thought.

> *Who does this girl think she is?* Richard thought. *She obviously doesn't know the first thing about tennis. Look at her flub that serve! Yet I could have sworn she told me at the office she had played before, many times. She must be trying to impress me. Maybe she thinks*

I'll take it easier on her at work if I think she shares my favorite hobby. Or maybe she's just plain scared. Could that be it? Do I really frighten people that much?

This is, in essence, an inner monologue. It lacks power and realism because it is not taking advantage of the third person distance, the ability to *relate* thoughts and feelings without having to quote them, so to speak. See how much smoother this passage reads when written mostly as indirect thoughts:

Who does this girl think she is?
Susan obviously didn't know the first thing about tennis, Richard thought, watching her flub a serve and nearly land on her face. She was probably just trying to impress him. That was why she said she'd played before, to make him think she was interested in his favorite hobby. But as he watched her gritting her teeth and gamely trying to return a serve, another thought occurred to him: She was scared. Scared of what? Scared of him? He was an imposing figure, and her boss. Richard shook his head. Thinking of himself as a frightening employer made him feel uncomfortable.

A Word about Dialect

Dialect, or regional words and speech patterns, are part and parcel of some historical novels and stories with distinctive regional settings. In order to give the reader a feel for a certain place and time – Yorkshire, England perhaps, or antebellum rural Georgia – a writer might create characters with those specific dialects.

When writing dialect, less is more, and more is often irritating, if not infuriating. In one exceptionally tedious historical romance (whose author and publisher will remain nameless), Scottish Highlanders were constantly sputtering nonsense along the lines of, "Ye shouldna gang...ye canna gang wi' me, m' bonnie lassie, or we'll a' be draggit awa' tae the Tollbooth." Such distorted language is hard to read and turns the reader away from the work, rather than toward it. In addition, the writer should have known that the dialect he was trying to convey is Scottish Lowland speech, not Highland.

When indicating dialects, tread lightly. A few well-chosen words, a familiarity with the speech patterns, and perhaps a few homey phrases ("Aye, they're dogs, every inch of them,") are all that are necessary to give flavor and spice to the writing.

Improving Your Dialogue —A Summary

Successful dialogue is so important that it's probably a good idea to practice writing it and rewriting it. The best dialogue is that which takes hours to craft and sounds as if it were dashed off in the odd moment.

As a general rule, the following can enhance your dialogue:

1. Make sure you have a good reason to use dialogue instead of narrative or indirect dialogue.
2. Clarify who is speaking to whom but do not let your characters call each other by name too often.
3. In conversations, your characters should usually speak in complete sentences, unless you are consciously trying for snappy dialogue.
4. Avoid stilted, staged dialogue.
5. Remember that people do not cease to exist when they are speaking. Show what your characters are doing and what your protagonist is thinking while they are talking.
6. Avoid heavy-handed dialogue larded with information for the sake of explaining things to your readers. Don't let your characters tell each other what they already know.
7. Use indirect discourse to surround and highlight important lines of dialogue or condense long discussions.
8. Use direct thought to express brief emotional outbursts, or if the character is addressing herself briefly. Use indirect thoughts to express a third person character's longer thoughts, reflections, and memories.
9. In dialect, less is more. A few well-chosen words or phrases are more effective than paragraphs of difficult-to-decipher jargon.

Of all the conventions, dialogue may just be the most demanding to master. Why? Because it takes so much effort to craft "speech" which makes a dramatic impact while sounding natural and uncontrived. Do not be disappointed if it takes you some time to sculpt your dialogue to the point where you know it works.

CHAPTER SEVENTEEN

CONVENTION: DESCRIPTIONS AND IMAGERY

PHYSICAL/SENSUAL DESCRIPTION

THROUGHOUT THIS BOOK we have spoken about the fictional dream and how to achieve it. Characterization, plot, POV and many other aspects of writing come into play to give the reader a sense that he is "living" the work. None of these factors is more important to the fictional dream, however, than physical description.

To prove this to yourself, imagine that you are reading about a character, say a young man named Ollie, walking in a Colorado mountain meadow in the summertime. Ollie is from the city, and this is his first close encounter with an alpine meadow. (Fortunately, he has no allergies.) How is Ollie going to react to the experience of walking in the meadow? Is he going to be so lost in thought about his upcoming graduation from college that he barely notices his surroundings? Or is he going to react to the meadow in a logistical way, determining how far across it is and where it lies in relation to his day's destination? No, Ollie is going to *feel* that meadow in every pore of his skin.

The Five Big Beautiful Senses

The most immediate task of the writer is to immerse the reader in the alternate reality of the fiction, and people tend to process reality in terms of the senses. This is what editors mean when they say, "Use more sensual detail." They do not want you to write a bedroom scene every other page; they want you to appeal to the reader's five senses, so that she sees, smells, tastes, touches and hears what you are writing about. That way, she can vicariously experience it.

This passage about Ollie's encounter in the meadow illustrates how sensual description can be used to involve the reader in the fictional dream.

As he stepped out of the green shade of the pines, the pink, red and gold of the meadow struck him. He had seen pictures of all these flowers before – rosy shooting stars, blue and white columbine and yellow asters – but he had never walked among them.

He ambled forward, almost afraid to step on the flowers, but he soon found they gave way before him, bending, bowing out of his path as he brushed his way through them. A cloud of fragrance rose from the bruised stems, a sweet, herbal scent that reminded Ollie of gingerbread. The tall shooting-stars nuzzled his hands as he walked, and he ran his fingers over their silken petals. How could he have lived so long and not touched wildflowers before? he thought.

Overwriting

The above passage omits sounds and tastes, and of course it is not necessary to include each of the senses every time you describe something. Indeed, it's easy to overdo physical description.

Too much emphasis on the realm of the senses often results in "purple prose" or overwriting. Overwriting, a form of literary hotdogging, occurs when a writer places her ego ahead of the good of the novel and the needs of the reader.

In writing, just as in sports, it helps to have a strategy, a reason for doing things a certain way. In Ollie's passage, the writer uses Ollie's reaction to the wildflowers to show the reader just how sensitive Ollie is. If there were no reason, however, to include such a rich description, the result could be downright ugly, perhaps something like this:

On each trip to the beach that month, Ellen ran through the wild waves of the ocean each day, digging her toes into the warm, white, wet sand. The ocean spray worked its way between her moist lips, filling her mouth with a salty taste. She loved the slippery feel of the water running down her arms and the sandpaper feel of the beach against her feet.

And the gulls! How free and daring they wheeled above her head, cracking open the pewter sky with their shrill cries, like black and white banshees screaming into the gusting wind.

Oh my! How much better off the writer would have been had he simply written, "Ellen walked down the beach, wading in the cool waves, listening to the cries of the gulls." How much happier the reader, too! When it comes to description, more can definitely be too much, and too much begins to create an unintentionally humorous tone.

The Seamy Side of Life

The world is not all wildflowers and ocean waves, of course. In fact, skilled writers often include some aspect of the grittier side of life – drugs, wars, crime, death, violence, perversion, sickness, madness and so on – as a means to exert pressure on the protagonist.

In order to create the fictional dream in a gritty scene or setting, the writer must still use sensory imagery to make the ugliness of his world come to life for the reader. If the reader is to believe in a scene in which the protagonist witnesses a murder, that murder must be believable. There must be the signs of violence – blood, cries of pain, suffering, body fluids, smells – all presented briefly and powerfully, not in tediously gruesome detail. It is just as easy to overwrite visceral physical description as any other kind.

The purpose of gritty realism is to disturb, shake up, grip or even frighten the reader, not to disgust him or sicken him or drive him away from the book. A successful visceral image is like a cigarette burn in the mind of the reader: small, intense and unshakable.

The horror writer Stephen King is a master of the visceral image. In his novel, *The Shining*, King describes a father, Jack, possessed by the evil spirit of an old hotel. Rather than kill his son, however, Jack drives the boy away. The spirit, enraged, causes Jack to split his skull with an axe, the shards of bone flipping through the air like shuffled playing cards. One does not easily forget such a striking comparison.

Sometimes the element of contrast can make a visceral detail even more disturbing. One talented beginning writer began his mystery novel with the discovery of a child's severed foot, wrapped in barbed wire, under the foundation of a porch. Such an image is at once repugnant and compelling, made even more powerful by the silent allusion to the innocence of the child.

Gritty imagery knows no genres. When it's needed, it's just as powerful in literary or mainstream fiction as in horror novels or murder mysteries. In the story, "The Grave," the great short story writer Katherine Anne Porter uses the graphic image of a dead, gutted pregnant rabbit to shock a young boy into the realization of the fine line between life and death.

It's Here. I Can Smell It

Writers have always emphasized visual images, more so perhaps in this day and age of the video than in any other. There is no doubt about the strong impact of visual imagery, but the most striking sensual images are those which arrive to the reader through the nose.

The human sense of smell has been described as the most primitive sense, as well as the one most in danger of disappearing in the future. Compared to dogs, pigs and other animals, man has a very poorly developed sense of smell, but what he does smell stays in his mind longer and more clearly than other sensory images. Smells are often associated with early childhood experiences: the sea-salty, fishy smell of the beach...the scent of new linens...the fragrance of wild strawberries.

With careful use of smell imagery, the writer has immediate control over the reader's most basic, primitive emotions and reactions. With the right images, the writer can easily shock or frighten the reader (the smell of death), disgust him (feces), delight him (cotton candy), make him feel wistful or nostalgic (Granny's lavender sachet) or make him hungry (pancakes on the griddle, coffee warming on the stove). In many cases, the effect will be stronger and more immediate than the most elaborate or elegant visual image.

In his short story, "The Emissary," Ray Bradbury tells the tale of a bedridden boy whose only contact with the outside world is his dog and the wonderful smells of the seasons that cling to the animal's coat. When the story takes a macabre turn, Bradbury uses olfactory images to such a great extent and with such sheer physical power that they almost become minor characters in the story.

The Use of Sensual Imagery to Define Characters

Sensual images are so powerful that skilled writers sometimes use such images to actually define or delineate their characters' personalities.

Perhaps one of the most striking modern examples of this technique occurs in the novel *Perfume* by the German writer, Patrick Süskind. His protagonist, Grenoille, is obsessed with smells, since his body has no scent at all. The entire novel makes use of a hypersensitive sense of smell to lead the reader into Grenoille's perverse psyche. This excerpt from the beginning of the book conjures up the stink of an 18th century city:

> The streets stank of manure, the courtyards of urine, the stairwells
> stank of moldering wood and rat droppings, the kitchens of spoiled
> cabbage and mutton fat; the unaired parlors stank of stale dust, the
> bedrooms of greasy sheets, damp featherbeds, and the pungently
> sweet aroma of chamberpots. The stench of sulfur rose from the

chimneys, the stench of caustic lyes from the tanneries, and from the slaughterhouses came the stench of congealed blood.

We don't necessarily recommend that your characters obsess over any of the five senses. Nevertheless, the more a protagonist is aware of his senses, the more he will appear to be aware of the world around him, and therefore that much more accessible to the reader on a very basic, primal, sensual level.

The Recurring, or Resonating, Image

When an image occurs more than once in a story it is called a recurring image. Often this image, usually an object, takes on far more importance than any other object in the story. It is called a "resonating image" because it symbolizes a theme or idea in the writing and adds depth, power and meaning to the story. The term "resonating" implies the strength of the image, which tends to permeate and inform the entire work.

Queequeg's coffin in *Moby Dick* is such an image. It appears several times throughout the book, suggesting a kind of fatalism, if not a premonition of a disaster to come. In the end, when Ishmael uses the coffin as a life-saver, it still represents the death of the crew, but in addition becomes an ironic statement about life and survival.

The green light at the end of the dock in *The Great Gatsby* by F. Scott Fitzgerald is another example of a resonating image. The light appears throughout as an image of the unattainable, the great future which is just always out of our reach. In a similar way, the grotesque image of a pig's head on a stick in *The Lord of the Flies* adds a feeling of growing horror and savagery to this story of innocent boys lost on an island. The horror builds to a climax when a boy is hunted down to replace the pig.

Horror fiction is replete with resonating images, and Edgar Allan Poe was a master of the technique. His stories, "The Tell-Tale Heart" and "The Black Cat," make use of strong, unforgettable images. One of the most famous images in the genre is found in H.P. Lovecraft's story, "Rats in the Walls," in which ghostly, ravenous rats appear to take over an ancient mansion. Eventually the reader discovers that the rats are merely fabrications of the diseased sensibilities of the first-person narrator, whose ancestors ate human flesh and who is, to some extent, a human rat.

A chilling image, mentioned only once, can also leave a strong impression on the reader and even help define a character. Looking to *The Great Gatsby* once again, the reader encounters a minor character, ostensibly a businessman, whose cufflinks are made from human molars. This gruesome detail alone lets us know what sort of "business" this fellow is in. Furthermore, it indicates what sort of people Gatsby is involved with and reveals how tainted his life really is.

Sometimes an act, instead of an object, can create a powerful image, as Jenefer Shute, author of *Life Size*, demonstrates in this description of an anorexic woman eating a spoonful of dessert: "...I treat myself to ground glass, delicate as spun sugar or shaved ice....As I swallow, the ecstatic friction begins: blood swells warm in the throat, spreading, savory, to the tongue. I smile and a hot gush escapes, meat red." The woman's mental connection between pleasure and agony is suitably painful to read.

The resonating image is more common in the short story than in longer fiction, since short works often need the power of a strong image to drive the plot forward. The beginning writer might well make use of forceful, recurring imagery to establish theme and a deeper meaning to his work. Again, the image must not appear "hokey" or contrived or "tacked on," but part of the natural fabric of the story.

In conclusion, remember that strong writing will almost always include powerful imagery, and most powerful imagery makes use of the senses. Creating effective images is almost a paradoxical task, since the writer must use the everyday sensory images that everyone is familiar with to present the reader with a mental picture which is new, fresh, original...yet intriguingly familiar.

CHAPTER EIGHTEEN

A BRIEF ENCAPSULATION OF ELEMENTS AND CONVENTIONS

FOLLOWING ARE SOME of the items we've discussed in the sections on elements and conventions of fiction. This list highlights and defines important terms that are often crucial to crafting a successful novel.

ELEMENTS

1. Characterization — The specific methods of creating a protagonist or other major character

2. Developed Character — Usually the main character (protagonist) who changes and grows over the course of the plot as he reacts to events in the plot

3. Stock, or Type, Character — A very shallow, undeveloped character that is basically a caricature or stereotype of a certain behavior, personality trait, race or position

4. Plot — The storyline of a piece of fiction; the events that take place during the story

5. Plot Structure — The way in which a plot is organized to ensure the development of the protagonist and the story

6. Compelling Event — An event which the protagonist must react to, whether he takes action, makes a decision, or refuses to act; (usually the first important event in a novel)

7. Conflict — The continuing tension or pressure arising from the compelling event which forces the protagonist to react initially and thereafter take action throughout the novel

8. Resolution — The confrontation and settling of the central conflict

9. Climax — The specific scene in which the conflict comes to a head and the resolution takes place

10. Denouement — The summation or declining action that occurs after the climax occurs and the conflict is resolved

11. Subplots — Minor or secondary storylines which enhance the protagonist or the major plotline

12. Secondary Characters — Major characters who serve to develop the protagonist and the plot

13. Setting: Place — The locale in which the plot takes place; place refers to broad settings (Atlanta, Georgia) or narrow ones (a diner in downtown Atlanta, Georgia)

14. Setting: Time — The time in which a plot takes place; time refers both to the time period (Elizabethan England) or the movement of time (chronological order and sequence)

15. Position — Exactly where and how characters are located in a specific setting at a given time; most critical at the beginning of a chapter or scene

16. Theme — The central idea behind the story; the insight about life which the story imparts to the reader

17. Voice — The distinct style or manner in which the protagonist or other character expresses herself

18. Tone — The distinct style or manner in which the author expresses herself through her writing in order to convey feelings or themes

CONVENTIONS

1. Contrivance — A writing technique which is obviously or awkwardly manipulated by the writer to achieve a predetermined, usually predictable end

2. Point of View (POV)— The perspective in which a story is told; the specific viewpoint of the character who observes the action in a story

3. Fictional Dream — John Gardner's description of the goal of a novel, i.e., to create an alternative reality in which the reader vicariously participates

4. Gingerbread — Certain techniques which add dimension to a novel, including frames, flashbacks, and prologue/epilogue combinations

5. Suspense — The manifestation of dread or stress in a reader's mind, resulting in the desire to gather more information

6. Tension — A character's internalization of stress, which urges that character to react or respond and drives the plot of the novel forward

7. Pressure — The stress that the writer exerts on a character to react or respond

8. Drama — Excitement, passion, or other strong, realistic emotion or sentiment engendered in the reader and rising organically from skillful writing

9. Melodrama — Sentimentality, or false emotion, engendered in the reader by the obvious manipulation of characters, events and images

10. Scene — A depiction of specific events, usually through the use of dialogue and actions; "showing" what happens to a character

11. Narrative — A method of relating general information or specific actions to the reader; "telling" what happens to a character; narrative often compresses time and neglects specific details of actions or conversations

12. Transition — One of several ways a writer can link one paragraph, scene or chapter to the next

13. Weight — The relative importance of various aspects of a novel *in*

the novel; weight usually determines how much emphasis a scene, character or storyline receives

14. Pacing — The speed or fluctuation of speeds at which a novel proceeds

15. Dialogue — The writer's attempt to render characters' conversation and other utterances on the page

16. Imagery — Descriptive language which allows the reader to visualize or feel the incidents, thoughts or objects in the novel; often incorporates allusions to the five senses or compares or contrasts one item with another

17. Resonating Image — A particularly powerful icon, symbol or description, especially one which occurs several times in the work and serves to develop character or theme

CHAPTER NINETEEN

FICTION WRITING FOR FOREIGNERS PURSUING THE AMERICAN MARKET

Getting an American Agent

Like any American fiction writer, the foreign writer will probably need to seek the services of an American agent if she wishes to have her work marketed in the United States. A first step is to secure the names and addresses of reputable American literary agents, many of whom are listed in *Writer's Digest* magazine, *The Writer's Market* and *The Literary Marketplace*. The next step is to write or call the agents and ask for their guidelines for making a submission, just as an American writer would do.

When submitting a manuscript to an American agency, be sure to follow their guidelines to the letter. This advice applies to Americans living abroad, as well as to foreign writers. If you have any questions about the guidelines or the agency, contact the agency in question and get clarification. Making a mistake when mailing manuscripts overseas could result in long delays and extra expense.

Also take care to include sufficient International Reply Coupons (IRCs) to cover the cost of a return letter, if the agency accepts the manuscript, as well as enough IRCs to cover postage for the return of your manuscript, if necessary. If you do not wish to have a manuscript returned, be sure to indicate to the agent in the cover letter that she may dispose of a rejected manuscript.

In calling an agent, be aware of the time zone differences between regions of the United States and other countries. For example, London time is five hours later than New York time and eight hours later than Los Angeles time.

Keep in mind that most American agencies do not find translators for works written in foreign languages. Therefore, if your mother tongue is not English, either learn to master the English language (as Joseph Conrad did at the age of 21!), or enlist the help of a very competent literary translator to translate your work effectively.

Visiting an Agent

While our agency has temporary accommodations for foreign writers and other short-term visitors, most agencies do not. When planning a trip to an American agent, remember that lodging, meals, airfare, and entertainment will be at your own expense. A kind agent or publisher might buy lunch for a first-time writer, but this would be a courtesy, not a requirement.

We are reminded of one disastrous incident a few years ago when an unpublished foreign writer visited the agency and arrived in the middle of the city's worst ice storm in ages. Our agency arranged for a representative to meet the writer at the local train station, but was unable to do so because the city was in a state of emergency. We managed to find him a room at the only downtown hotel which still had a few vacancies – fortunately within walking distance of the train station. The foreign visitor was grateful that we arranged a room for him so he didn't have to spend the night on a couch in the station.

The next morning an agency representative picked the writer up at the hotel and took him to our agency accommodations for visiting writers. Things went downhill from there. The day we met him, our visitor handed us the bill for his hotel room, expecting us to pay. He also expected the agency to provide him with free meals and entertainment, as he had not made arrangements of his own. To further complicate the issue, we had set up an appointment for this writer to meet a New York publisher, from whom he also expected free room and board.

Had this visitor been an established, successful writer, he would have received red carpet treatment. However, he was a new, unproven writer whom we had provided with excellent marketing opportunities. Because of reasons known only to himself, this visitor chose to take advantage of the agency's hospitality instead of the business offer.

Is Your Manuscript Suitable for the American Market?

American fiction and the fiction from other countries are two very different animals. Although each influences the other, they can be seen as two distinct styles. Indeed, fiction varies from region to region and age to age, and Asian fiction is as different from European fiction as the works of a Southern writer such as William Faulkner are from the works of Northeastern writer J.D. Salinger. For the sake of simplicity, we have divided contemporary fiction into two handy parcels – American and Comparative (including anything other than American fiction).

When writing, you might do well to consider the market you want to reach – American, European, South American, African, Asian, and so on – and write accordingly. If you wish to write for the American market, consider studying successful American writers. It might be beneficial for you to read at least half a dozen American novels in the category you'd like to pursue before attempting to write for that market. Keep in mind that the U.S. literary market is very genre- and category-oriented, as mentioned earlier in this book. Be sure to target your writing to a specific audience, such as readers of literary fiction, trade fiction, or romance, horror and other genre fiction.

Another way to acquaint yourself with American writing is to attend college or university seminars whenever American writers, publishers or agents are speaking. This will give you insight into writing and marketing for an American audience: what they expect, what they are used to, what they might find intriguing.

Wherever you live, take advantage of your country's local color, history, landscape, climate and customs. Most Americans are only several generations removed from emigrant stock and are often eager to "learn about their roots" or be exposed to different cultures. For example, we are currently marketing a novel in the tradition of "magic realism" by a Greek writer who brilliantly captures the people, places, history and mindset of her native country.

Differences between American and Comparative Fiction

In a previous section, we discussed the differences between classical European and American writing styles. Of course, these descriptions make abundant use of generalizations, but in many cases these divisions between American writing and the styles of other countries hold true. None of these styles is either "right" or "wrong," but simply a reflection of the tastes and interests of very different reading populations.

Comparative Fiction

In general, the works of European, Russian, South American and other Comparative writers tend to focus on the intellectual, political and philosophical climate of a country, or on these aspects of the life of their characters. Characters in Comparative fiction are often receptacles of ideas and concepts, and are not necessarily what one might call "realistic" or "representational."

On the other hand, conventional American writers, in the main, focus on developing believable characters who undergo a personality change, usually for the better, in the course of a novel. Thus there is a strong emphasis on characters' emotional response to events, as opposed to their intellectual response. In American genre fiction, plot is often as important as character development, while American literary writers tend to concentrate on the interior lives of their characters.

The works of Comparative writers are often more cerebral, and hence more emotionally distant, than those of American writers. The language is often lush and lyrical, and characters and plot are less developed. Philosophical ideas and intellectual concepts are often analyzed at length and in depth, and language itself is often manipulated for its intellectual impact, as in the works of Umberto Eco, Günter Grass, Milan Kundera and James Joyce. Political themes are popular with Comparative writers, and often their novels are a sort of satire or expose of a particular regime or government. That is the case with Grass's novel, *The Tin Drum,* and parts of Kundera's work, *The Unbearable Lightness of Being.*

The works of European and other Comparative writers are frequently in the omniscient point of view, which offers the broadest range of control for the writer. Comparative writers sometimes seem like puppet masters manipulating a large cast of characters in an intricate landscape. What the writer gains in control and scope he sometimes loses in the reader's lack of emotional involvement, since, as we have discussed, the omniscient POV is one of the most distant and cerebral.

Works by Comparative writers are often more inventive and, in a way, more wildly imaginative than those by American writers. Comparative writers, for example, sometimes include puzzles or games as part of their novels, even when such devices are not integral to the story. This is evident in the works of the Spanish writer, Jorge Luis Borges, as well as the 18th century English novelist, Lawrence Stern.

Another form of this gamesmanship is the testing of the reader. Umberto Eco, for example, in *The Name of the Rose*, purposefully wrote the first 100 pages of the work in a difficult-to-read style, as a "penance" for the reader. Although these works have found some popularity in the United States, most successful American writers would think twice about intentionally throwing roadblocks or diversions in the way of their readers.

Another example of inventive Comparative writing is the school of "magic realism," a term often associated with the Colombian writer Gabriel Garcia-Marquez and his novel, *One Hundred Years of Solitude*. In this piece, strange events happen without explanation or reactions from the characters:

A 16th century galleon appears in the jungle; inexplicable explosions of animal populations occur in the streets of the city; and the murder and abrupt, subsequent disappearance of thousands of people take place. Czechoslovakian novelist Milan Kundera and Italian writer Italo Calvino also make use of magic realism, which tends to produce a highly stylized sort of writing. At its best, magic realism is intriguing and dreamlike, while at its worst it is confusing, distant and inaccessible.

American Fiction

While magic realism is not unheard of in American letters (some of the novels of Toni Morrison and John Barthelme include magic realism), American fiction writing in general places less emphasis on invention, language play and the intellectual exploration of ideas.

Experimental and innovative novels aside, there are basically two kinds of novels written by Americans for an American audience: commercial and literary. While the goals and markets of these two kinds of novels are different, they frequently have one major aspect in common: They use a fully developed character as a protagonist.

Commercial novels include mass market and trade fiction meant for a broad audience, as well as genre fiction such as horror, romance, mystery, science fiction and fantasy novels. While the basic intent of these novels is to entertain, many also reveal thoughtful insights into the human condition and the vagaries of life. Most of these feature a contemporary setting, but some romances and fantasies are set in the past, while science fiction and futuristic novels almost always reach beyond the present.

Most commercial novels, to some extent, investigate the feelings and thought processes of their major characters, and are primarily attached to the POV of the protagonist. Some are in the first person, usually fictional memoirs and detective mysteries, and some use an omniscient narrator. There is usually a strong emphasis on plot in these novels, and the action is often fast-paced, rising and somewhat episodic. The popular novels of John Grisham, Tom Clancy, Danielle Steele and Stephen King fall into this category.

American literary novels today are influenced by many sources, including those from European, South American, African and Asian writers. Typically, however, American literary novels often owe much to the writings of Steinbeck and Hemingway at their best, or bear the mark of the great Southern American writers: William Faulkner, Eudora Welty, Flannery O'Connor, Carson McCullers, Alice Walker and Truman Capote (best known for his novelistic nonfiction).

These styles emphasize character development and the exploration of human nature, that is, what makes people tick and why. There is far less emphasis on plot, and whatever events take place in the novel seem to rise organically from the characters themselves. In the main, American fiction is far more oriented toward gaining an understanding of people than of expressing ideas or making statements. American writing tends to be more personal, more intimate, more emotionally moving and far less political than the more cerebral, philosophical works of Comparative writers.

We have discussed the strong, powerful, hard-hitting prose of Steinbeck and Hemingway earlier. It has been called "simple" writing because it is straightforward and under-embellished, but it is certainly not simplistic, nor is it devoid of description. The first few chapters of *The Grapes of Wrath*, for instance, capture the plight of the "Oakies" with great power and economy.

The "Southern" style of American literary writing is, as its name implies, usually employed by writers from the Southern states or African-American writers with a Southern heritage. The Southern style in general draws on elements of regional folk-tales and legends, and often features eccentric or isolated people in slightly dangerous, unusual or deteriorating circumstances. Thus we call much Southern literature "Southern Gothic" because of its air of decay and eminent doom. The short story, "A Rose for Emily," by William Faulkner, is a good example of this style. Tension between the races and the sexes are also common elements in much Southern fiction.

Southern Gothic is not an easy style to affect and can easily collapse in a heap of cliches in the hands of an unskilled or unknowledgable writer. At its best, as in the works of Faulkner, McCullers and Walker, Southern fiction is rich in characterization, insight, lyrical descriptions, and a haunting atmosphere that evokes impending destruction and man's inability to escape the inevitable.

A Decision to Make

Of course, many Comparative writers have "broken into" the American market, usually in the area of literary novels. The readership of this market is usually highly educated and more open to fiction which might seem unfamiliar or inaccessible to other readers. Therefore it's up to the writer to decide whether to pursue a wider, more popular audience by writing in the "American style," or to go after a smaller, more open-minded literary au- dience interested in inventive, philosophical, intellectual writing. In either case, only the most effective, well-crafted fiction will succeed, such as the ones listed below.

SOME FOREIGN NOVELS WHICH HAVE BEEN SUCCESSFUL IN THE UNITED STATES

1. *The Name of the Rose*, Umberto Eco
2. *The Unbearable Lightness of Being* and *The Art of Laughter and Forgetting*, Milan Kundera
3. *The Tin Drum* and *The Dog Years*, Günter Grass
4. *Perfume*, Patrick Süskind
5. *One Hundred Years of Solitude* and *Love in the Time of Cholera*, Gabriel Garcia-Marquez
6. *Like Water for Chocolate*, Laura Escoval
7. *Time's Arrow*, Martin Amis
8. *A Bend in the River*, V.S. Naipal
9. *The Guest of Honor*, Nadine Gordimer
10. *Midaq Alley*, Naguib Mahfouz
11. *The Lover*, Marguerite Duras
12. *The History of the World in Ten and a Half Chapters* and *Flaubert's Parrot*, Julian Barnes

CHAPTER
TWENTY

SCREENPLAYS AT A GLANCE

The bulk of the manuscripts that the agency receives are novels, and therefore we have emphasized novel-writing in this book. With the growing influence of film, many writers are switching from trying to write novels to trying to write screenplays. While the number of screenplay submissions we receive does not equal the number of fiction manuscripts, the volume is increasing. Unfortunately, our screenplay submissions contain more mistakes than any other type of manuscript.

The screenplay works in an entirely different manner than the novel. Because the two media – cinema and print – rely upon separate elements to render a story, one should not expect to be able to translate a work literally from one medium to the other.

Nearly every week the agency receives at least one inquiry from a fledgling writer who invariably says, "It's a book but it could be a great screenplay." In previous chapters, we have discussed the drawbacks of writing a novel in a cinematic style. Just as some would-be novelists do not understand the way a novel works, many writers who are attempting to write a screenplay for the first time don't understand that there are conventions to screenwriting as well.

Mozart Did It, So Why Can't I?

Most beginning musicians would no more sit down at the piano and say, "I'm going compose a concerto," than they would retire to the garage and try to build a rocket engine out of spare lawnmower parts. For some reason, however, many first-time screenwriters (just like many first-time novelists) believe that if they've seen a movie (or read a book), they can write one. And just as those novelists who have not spent time learning how to make fiction work inevitably stumble, so does the screenwriter who has not yet taken the time to study and understand the craft of the screenplay. Having watched lots of television or many movies does not in itself qualify you for the art of screenwriting.

THE SCREENPLAY PROPOSAL

As with non-fiction submissions, the screenplay relies upon the success of its presentation as much as upon the work itself. The screenplay proposal should include the following: a treatment, a marketing prospectus, and a properly formatted screenplay.

When we review a screenplay submission, the first thing the agency checks is whether or not the writer has properly presented his proposal. The mistakes are frequent and obvious, and they serve to separate the amateurs from those with professional potential. If the writer has not followed the proper guidelines, then we can do little with the submission, no matter how good the idea, except ask the writer to do his research and learn how to put a screenplay submission together properly.

Let's examine the three components of the proposal in more detail.

1. *The Treatment*

Perhaps the most important aspect of the screenplay proposal is the treatment. Even more than the screenplay itself, the treatment is the vehicle necessary to sell your story to the producer. With the mountain of screenplay submissions producers receive, first judgments are frequently based on the treatment alone. If the writer fails with his treatment, his screenplay is not likely to be read.

A treatment is the camera's eye view of the central action of the script. It may or may not include dialogue. It is similar to the synopsis of a novel, though it is usually longer. Producers will examine your treatment to make sure that the story is appropriate for your genre and for your target audience.

Here's an example of a treatment put together and sold by the agency. The story, *The Rescue of Jennifer Lynn*, is intended for a made-for-television movie.

This treatment is effective because it is brief, fast-paced and tightly focused on the events in the screenplay. Note how snatches of dialogue are included to indicate the natural-sounding, easy-to-follow dialogue of the screenplay and whet the reader's appetite for more. The treatment also has the good fortune of being about a timely topic.

THE RESCUE OF JENNIFER LYNN

"The foster care system should exist for the benefit of
the children, not the children for the benefit of the
system."

(Gerry Schmidt before the Texas State Senate)

When there's too much wheat, the farmers are paid not
to grow it. When too many deer roam the fields and
forests, it's declared open season. But what's to be
done with the many thousands of neglected children? We
can't pay parents not to have any more. We can't shoot
them. Instead, we simply lose them in the shadow world
of the foster care system.

Every day, innocent children are lead into a system
that shuffles them between unfit parents and strangers.
In this world, the only thing that is black and white
is the certainty that, if a meal is served, it won't be
with love. In this world, the joys of childhood are
lost somewhere in the struggle of staying alive. This
is a place that most of us will never enter because if
we do, we will see these shadow children. Then the
question becomes our own. Each one of us must ask
ourselves, "What will I do?"

Joy and Gerry Schmidt entered that world where, as the
saying goes, even angels fear to tread. The Schmidts'
reward: a four-year old, blonde-haired, blue-eyed
beauty named Jennifer Lynn. This is their story. A
true story of struggle, hope, triumph, joy and, most of
all, love.

WHEATEN, TEXAS

A montage of happy, positive, sunlit scenes give us a
sense of well-being as children at play are laughing
and neighbors are talking across white picket fences.
All is right with the world, at least when that world
is on the right side of town.

In the backyard of a broken-down house, the sun is not
shining as brightly. We sense an uneasy feeling about
the unkempt, still grounds. Our eyes catch a movement.
It is a small, half-dressed child whose dirty face is
streaked by the secretions of a runny nose. We watch
as the child crawls across the yard, then drinks from
the dog's bowl.

--2--

A man, who is watching from the doorstep, walks over
and kicks the child repeatedly. He takes the cigarette
from his mouth and holds it against the child's arm.
His other hand, tight against her mouth, muffles the
little girl's screams.

A neighbor watching from her window dials 911.

Jennifer Lynn is seemingly rescued from a life of
terror as the child welfare system rushes to her aid.
The next few days bring a flurry of adults into
Jennifer Lynn's life, who leave as quickly as they
entered. Within a week, Jennifer Lynn is processed and
placed with the Millers, her first foster care family.
Justice has been moving quickly, too, and Jennifer's
father, Michael, pleads guilty to child abuse and is
locked up in the county jail. Debbie, Jennifer Lynn's
mother, undergoes a brief investigation by state
officials and then returns home to care for her one-
year-old son, Jimmy.

At the Millers, Jennifer Lynn meets their neighbor, Joy
Schmidt. Joy, a woman who believes that people will do
the right thing simply because it is the right thing to
do, instantly falls in love with Jennifer Lynn. Joy's
safe, comfortable world begins to crumble when she
learns that Jennifer Lynn's scarred and bruised body is
a result of the beatings she had received. "I hope
that man rots in jail," is Joy's first response to
Michael's incarceration. Joy's love for Jennifer Lynn
is returned openly and freely, and Joy convinces her
husband, Gerry, that they should adopt her.

The Schmidts hope to spare Jennifer Lynn the trauma of
the foster care informal six-month rule that will force
Jennifer Lynn to leave the home of the Millers and be
placed elsewhere. The Schmidts visit Larry Leanman of
the Foster Care Department and inform him of their
desire to adopt Jennifer Lynn immediately.

Larry personifies the big fish in a little pond and
enjoys intimidating and controlling people. His
department is run efficiently and has the highest
rating in the state for placing children in foster care
homes. Since the state pays only for the children in
the system, Larry Leanman keeps his department revenues
healthy by keeping captive the children already in the
system.

--3--

At first, Larry tries to dissuade the Schmidts from
adopting "that" kind of child, who brings with her
pain, confusion, trouble and years of therapy. The
Schmidts, however, remain firm in their decision.

"I promised Jennifer Lynn that she will be coming home
with me," Joy says as she shows Larry a picture of her
two children. "I told her a new brother and sister are
waiting for her." Larry congratulates the Schmidts for
their strong conviction and dedication and promises to
expedite the process.

Kathy Brown is the caseworker assigned to assist the
Schmidts. Larry instructs Kathy to go through the
motions but voices his doubts about the Schmidts'
commitment to actually going through with the adoption.

"This is just a Christian crusade that will pass when
they realize what they're in for," says Larry.
"Besides, if people start adopting these kids, we'll be
out of a job."

When Kathy realizes that the Schmidts are, indeed,
serious, she works to make it happen. However, Kathy
finds that all the paperwork she submits on the
adoption of Jennifer Lynn finds its way back to her
desk marked "incomplete." The adoption process comes
virtually to a halt and Jennifer Lynn is taken from the
Millers and placed in her second foster care home.

When the Schmidts learn of Jennifer Lynn's new
placement, they frantically try to reach her to explain
that they have not deserted her. They are told by
officials at the Foster Care Department that they are
not permitted to have any contact with Jennifer Lynn
and that their relationship with Jennifer Lynn is
disruptive to her.

An angry Gerry Schmidt storms into Larry's office and
questions him about the restrictions placed against him
and his wife. Larry plays dumb and promises that he
will look into the problem. Kathy, overhearing the
exchange, realizes that the hold-up on Jennifer Lynn's
adoption is not a matter of the system's red tape but
Larry's deliberate attempt to prevent it. Kathy finds
herself faced with the decision of remaining silent and
keeping her job which, as a single parent, she cannot
afford to lose, or blowing the whistle from the
unemployment line. She decides to silently help the
Schmidts and arranges a secret meeting with them.
Kathy runs through a list of ways to beat the system.

--4--

"You're gonna have to put up a hell of a fight for this
little girl," Kathy warns them. "It's gonna cost you
lots of money and loads of heartache."

"We've got the money," Gerry answers. "We can take the
heartache."

The fight between the Schmidts and the system begins.
The Schmidts' attempt to attract the attention of
numerous state appointed and elected officials. None
seem interested or able to do anything to help Jennifer
Lynn. When these efforts fail, the Schmidts take the
case public with petitions signed by friends and
neighbors.

Armed with the signed petitions, Joy visits the local
newspaper where she meets reporter Dave Lindor, who has
the soul of a Lou Grant with a body that is not far
behind. Dave listens intently to Jennifer Lynn's
story.

"Somewhere between here and there is where the truth
lies," Dave concludes. "You seek it out, Mrs. Schmidt,
and, in the meantime, I'll report the story."

Kathy becomes Dave's anonymous "inside source" via the
telephone. Since he does not know her real name, he
nicknames her "Murphy," because he thinks she sounds
like Candice Bergen.

It is not long before Kathy's calls to Dave are more
frequent and of a more personal nature.

The reporting of Jennifer Lynn's story changes from
factual journalism to an emotional cry to help free
Jennifer Lynn. An entire city throws its support
behind the Schmidts' efforts to adopt Jennifer Lynn.
Bumper stickers, posters, and billboards read, FREE
JENNIFER LYNN: A Prisoner of the System. Gerry passes
out POW bracelets with the inscription: "Jennifer Lynn
4/21/86" which people are to wear until Jennifer Lynn
is freed.

While the townspeople are rallying around the flagpole
and lawyers are filing motions for legal custody,
Jennifer Lynn becomes further lost in the shadow world.
She is removed from her fifth foster home and
"mistakenly" placed in the custody of her natural
mother, Debbie.

--5--

Debbie, suffering from the public humiliation her
daughter's story has caused her, punishes Jennifer Lynn
by tying her spread-eagle to a bed where Jennifer Lynn
remains both day and night. Debbie releases Jennifer
Lynn only long enough to satisfy the caseworker who
visits daily to check on Jennifer Lynn's progress. As
the days pass, the caseworker's visits are less
frequent. Within a week, they stop altogether.

Only Larry and the now former caseworker know the true
whereabouts of Jennifer Lynn.

Michael, still in prison, learns of the Schmidts'
struggle to adopt his daughter and contacts Joy,
requesting that she visit him. Joy immediately drives
to the county prison where she expects to find an ogre.
Instead, she finds sitting before her a soft-spoken,
eighteen-year-old boy. His brown eyes are more like
those of a puppy than a child abuser. To Joy's
surprise, her hatred and fear give way to compassion.

"My parents did worse to me than I did to Jenny,"
Michael begins, "but that's no excuse for what I did.
God knows that her momma's no good either. But now,
you bein' a Christian woman and all, I gotta chance to
make it right." With that said, Michael hands Joy a
piece of paper. "My lawyer said this should help you
get Jenny. I'm givin' her up and this here paper says
so. It also says you and your husband should be the
ones to get her."

Throughout Joy's struggles with the Foster Care
Department, the legal system, the mounting bills, and
her career, she manages to visit Michael twice a week.
It is because Michael did the right thing for the sake
of doing what was right that Joy's faith is restored
and her strength renewed.

Michael comes to trust Joy, and slowly his story of
being a child lost in the shadow world unfolds.
Through Michael, Joy is able to understand more fully
the cycle of child abuse and learns ways in which she
can help Jennifer Lynn.

While the Schmidts are rejoicing over the progress made
regarding the adoption, they receive a phone call from
Kathy who has just discovered that Jennifer Lynn is in
the custody of Debbie, which is contrary to what the
official records report. Kathy believes she knows who
is responsible for putting Jennifer Lynn with her
mother but declines to give any names until she checks
it out.

--6--

"I don't think you're going to win this one," Kathy
says, "Jennifer Lynn's mother is going to fight for
custody, and I'm ashamed to say the foster care
department is supporting her."

That evening, while Kathy is working late, she searches
Larry's private office. She find Jennifer Lynn's file
and makes a complete copy. As she is refiling the
information, she is interrupted by Larry. Kathy gives
a lame excuse for being in his office and quickly
leaves the building.

From then on, the work place for Kathy becomes
unbearable as she receives a continuous barrage of
petty complaints from her superiors.

The Schmidts' day in court is fast approaching. Even
though Michael has given up custody to the Schmidts,
the lawyers do not see much hope for the child to be
taken away from her mother. The Schmidts are advised
that the Foster Care Department plans to prove in court
that the Schmidts are an unstable, holy-rolling couple.

In desperation, Joy waits outside the city building for
Kathy to leave work. Unbeknownst to Joy, reporter Dave
Lindor is also waiting for Kathy.   Dave has fallen in
love with Kathy 'Murphy' Brown even though he does not
know what she looks like. He has stood in front of the
city building for the past week, trying to match a face
with the voice. And now Joy was going to lead him to
his Murphy.

Kathy, who fears someone will learn of her involvement
to free Jennifer Lynn, tries to avoid Joy, but ends up
agreeing to speak with her over coffee. Joy begs Kathy
to testify in court against the Foster Care Department
but Kathy refuses. "I'm afraid," Kathy whispers
looking around, "not only for my job by for my own
safety. I'm being watched."

And indeed she is, by both Larry and Dave. However,
Dave is not as interested in what was being said as he
was in Kathy's appearance, which he finds very
appealing.

Finally, the case of Schmidts vs the Foster Care
Department is heard in court. Things are not going
well for the Schmidts as their personal life is made
public. All objections by their lawyer are overruled.
It becomes apparent that the judge is biased on behalf
of the system. The first day in court ends with the
allegation that the Schmidts abuse their two children.

--7--

Jennifer Lynn's mother weeps as she expresses her fear of losing her daughter to those kind of people.

Dave's report of the day is biting as he calls for the judge to "clean his eyes and heart out."

Kathy, who decides she must do what is right, confronts Larry with a copy of his personal file on Jennifer Lynn.

"I know what's going on," Kathy says, waving the file before him. "The police are already on their way to take Jennifer Lynn from her mother and you'll be the one who will have to answer why we didn't protect this little girl. It was you that sent her back there. It was you who stopped her supervision. It was you who lied about her whereabouts. It's going to be you who pays. You and poor little Jennifer Lynn."

Kathy hands in her resignation. She then places a call to Dave and relays to him her confrontation with Larry and the information she has obtained.

"This isn't good," Dave says.

"What are you talking about?" she questions. "This will make the Schmidts' case."

"But it could hurt you," he answers.

Dave tells Kathy that she is in trouble and convinces her to meet with him at the news room where he can keep her safe. Kathy drops her daughter off at her mother's, then heads for the DAILY PRESS building.

While Dave and Kathy are meeting for the first time, Kathy's apartment is being ransacked and the Schmidts are explaining to their children that Jennifer Lynn may not be coming home to live with them.

The following day, a malnutritioned, burned and bruised Jennifer Lynn is brought into the courtroom. She has not spoken a word in weeks. Kathy, Jennifer Lynn's ex-social worker, and the police all testify against the Foster Care Department.

Finally, after 18 months of struggle, the court frees Jennifer Lynn. As Joy and Gerry hug their new daughter, Jennifer Lynn whispers, "Can we go home now?"

--8--

Reporters from all over the state question the Schmidts as they leave the courtroom. Joy, who is carrying Jennifer Lynn in one arm, stops and raises her free hand. "See this bracelet?" she says, "I'll wear it until all the Jennifer Lynns are free."

In the background, we watch as Debbie is being escorted out by the guards. We also catch a glimpse of Kathy and Dave holding hands.

We leave this triumphant scene and move into the same backyard where we began. It is still unkempt. The eerie shadows play upon the cool ground. Our eyes catch a movement. It is Jimmy, Debbie's other child. We watch as he crawls from the tall grass and heads toward the dog house.

The story is not over.

We hear a child's joyful laughter as the faint images of Jennifer Lynn and her new family playing together in their backyard become visible, superimposed over Jimmy. The striking contrast between these two realities gives us hope that we can, indeed, bring a shining light into a world of shadows.

THE END

2. *The Prospectus*

Who's going to see this movie? This is the key question behind the marketing prospectus. A producer needs to know more than what the story is about; he needs to know who the intended audience is, which type of production company is most appropriate, and how much money would need to be budgeted.

While at this point the prospectus does not need to be detailed and need cover no more than a single page, it should provide all the vital information a producer needs to know about the film. For example, the prospectus should include the intended audience. Is this script intended to be an animated movie for a children's audience? Is this script for a high-budget action movie aimed at a male audience? Is this script for a made-for-TV movie aimed at an elderly audience?

Once the audience has been determined, the prospectus should reveal information that will let the producer know what type of production company would be most appropriate. This will depend in large measure upon where the writer intends the filmed script to appear. Is it a prime time made-for-TV movie? An after-school special? An independently released art house film? A low-budget, straight-to-video action picture? Or a studio feature?

The writer needs to estimate the budget. Is this intended for television or cinema? Low budget or high budget? A certain give-away of a writer who doesn't know his craft is the writer who has a 12-million-dollar budget for an after-school special.

Producers look at the bottom line. They need to take into account more than the screenplay itself when reviewing a script, and this is where the prospectus comes in handy. They look at the genre, the intended audience, the budget and more, and if the prospectus is carefully presented, it can help you sell your story.

3. *The Screenplay Format*

A screenplay, to begin with, has to look like a screenplay. Many people, from producers and directors to actors and set designers, will need to look at the screenplay. A standard format has been adopted so that, just from looking at the page, each individual can determine what he or she will be responsible for during the course of filming a scene. The screenplay's specific, unique format bears little room for variation, and it is extremely important that you learn the proper guidelines.

The narrative is usually set off by approximately one and one-half inch margins on either side, and dialogue by two and one-half to three inch margins. For complete formatting guidelines, consult *How to Write a Screenplay* by Syd Field.

Below is an example of a page taken from a horror screenplay entitled *The Congregation* by John Russo, the screenwriter for *Night of the Living Dead*. This page will illustrate the proper format for a screenplay.

```
                                                              28

    15.   INT - MEREDITH'S OCCULT SHOP - DAY

          Meredith Brewster and Morgan Drey are in a "seance
          area" in the back of the shop, seated at a small,
          round table with two lighted candles between them,
          giving off a flickering, orange cast.

          Meredith is peering intently at Tarot cards that
          she has dealt from a deck.

                          MEREDITH
                    Your fiancee is unhappy with
                    you.  She senses that she may
                    not be the only woman in your
                    life.  You teach at a college
                    where voluptuous young women
                    abound.  For some of them you
                    would make quite a desirable
                    father figure, Dr. Morgan Drey.

          She looks up at him, flashing a facetious smile.

          He shakes his head, amused.

                          MORGAN
                    Once again, Meredith, I must
                    say that there is nothing
                    particularly magical in your
                    observations.  It's all good,
                    logical conjecture, based on
                    what you already know about
                    me.

                          MEREDITH
                    What sort of things would you
                    like me to tell you about your-
                    self?

                          MORGAN
                    Nothing.  I don't want to hear
                    anything about myself.  I want
                    to hear about you.  That's what
                    I need for my book, remember?

                          MEREDITH
                    I forgot about the book.

                          MORGAN
                    Well, I didn't.  The publisher
                    won't let me.  I'm on a tight
                    deadline.
```

Besides the layout of the words on the page, we examine a screenplay submission to make sure that the script contains the proper use of narrative and dialogue. Unfortunately, many beginning writers fail to understand how to tell a story through appropriate scenes. The mistakes fall within a broad spectrum. We have received screenplays written almost entirely as dialogue (with virtually no narrative to convey description of characters, setting, or action, and without separating the story into individual scenes) and screenplays written in large chunks of narrative description (where the action is summarized and dialogue is not used to progress the conflict or reveal character).

The novice screenwriter should also take into consideration the length of his script. We received one 180-plus page screenplay from a writer who was completely unaware that his screenplay, if filmed, would have a running time of over three hours. As a general rule of thumb, you should consider one page of script equal to one minute of screen time.

When writing for television, you need to keep programming restrictions in mind. You must conform to the programming formats (half-hour sitcom, one-hour drama, two-hour made-for-TV movie, and so forth). A made-for-TV movie, for example, fills two hours of network air time. A two-hour television movie will have a running time of approximately 90 minutes (subtracting time for commercials), and thus the script would need to be approximately 90 pages long.

Unless you are a writer with the stature of a Stephen King or a Jackie Collins, it is not very likely that your script for a mini-series or a movie of more than two hours will be produced. If you cannot write a script that will fill an appropriate time period, it is more than likely that you have chosen the wrong medium in which to work.

With cinema, you have a little more leeway, but you should understand that the average movie lasts approximately one hour and forty minutes. At roughly one page of text per minute of film, this translates into approximately 100 pages for the length of your feature film script. Even a star with as much power as Kevin Costner had to struggle to get *Dances with Wolves* made, due to its three-hour plus length. It is very unlikely that a beginning screenwriter will have a producer option a screenplay that is much more than 135 pages long.

Finally, always remember that you are not the director. Do not indulge yourself by including camera angles and tracking shots throughout the script. Your job is to write the story, primarily in dialogue, so that the director can film it.

CONVENTIONS OF SCREENWRITING

The approach to screenwriting is somewhat backwards compared to other fiction writing. Whereas we tell the novelist, "Know your conventions," we tell the screenwriter, "Know your form." You have to be dressed for the part, so to speak, before your treatment/screenplay can be judged for its story merits.

Once you've come to understand how the screenplay proposal needs to be put together and can write toward that end, then you should begin work on the screenplay itself.

The conventions of the film medium differ in many ways from those of the novel. Understanding the ways in which a screenplay functions is critical to making your work successful.

1. *Dialogue*

A screenplay is basically a script: Dialogue is the single most important element. If you are unsure of your ability to write natural-sounding dialogue, then the screenplay form is probably not for you.

Dialogue has to convey character. Unlike the novel, you cannot go into the characters' minds for their thoughts and insights. The dialogue has to show who the characters are and what they are feeling. How a character speaks will also reveal much about the character. Does she stammer nervously? Or does she speak with rapid-fire bravado?

Dialogue can also be used as a means of exposition, setting up the future action of the script, or explaining important aspects of a character's background. A writer should take pains, however, not to write too much dialogue as exposition, as this type of writing becomes stilted very quickly.

Dialogue should also move the story forward. It is essential to avoid "chitchat." If the dialogue is not somehow progressing the plot or creating conflict, then chances are it needs to be cut from the screenplay.

Although writing dialogue for the screen is different from writing dialogue for the novel, there are many pitfalls to avoid, no matter which medium you are working in. *Potential problems* involving dialogue have been discussed in depth in previous chapters.

2. *Narrative*

While the screenplay is primarily composed of dialogue, the narrative elements are an important function of the script. The narrative establishes the scene and provides important information for the director. The narrative should be written in the present tense.

The first responsibility of narrative is to establish the scene, from the physical setting to the characters. Directors will need to know if the scene is interior or exterior, day or night. They will need to know what the setting is, whether it's the kitchen of a four-star restaurant, an old cottage overlooking the sea, the backyard of a suburban house, or any other place that you can imagine.

The use of some concrete, descriptive details will further establish the scene and reveal character. Is the kitchen immaculately clean and modern, or does it have cracked linoleum and peeling wallpaper? Your details will help to clarify the setting.

The narrative should also establish which characters are in the scene, from JEFF, the chef, to MARTHA, a retired school teacher, to BILLY, a spoiled 9-year-old. (Note that you place the character's name all in caps when it first appears in the script, and when indicating dialogue.) Strong descriptive details can also help to clarify characters. Is Billy wearing a little sailor's uniform or prep school clothes, or is he dressed in baggy shorts and a baseball cap turned backwards? Your narrative details, although brief, should be used to reveal information to the director and actors.

Narrative is also an important device for describing any action that is critical to the scene. For the most part, you don't want to orchestrate the action; that is the director's and the actor's job. However, if Billy, our spoiled nine-year-old, throws a baseball through the window of his stepfather's study, then that action has to be described in narrative in the course of the screenplay.

Be sure not to write too much in narrative. Narrative is used to describe the actions of the characters, but these movements should be summarized in short paragraphs. Narrative is also frequently used as a transitional device from scene to scene. If you find yourself writing pages of narrative, however, you might want to consider trying your hand at a novel after all.

3. *Visual Medium*

Cinema is a visual medium, and so you should always render scenes with that in mind. Unlike a novel, where a character's thoughts, insights and feelings are of primary importance in rendering a story, you have to rely exclusively upon what can be seen.

Kate, a teenage girl, might think that Josh, the new boy in school, is cute, but you don't want to write "Kate thinks Josh is cute." Instead, you will have to think of a way to show that Kate thinks Josh is cute, perhaps by the way she stares at him. Perhaps she will admit it in dialogue to a friend.

Visual images also apply to characterization. A character might be politically active, but unless you find a way to show this information (through campaign posters, buttons, bumper stickers, or a debate, perhaps) on the screen, then it does not belong in the script.

Because we rely heavily upon the sense of sight in our own lives, the screenplay is a natural for many people. Nonetheless, it is surprising how difficult writing can be when you are restricted to revealing character only through an external set of details that relies almost exclusively on only one sense.

4. *Dramatic Structure*

A screenplay relies upon dramatic structure to build suspense and create tension and pressure. Each scene has to build upon the next, gathering momentum, much like a set of dominoes knocking one down after another. If one domino is missing from the chain, or if there is no conflict to start the dominoes falling, then a screenplay will lack the drama necessary to achieve success.

A feature film screenplay generally has three acts, with each successive act hinging on a plot point, or "hook," that sends the action in a new direction, in the process escalating the conflict by intensifying tension and pressure. (See the section on hooks in Chapter Seven.) The oldest story in the world, perhaps, follows this three-act structure: Boy Meets Girl, Boy Loses Girl, Boy Wins Girl Back. Watch any movie today, and you will find that it almost invariably boils down to that simple three-part structure.

In previous chapters, we have discussed in depth ways in which it is possible to create and build suspense, conflict and tension, the underlying principles of all fiction, regardless of the genre.

IN CONCLUSION

While this information should help the beginning screenwriter get started, it is by no means meant to be all-encompassing. Plenty of good books are available on the subject of screenwriting, covering the topic in more depth than we will be able to address in these pages. We encourage writers who are interested in writing for film to go to their local bookstore or library and read as much as possible on putting together a treatment and writing in the appropriate manuscript format for screenplays.

The competition is fierce, and if you don't understand the form of the screenplay and the screenplay submission process, the likelihood of selling your work is very small indeed. But, if you learn your craft and set your mind to it, you may one day see your work come to life in front of you.

CHAPTER
TWENTY ONE

PUBLICITY

A S A NEW WRITER, you now have a working idea of the literary marketplace and the conventions of novel writing. You feel good about your new understanding and are ready to put to use everything you have learned. With commitment and diligence, you will eventually realize your dream and graduate from being a new writer to a published author. The new swimming pool may soon be yours.

Now let's take a look into the future and see what's in store for the new author.

You have finished writing your book, it's been sold and in a few short months it will be heading for the bookstores. The hard work is done! Right? Wrong. It's just that *that* part of the hard work is over. You still have ahead of you the very tedious task of promotion and publicity. Many newly published authors are in for a big surprise when they discover just how much time, energy and savvy is needed to drum up publicity for their work. And there's nothing the newly published author needs more than publicity for his book.

This need for publicity will demand that you wear another hat – that of a publicist. You will find that as a newly published author you will have to promote yourself and your work at every turn. As you and your work get better known, your life will change, especially where the public is concerned. They will envy you, admire you and hold you slightly apart from the crowd. Perhaps this is justified, because just about everyone has a story to tell and wishes he or she could tell it in book form. You have, against the odds, accomplished the very difficult task of getting your book published. You have successfully entered into a strange new world that to most is as foreign as the planet Mars. This world, however, has both its ups and downs. When you get your first negative review or publicity, you will understand exactly how far that "down" can be.

What is publicity anyway?

Publicity is anything that will place the author and his book before the consumer, the booksellers, reviewers and the public at large. It is free of charge and normally promulgated through the media in the form of "news." In general, the author is in charge of publicity (which, though nominally free, can be very "expensive" in terms of time and effort). Publishers generate some publicity for the new author, and are helpful in offering tips and suggestions. Publishers also have a promotional budget, and will promote your book through advertising and other means, which must be purchased.

In many ways, authors of nonfiction books have an easier time securing media attention, especially if their book is of a timely nature, than do the authors of fiction. The reason for this is simply the nonfiction authors' expertise in a certain subject. For example: Dr. Jane is a psychologist who specializes in the treatment of abusive spouses. Her first book, entitled *Why Men Kick the Wife and Pet the Dog,* was recently released. Joel, a science fiction writer, had a novel, *Out There,* released at the same time. Both newly published authors live in the same town, both have the same publisher (different imprints), and media packages were sent out on both authors. Joel gets a nice write-up in the local newspaper while Dr. Jane is booked on every TV and radio talk show and has signed up for a lecture tour. All the daytime talk shows have invited her to be their guest, and she's even offered a half-hour radio talk show of her very own. In the meantime, Joel is going from bookstore to bookstore, trying to arrange a booksigning. He is also rather upset because he feels his publisher has given him a raw deal by not making him a celebrity like Dr. Jane. The truth of the matter is that abusive spouses happens to be the hot topic of the week, and Dr. Jane has both the book and the qualifications to make for an interesting interview. It was not difficult for her to obtain adequate publicity; for Joel it will be a continual struggle.

Joel, you and other newly published authors can build upon the success of getting your book publicized by gaining media attention. Here are some guidelines for doing just that.

1. Media File. Create a file of your media contacts, that is, everyone you speak to at radio and television stations; newspapers; magazines; other publications; bookstores; literary organizations, and anyone else who can promote your book. Keeping track of all this material may be a little time-consuming; however, if you put in the effort now, the work will be easier the next time around. You may even wish to start creating your media file before your first book is sold, putting together a list of contacts in key media.

This information is helpful to your publisher and your agent. It also shows them that you have done your homework and have a good idea of what it takes to stir up some publicity.

The file should include the following information. *Radio and TV*: the name of each likely show, the host, your contact, the program director; the station's call letters, address, phone and fax number; the date of the last contact, why you called and what the response was. *Publications*: the name of the newspaper or magazine you contacted and the name of the section or feature (Lifestyles, Regional News, Book Reviews, and so forth); the editor (contact), the managing editor, the senior editor; address, phone and fax; date of last contact, purpose of call and response. (See the media file chart in the appendix).

2. Put media contacts in your address book or rolodex.

3. Create a media calendar. If you are scheduling interviews, a media calendar will help you keep track of the dates and times of the interviews and how they went. The calendar should include the day, date, time and length of the interview; the station's call letters or the name of the publication; the name of the person conducting the interview; address, phone and fax and room for comments on how you did on the interview and how you might improve the next. (See the media calendar chart in the appendix.)

4. Publicity Photos. If you have not already done so, have publicity shots taken. The preferred size is 4x5. When sent to the media, these photos are not normally returned, so arrange to purchase the negatives from the photographer. That way you can get a supply of photographs made whenever you need them. Also work out an agreement in writing, signed by the photographer, in which he states that you own the photographs and are allowed to use them for publicity and promotion without restriction.

The publisher usually requires a photograph of the author for the jacket of the book, so you should have some extra shots taken when you are getting your publicity shots. Have a roll taken in color and a couple of rolls in black and white. Take at least two changes of clothes to the studio, one casual and the other dressy. Certain poses, such as hand(s) to chin, arm wrapped around bent knee, are typical of authors' pictures. Although these may not be the "look" your publisher would like you to have, they are often effective, so do no hesitate to take a few of these typical shots.

Also take a few full body shots, although most of the time only head and shoulder photographs will be required. Try a few shots that are out of the ordinary, perhaps with a prop or in an unusual pose. They may just work. Ask the photographer if the studio will do your make-up and style your hair. You may wish to take advantage of this service if it's available. However, you may not feel like yourself and therefore may not be comfortable with your new look during the shoot. Your distress will show in your photographs.

While posing for photos, try to relax and enjoy yourself. A professional photographer will find a way to get you to loosen up so you will look your best. Since your picture is going to be seen by thousands of people, including family and friends, this is not the time to conserve money by having your photographs taken at the photo booth in the mall.

Interviews

Interviews in newspaper and magazines and on radio and television are your main source of publicity. Interviews are arranged by you, not your publisher. They are extremely important to the sale of your book, since they will help the public determine whether or not your work is of interest to them. Your personal warmth, charm and intelligence will go a long way to persuade people that yes, indeed, yours is the book for them. The information in this section will help you arrange and prepare for several different kinds of interviews.

Let's say you've landed an interview with your local newspaper. (This is normally not too difficult to achieve, since most hometown papers are just as proud of you as you are of yourself.) Before the interview, contact local bookstores and let them know you are about to be interviewed. Inform them that you believe the newspaper will mention the name of any bookstore which is sponsoring a booksigning for your new book. (Most newspapers are willing to extend you this courtesy.) Ask the bookstore managers if they are interested in arranging a signing for you at their store. The bookstore gets free publicity, you get free publicity, and the newspaper gets the credit for helping your new career.

Next you'll need to do some research about local radio and television programs that interview authors. Call the program manager of the station and very briefly tell him about your book. Then send him the book, a copy of the newspaper article, and a list of bookstores where you have had or are going to have a signing. Don't forget to request to appear on a particular show. After all, you are not only a published author, but an authority who can offer listeners some insight into what it takes to get published. In Joel's case, he could entertain the listeners with some interesting facts that his research for the book had uncovered, especially the information he had unearthed on aliens from "out there" and government cover-ups regarding those aliens.

After a week or so, give the program director a follow-up call. Did he get the book? Did he get a chance to look it over? (Don't be disappointed if he only scanned the book. These people have precious little time, and reading your book is not one of their top priorities. Whether or not they have actually read the book is of little consequence. The purpose of sending the book to the program director was to help you get a shot at being a guest on the show.) Ask him if he would like to schedule you for the show.

If the answer is no, politely ask why. If you don't ask, you will go away feeling hurt and dejected. With few exceptions, newly published authors tend to take "no" as a personal rejection, but interviews are normally declined because of scheduling conflicts, time constraints or book topics which are not suitable for that particular program's listeners. End the conversation on a high note; you want to keep the door open. Maybe once everyone else in town is interviewing you, the program director may find the time to have you on.

If the answer is yes, you're in clover. No matter whether your interview is for radio, TV, or print, the following information and tips will help insure that the interview will be successful and you will come across as an old pro, not a nervous first-time interviewee. Remember that, when giving an interview, nothing is really "off the record," so don't say anything that you don't want to read about.

What to Do for All Interviews

— Write down the day, date and time of interview.
— Prepare yourself for your interview. If it has been a while since you last read your book, read it again.
— Make a list of questions you think the interviewer may ask.
— Make certain you can summarize your book in a few sentences.
— Always be courteous to the person conducting the interview. No one could possibly be more important than him or her at that moment, so give the interviewer your full and undivided attention.
— Do all interviews with a smile on your face and a song in your heart. Put energy and spirit into the interview. Make the interviewer and the people who are listening to you (or reading your words) glad that they are addressing them.
— This may be difficult, but keep the exaggerations down to a minimum. Stick to the truth and you'll never go wrong.
— Always have information on where the book can purchased. Most publishers have an 800 number. Before the interview, ask your host if he wishes to give out that number or if you should mention it during

the interview. If a bookstore is not carrying your book, remind your audience that they can ask the bookstore to order a copy from the publisher.

— Give yourself a few seconds to formulate each answer, then speak clearly and confidently. Include a short anecdote where appropriate. Remember to occasionally refer back to your book. Use introductory statements such as, "As I say in my book" or "when I was writing my book."

— Stay focused. Answer the question. It is very easy to get distracted, and once this happens, you may start to ramble and stray from the topic. While this may be acceptable and expected from a politician, it is not acceptable from you.

— Be persuasive. Take every opportunity to create a need for people and then answer that need with your book. Remember that being persuasive involves a great deal of tact and diplomacy.

— Keep your publisher informed of all publicity. Send them a copy of all written material that has appeared on the book.

What You Should Never Do When Being Interviewed

— Although the interview is a way of generating publicity, it is not a free commercial, so don't treat it as such. Haughty or smug behavior is presumptuous and highly insulting to the interviewer. You will appear as an opportunist.

— Do not use annoying sounds such as "um," "huh," "ah," or "uh." Be careful not to overuse such filler material as "well," "like," and "y' know," for example: "I said, like, you know, do you want to go or not?" or "Well, like, well, I'm not sure. Uh, like, whadda you think?" If you think those sentences read funny, they sound even more ridiculous over the radio or television and don't make you appear very credible as an author, if the show is airing live and unedited.

— Do not get so caught up in listening to yourself that you overstate your importance. Allow the host to direct the interview. Add a touch of friendliness by referring to your host or interviewer by name from time to time, even during an interview for a paper.

— NEVER be late or forget that you have an interview. Nothing upsets a host more than your irresponsibility, and being late or not showing up at all is extremely irresponsible. There's no quicker way to kill an opportunity than by being undependable.

— NEVER criticize, poke fun at or take a combative stance against your interviewer. You are a guest, and the audience is paying attention to your words because the interviewer has earned their attention. It's best to keep him on your side.

Newspaper and Magazine Interviews

Usually a publication (especially local papers) will send a reporter over to your house or office to interview you. The interview on average lasts between one and two hours. The angle on the story is normally along these lines: Local writer, after years of rejection, finally realizes dream of having book published, or hometown boy/girl does good. Therefore the questions are light and easy. "What's your book about? Who's your publisher? How many rejections did you receive? When did you first discover you wanted to be a writer? Who was your inspiration?"

If your interviewer does not ask the name of your publisher, remember to give it. Also give them your publisher's 800 number for ordering copies of your book. If you are so inclined, you may wish to mention your agent and the wonderful job she has done for you.

Ideally, you would like your interview to be a feature story, which means it would occupy a place on the front cover or other prominent position in a newspaper, often in the style or regional section, or appear as a feature magazine article. Most magazines and many newspapers include color photos in their features. Unfortunately, you have little or no say as to whether or not your story will be a feature, and no say whatever on placement. Ask the reporter how much space he's been given. Speak slowly and clearly so the reporter has time to take notes. Many reporters use a tape recorder in conjunction with taking notes. Spell your name to the interviewer as you wish it to appear in the article. If your name is unusual, spell it extra carefully.

If the publication wants a photograph, they normally send a staff photographer to take one. Most of the time the interview and the photographs are done separately, so you may have to schedule two different times or days. Preferably you would like to have a picture of you reading your book, or surrounded by copies of your book.

If the paper or magazine representatives do not mention a photograph, ask if they will require one. If they say no, give them a black and white publicity photo anyway. Ask when the article will appear, but do not bother asking to see a copy of the article before it is printed. It is the policy of most publications to decline that request, probably because reporters do not want you to censor or change their material.

Remember to give your interviewer a signed copy of your book and thank him for taking the time to interview you. After the article appears, write a nice note to the interviewer and the administration of the publication, telling them how pleased you are with the article.

Be forewarned that the article may not read exactly how you thought it would. Your good quotes might not make the article, and what quotes did make it might be taken out of context. Before you become convinced that the world sees you as an idiot, rest assured that is simply not true. Chances are you are the only one who sees yourself that way, based on one article. You may be overly sensitive because it is your first article. It's not easy to read about yourself. It seems as if, no matter how many times people write about you, no one really gets it right.

Let your frustration go. Do not get adversarial with a newspaper or magazine. After all, it is the publicity you are after. Publicity translates into book sales, and that must make both you and the publisher very happy. Selling books is the name of the game.

However, if the publication has made a gross mistake (such as giving the incorrect name of the publisher or title of your book), then politely bring it to the interviewer's attention. You will receive a correction. The agency once had a recent book release mentioned in a local paper. This was fine ...except that the book editor made three mistakes in four lines. Needless to say, we were upset and rightfully so.

If your local paper is not the hometown paper of your youth, make certain you contact your hometown paper. They are particularly generous and flattering of their own. If the hometown paper is located far from you, the interview can be conducted over the phone and you can send them a photo.

Newspapers outside your local area may not wish to do a personal interview; however, they may announce the publication of your book. To encourage the paper to do so, send them a one-page or shorter press release and a publicity photo. Ask them to send you a tearsheet (the newspaper page featuring the article) should they run the article. Follow up with a phone call and ask if they ran anything on you. If they did and it is the paper's policy not to provide tearsheets, ask how you can get back copies.

Magazines – local, regional, and national – are another avenue for publicity. Many large cities have "city" magazines which feature stories about city writers. Company, university and college publications may also be interested in feature articles about their employees and alumni who have published a book.

If you know a major article is going to appear on you, you may wish to pre-order additional copies of the newspaper or magazine. To order 100 or so is not unreasonable. You'll need copies for friends, family, framing and for use in any way possible to generate more interest and publicity in you and your book. This is not a matter of ego; this is a matter of creating success for yourself. Be smart. Push yourself, because no one else is going to do it for you.

In our office we have, hanging on our walls, the history of our success. We have framed many of the articles which have appeared on the agency, ourselves, our clients and any special accomplishments that we have been personally involved with. For us, these articles are daily reminders of just how far we have come and help us focus on where it is we want to go. The articles also give the newer members of the staff a strong sense that they too can accomplish their goals by seeing how success builds upon itself.

Radio Interviews

Radio is sometimes a little difficult at first. Since the interviews are often done over the phone, you may not have the opportunity to talk with or see you host prior to the interview. Nevertheless, the interview must sound personal and warm. In this situation, nothing substitutes for broadcast experience, but until you gain some, you may find the following information about radio interviews helpful.

Radio interviews can last anywhere from a few minutes to an hour, depending upon the format and purpose of the program. There have been many times when our office has been contacted to do live interviews that lasted about two to three minutes. Our insights into publishing or comments on a recent release either precede the news or set the tone for a talk show. This kind of interview is normally set up with little notice and is done over the phone. Be sure to ask the program director the length of the interview and the type of audience to whom you will be speaking. This will help you prepare what you want to say and have ready answers to anticipated questions.

Interviews that are conducted over the phone are rather convenient because you can do them in your pajamas if you so desire. Once you have a few of these interviews under your belt, they become surprisingly easy to do.

First of all, make sure the interview is conducted in a private, quiet room of your home or office. Have someone present to keep the dogs from barking and the kids from screaming. You may wish to have your call forwarding disconnected so you are not interrupted or distracted by the signal. Avoid cellular or cordless phones, which are prone to produce static, and do not listen to the radio while the interview is in process.

The station will call you a few minutes before you are to go on the air. Normally you will be put on hold and allowed to listen to the station's programming. Your host may speak with you for a few seconds before the show, but most likely you will hear your host introducing you and saying a few words about your book. This is your cue to get ready to go on the air.

If the show is taped to air at a later date, the audience will not be asked to call in with questions for you and the station will probably edit your comments. Recently we did a taped interview on European publishers and authors. The host interviewed us for almost forty-five minutes, then edited our comments back to about a twenty-eight minute segment.

If the show airs live and it is a call-in show, you must be ready to answer questions from the listeners. These questions can range from astoundingly astute queries to questions that have nothing to do with the topic at hand. Calls are normally screened and a remarkable job is done to screen out the "crazies." However, if an unbalanced caller does get through, it is your job to skillfully and graciously answer his question or avoid it. If the caller gets out of hand or strays from the subject matter, it is the host's job to either disconnect the caller and move on to another, or tell the caller that his question is not appropriate. You must ALWAYS be sincere, warm, and considerate.

Sometimes you will be asked to go to the studio for the interview. We at the agency prefer this arrangement over telephone interviews because we actually get to see whom we are working with. When you are able to meet your host, the program director and the staff face to face, your are no longer just another interviewee: You become a real person. The time spent making this contact can help you in the future, especially when your second book is published.

The radio studio is an interesting place. We have conducted interviews in a station that was no bigger than a closet, and in others that were as spacious as a boardroom. In some stations, only the interviewer was present; others were highly staffed right down to the receptionist who requested that you sign in so the guard could escort you to the correct studio.

Once inside the studio, you will sit in front of a microphone. Most likely a sound check will be done to test the level of your microphone. The host will talk to you for a few minutes, then you are ready to go. When they open up the show to call-ins, you will need to put on your headphone so that you may hear the questions. Should your mouth become dry during the interview, a sip of a lukewarm beverage is the best cure. Liquid that is either too hot or cold could cause your throat to constrict and make your voice sound a little strange. (A local actress known for her radio work drinks nothing but flat Diet Pepsi during a taping session.) And, since you may be a little nervous during the interview, it would be wise not to eat too much before the show. Besides, you don't want to risk making any embarrassing body sounds.

Check with the program director before the show to find out if they can give you a tape of the program. If it is against their policy to do so, have a friend or family member tape the program for you. Reviewing and studying the tape is a valuable tool in helping you refine your radio interviewing skills.

Television Interviews

If you think it is difficult and strange to read about yourself or listen to yourself, just wait until you see yourself on television. Everything seems magnified, and you may find yourself being hyper-critical. However, by adding the following to the preceding suggestions, you can make the shock of seeing yourself on the screen a pleasant, enjoyable experience.

Usually the top television shows require a pre-interview before scheduling a taping. This gives you an added burden: You must convince the producer that you are the right person for the show. A professional appearance that includes looking good, speaking clearly and being knowledgeable is of the utmost importance.

Being a guest on a top-rated show could give your career a momentous boost in the right direction. Therefore you must choose your wardrobe with great care. We advise you to play it safe and dress conservatively. Do not wear outlandish prints, plaids or checks. Extremes, such as dark blues, browns, black or white is not desirable for women. Bright, flashy colors, such as red, should be used only to accent your outfit. If you are wearing slacks, make certain the socks or stockings you wear are long enough to prevent your leg from showing. Check to make sure that your shoes do not have holes or heavily worn spots in the soles.

Inquire if the studio will do your hair and make-up. The top shows usually provide this service, but most local shows do not. The day of the show is not a good time to try a new hair color or hairstyle or to experiment with cosmetics or attire. If you are uncertain about your "new" look you will not be comfortable and this will show.

The program will advertise your book in at least one of the following ways: You or your host will mention the book; the cover will be flashed on the screen; or the host will hold up the book in front of the camera. If your name and the book's title are to be flashed upon the screen, request that you check both for accurate spelling.

While you are being interviewed, you may have a tendency to look into the camera. Do not do this. Address your answers and comments to your host as if he were the only person in the room. If the show has a call-in format, you may look directly into the camera as if you were talking to the caller.

Do not slouch back in your chair. Sit up. Look alert. Lean forward slightly to give the appearance that you and your host are engaged in an interesting talk. Use a conversational tone, but speak just a little slower and more clearly than you normally would.

One of the first television interviews that was conducted on our agency was both good and bad: good in that it became a learning experience and helped all of us hone our skills...bad because our hand gestures ran amok. While hand gestures are normal in ordinary conversations, on television they are distracting. Keep them to a minimum. It's helpful to practice talking in front of a mirror, using no hand gestures.

Remember to find out when the show is going to air. If the station is unable to provide you with a tape of the show, you should have plenty of time to arrange to tape it yourself. Once again, study it.

Other Means of Obtaining Publicity

No area should be left unexplored when it comes to creating publicity for your book. The following list includes some proven means of selling books.

Literary Conventions

These can provide useful publicity for the new author, whether you are an invited guest or attending on your own, seeking out the media. If you are a speaker, mention your book at some point during your presentation. You also may be able to arrange a booksigning in advance. Check with the organizers.

If you are an attendee, give the media a handout that explains your book(s) and try to tie your book in with the needs of the convention. For example, imagine you are attending a science fiction convention and recently there has been a big interest in the planet Mars. As fate would have it, that just so happens to be the planet where the action in your novel takes place. Let the media know this and make yourself available to talk on the subject.

Workshops and Seminars

There are many writer's workshops and seminars being held across the country each year. You will need to contact far in advance groups and organizations that sponsor these events and let them know you are available to come as a guest. If you are invited as a speaker, a fee of some sort is usually paid to you. Often writer's groups cannot afford what you may feel you are worth, but there is always room for negotiating. Normally the books you are able to sell and the contacts you make are in the long run more valuable then the extra hundred or two hundred dollars you may have wanted. Re- member to have the organizers schedule a booksigning for you.

Churches and Other Organizations

Contacting your church, college alumni association, your high school newsletter and other clubs and organizations in which you hold a membership are all valuable sources for promoting your book. Check into these often overlooked sources to see what they can do to help you.

Libraries

Send a flyer or an article on you and your book to all area libraries. Mention in a cover letter that you are available to lecture or perform a reading from your book. Also give them your publisher's 800 number or the mailing address of where they may order copies of your book.

Book Reviews and Awards

Work with your publisher in securing reviews and being nominated for awards. These kind of accolades help in future marketing of your book and your next work.

Friends and Relatives

The people you know and love best can be a big help to you in terms of publicity. Your family, friends and co-workers will often rally to your side, buying copies of your book and throwing small "booksigning parties" for you, their favorite author. Don't forget, word of mouth is a powerful marketing tool, and chances are your friends and relations will be only too happy to tell their acquaintances about your book. Be sure to politely encourage them to do so.

It may be interesting to note that once the "newness" of being in the limelight has worn off, it may become somewhat unexciting and even a bit tiresome to give yet another interview. In one day, we had twenty-six interviews to give. Each time we had to sound cheerful and informative, even though we felt as if our tongues where going to fall off and maybe even wished they would, just so we could get a break. But, just as writing consists of re-writing, promoting one's book consists of giving interview after interview.

IN CONCLUSION

It is our wish that all of you who read this book meet with success that far exceeds even your wildest dreams. If this book has even in the slightest way helped you along in your writing career, then your success is our success. We would like to hear from you. Let us know your ups and downs, your joys and frustrations in this brave new world of publishing that you have chosen to be a part of. Perhaps in our next book we can address the concerns of the new, soon-to-be published author.

Good writing!

Cynthia Sterling
Megan Davidson
Lee Shore Literary Agency, Ltd.
440 Friday Road
Pittsburgh, PA 15209
Phone: (412) 821-0440
Fax: (412) 821-6099

APPENDIX ONE

COMPLETE SYNOPSIS

Permanence

By Vincent Zandri

SYNOPSIS:

Permanence is not a happy novel, nor is it a novel that boasts
mortal strength amidst profound adversity both real and imagined.
This novel is a tragedy--a simple, familiar tragedy of death,
lost love and failed human endurance in which a woman's very
"humanness" makes her the slave of Providence and fate. But
more specifically, Permanence is the contemporary, first person
account of Mary Kissmet, a twenty-nine year old woman made to
cope with the accidental drowning of her two year old son.
A relatively brief story of 57,000 words, the novel is divided
into three parts or books. Namely, "Water," "Smoke" and "Fire."
A separate epigraph (the first by Douglas Glover, the second
by Ernest Hemingway and the third by Max Frisch) is presented
at the opening of each book and is utilized as a thematic thread
for tying the novel together.

   Logically, Book One is concerned with disclosure. Much is
revealed of Mary Kissmet's past including the childhood
cataclysms that will later mold, dominate and even haunt (in

PERMANENCE/ZANDRI   2
the form of "demons and voices") her adult existence. Mary

is the product of a workaholic father and is raised by a mother

who must complacently bear her husband's compulsions and

obsessions. At ten years old, Mary becomes the sole survivor

of a house fire set by her father--the insane result of his

failure and bankruptcy of his construction business. In turn,

Mary is raised by an aunt and uncle throughout her teen-age

and college years.

     As an attractive young adult, Mary becomes a successful travel

agent, despite her distaste for going anywhere, preferring

instead to remain in "the safety of her own home." She marries

an engineer named, Jamie. Together, the two have a child whom

Mary will namelessly refer to as "baby" even when the boy becomes

a toddler. Be it maternal obsession or harmless use of nickname,

one thing is very apparent: Mary's persistent use of "baby"

as her child's name is a sign that, like her father before her,

she is subject to compulsions and obsessions.

     The story opens fourteen months after Mary's baby accidentally

drowns in the bathtub. She believes baby's death is the result

of her negligence--she left baby alone in his bath "for only

a few minutes. But baby was old enough to sit up on his own

. . ." The loss of the child has also resulted in the breakup

of her marriage--"I can't imagine replacing baby," exclaimed

Jamie, "so what's the point of you and me?"

     Mary has been left alone to make sense of a life that, at

only twenty-nine years, has realized the separation or loss

of every family member both immediate and extended. But she

PERMANENCE/ZANDRI   3
finds some solace in the memories she has formed of the life

she shared with baby and Jamie. A collection of family

photographs taken before baby drowned reveal cherished moments

captured in time, free from the effects of Providence or fate

and therefore rendered permanent. These are photos of baby's

"short, happy life." "There is baby playing in baby's first

snow fall, baby wrestling on the floor with his father; there

is baby eating spaghetti and baby covered with spaghetti. 'Look

closely,' insists Mary. 'Eventually there is no more baby.'"

Mary elects to see a psychiatrist "whether she needs one

or not." This self appointed "restitution" serves as a

penance--a process Mary believes will relieve her of the intense

guilt she attributes to the loss of baby and Jamie.

The psychiatrist is a man who never smiles, rather a man

who wears a perpetual frown of indifference that ironically,

Mary finds mysteriously attractive. In doctor, Mary discovers

a middle-aged man of confidence and understanding. Like baby,

she will refer to her doctor throughout the novel simply as

"doctor," as though denying his "humanness" for a thing to be

cherished like a lifesaving medicine or a newly found faith.

Beside mental alleviation, Mary also discovers a physical

satisfaction in doctor. At the end of her weekly one hour

session, the two make love. Eventually, Mary becomes pregnant

with his child--a pregnancy she will maintain through the first

few weeks, but will keep hidden from doctor throughout the novel.

Book Two, "Smoke," concerns itself with the maturity of

doctor's professional and personal relationship with Mary.

PERMANENCE/ZANDRI   4
The section commences with an explanation from doctor about

his ensuing trip to Venice, Italy where he is to deliver a series

of speeches at a psychiatric conference. Panic stricken at

the thought of being without doctor for even a few weeks, Mary

despairs. She has come to depend upon doctor for emotional

and physical sustenance. But doctor, having fallen in love

with Mary, invites her to accompany him. Mary might have a

fear of travel, but she is more frightened of being left alone

without doctor. With very little deliberation, Mary agrees

to go with him.

    A series of adventures and misadventures follow beginning

with the loss of an engine during the transatlantic flight to

Europe. An emergency landing ensues in Italy and the two, along

with the other passengers, emerge unscathed, at least physically.

From there, Mary and doctor proceed to lose themselves inside

romantic Venice. Although he visited the ancient city years

ago, Doctor has no way of gathering his bearings. By the time

the two discover the location of their hotel, Mary is emotionally

exhausted. In fact, Mary's emotions seem all the more delicate

when, that very night, doctor proclaims his love for her while

making love in a room that overlooks the Grand Canal. Although

Mary has suspected his feelings for her which has culminated

with their love making, she cannot bear to hear doctor say it.

She cannot imagine the idea of replacing the love she had for

baby and Jamie.

    Then Mary discovers this: doctor is physically ill. He chokes

easily when swallowing little bits of food and even liquid.

PERMANENCE/ZANDRI   5
"Doctor," Mary says, "is losing weight he can ill afford to
lose." It becomes clearly evident when Mary and doctor are
involved in an auto accident in Florence, that doctor is not
at all well. "He bleeds too easily," Mary observes of a gash
that runs from doctor's bottom lip to his chin.

Mary overhears a conversation between a Florentine physician
and doctor in which the presence of his illness is confirmed.
Now that Mary is emotionally attached to doctor, he, like all
the others, threatens to abandon her.

But it is during this period in Italy when doctor persuades
Mary to reveal the **true** story of baby's drowning and subsequent
death. Mary's explanation is a detailed account of the moments
before, during and after the horrific incident--an incident
that seems like an accident, but that is the result of Mary's
negligence.

In Book Three, Mary and doctor come home. The book opens
with an emotional account of Mary's abortion of doctor's child.
Then, weeks later, she witnesses the terrible truth about
doctor's sickness. "My cancer," he assures Mary, "has not spread
beyond my throat and mouth." According to doctor, there is
a 94.4 percent chance that he will survive the ailment ("the
remaining 5.6 percent is left up to Providence or fate").

But there's more.

The perpetual frown doctor had maintained throughout the
book has been replaced with a permanent smile, now that a portion
of doctor's jaw has been removed and the corners of his lips
sewn closed (in a way that seems they may split open if doctor

PERMANENCE/ZANDRI   6
should suddenly laugh or cry). In spite of her need for doctor,

Mary becomes repulsed by his appearance. But the revulsion

will be short lived, since it is not long before Mary's worst

fears are confirmed and doctor dies.

With doctor's death comes Mary's complete loss of rationality

combined with a desire to self destruct. This inevitable, final

act of violence will mirror her father's, since Mary sets fire

to her home. The fire is all consuming, except for the bath,

where Mary has allowed the bathtub to overflow onto the floor

while she waits for the people to come for her, including her

ex-husband, Jamie, "through the water and the fire."

Throughout this summary I have attempted to convey some of

the events that shape and re-shape Mary Kissmet's burden--a

burden of guilt, loneliness and "humanness." But I have taken

a great risk. In synopsis form I cannot relay the true

psychological importance of this novel--the actual madness that

fuels Mary Kissmet's decision to let her child drown, or why

she becomes romantically involved with her psychiatrist or how

she feels when she aborts his child.

Permanence, on the surface, may be a novel about the death

of a boy and how his mother deals with that destruction. But

Permanence is also a psychological thriller and a romantic novel

told in the form of passages rather than chapters in order to

relay optimum action and tension. Images (the most familiar

being fire and water as well as Providence and fate) are repeated

throughout the novel in order to provoke rhythm and to establish

a familiar, trance-like tone and quality. This may be a sad

PERMANENCE/ZANDRI   7
story, but <u>Permanence</u> is never boring, never without consequence.

I hope you find this a readable book that remains accessible

to everyone.

APPENDIX TWO

ONE-PAGE SYNOPSIS

Approx. Word Count: 110,000
Category: Historical Romance

SYNOPSIS

ROAD TO THE ISLES
By Megan Davidson

The year is 1715. The place: Glasgow, Scotland. Abby Field, a proper English lady, is left widowed and destitute by her gambler husband. Tantalizingly beautiful and full of spirit, Abby is thrust into the company of a Highland rebel, Calum Og MacDonald, a fugitive from a recent uprising against King George. The fiery red-haired roguish Gael, it seems, is the only person who can lead Abby to her young daughter, held captive on a remote Scottish island.

Together, Abby and Calum travel the "road to the isles," the only path linking the south and north of Scotland, while enduring hardship and heartbreak. Love and passion blossom between them, but they have many an obstacle that lies in the way of their happiness: Calum's grief at finding his family destroyed, Abby's quest to rescue her daughter, and a demonic English officer bent on crushing Calum and all the Jacobite rebels.

Abby finds herself shedding her genteel English manners and adopting the earthy, simple life of the Highland Gael, as she becomes engulfed in a love so pure and intense she is willing to risk her life for it.

APPENDIX THREE

CHAPTER-BY-CHAPTER OUTLINE

SYNOPSIS

The following is a fictionalized account of the life of
the Lady of the Mercians, Aethelflaed. This queen, daughter
to Aelfred, the Great, was a fascinating person. She was
responsible for pushing the Vikings out of England, and for
the uniting of smaller countries into a large unit that has
remained strong to this day.

Like other women before and after her, Lae has been
forgotten by history though she was so much a part of it.

The story was heavily researched. Fact is so much more
exciting than fiction in some cases.

WARRIOR QUEEN: VIKING SLAYER

BOOK I -- 893 A.D. through 899 A.D.

Chapter I

A trip into enemy territory by Aethelflaed, Queen of
Mercia, has ended with a tumble to the ground. Lae, as she
is called by her husband and family, lies on the ground
encased in the arms of a Viking warrior. Waiting to regain
her breath and her composure, she is angry with herself for
underestimating the Vikings. Lae had made many trips into
Danelaw to spy. All were without incident until the arrow
whizzed past her today. She found that their blacksmiths
were making armor and swords, and she was on her way back to

Page Two

Lundenburh to tell her husband.

Aethelflaed, a queen, is wife to Aethelred and daughter
to Aelfred the Great, King of Wessex. Lae had been trained
in warfare from the time she had been a child, and now she
found her self on the ground in a compromising position.

Her capturer is Eiric, son of the chief of the Vikings
at Beamfleot. Lae is upset to find that she is attracted to
this brash and laughing Viking who taunts her. Since they
are not at war, yet, she is able to ride away from him, but
not before she insults him verbally.

Lae crosses the bridge over the Thames that separates
their two countries and rides back to the fortress that she
has called home for the last few years.

Arriving home, Lae finds her husband looking at the maps
in preparation for war. Her brother, Edward, and father,
King Aelfred, arrive to discuss the joining of armies of
Wessex and Mercia to push the Vikings from the British
Island. Lae discovers that her brother's spies have seen her
in Viking territory, and he tells on her. She angrily tells
the men in her family that she can do whatever they can do,
and she will. She hates the Vikings. She has been trained
as a warrior, and she will act like one. The men agree, then
settle down to ask her what she has seen on her spying trips.
The men in her life, her husband, her father, and her brother
raise their bowls of mead to hers in a vow to begin the push
to rid the Island of Vikings.

Page Three

Chapter II

    Lae and Prince Edward, her brother, ride into a village in his own country of Wessex. He stops at a hut that houses his former mistress and his illegitimate son. His wife has had nothing but weak children, and King Aelfred orders Edward to get the one healthy child that is his. Edward's original plan was to take the boy without the mother, but she pleads with him to allow her to go along with the child as his nurse. Egwinna is intelligent, persistent, and fights for her son. Edward agrees that she may accompany the boy to Mercia where Aethelstan, his son, will be reared as royalty by Lae. Lae mentions that her young daughter, who is about Edward's son's age, needs a nurse as well.

Chapter III

    While staying in a church overnight on the way to Mercia, the Vikings attack Lae and Edward. While Edward and his men are fighting the enemy in the woods, one Viking comes into the church and kills the priest. Edward has left. an older knight with Egwinna and Stan to protect them, never expecting any problems inside the church. After fighting with the Vikings and killing them, Edward returns to find Egwinna holding a bloody sword. Egwinna explains that she had heard the priest scream, and she had hidden Stan. The Viking had killed her protector and in desperation, Egwinna had grabbed the downed knight's sword. She had sliced into

Page Four

the Viking, nearly severing his arm. He died from loss of blood. Lae is impressed with this shepherdess, as is Edward.

The rest of the trip was uneventful. Egwinna meets Lae's daughter who is a screaming, kicking child. Egwinna is horrified to discover that the child is a monster, and she is supposed to care for her. Her instructions are to make the girl as sweet as her own son, Stan.

Chapter IV

Egwinna works hard to ignore the screaming child who is in her care. Her own son, Stan, cannot tolerate his cousin because she kicks him, hits him and in general makes his life miserable.

Through her own natural ability as a mother, Egwinna learns to break through the wicked little girl's screams to control her.

Egwinna overhears her future being discussed by Edward and Lae. She learns that Edward's wife is coming to visit and that Egwinna is to be sent away without her son. Never having been separated from him, she panics.

Chapter V

That night Egwinna takes Stan and runs away. Knowing that she would be found in her own village or anywhere in Wessex or Mercia, she decides to run away to East Anglia. She crosses the bridge from Mercia into what she thinks is

Page Five

East Anglia, but in reality it is Danelaw. She hides in a
sheep shed, falling asleep in the hay, her son wrapped in her
arms.

The next morning, a trio of Vikings finds her. Eiric,
who is the same one who had captured Lae, runs his sword into
the hay where Egwinna had hidden her son. Eiric had expected
to find a lover, not a child. He asks who she is, and
Egwinna blurts out her story. She finds that Eiric is
attracted to her, but she has nothing but fear of him.

Edward and Lae ride in to Danelaw with an army to take
Egwinna back to Mercia. She chooses to return with Edward in
order to care for her son. Edward intrigues her.

Chapter VI

Lae meets with Egwinna to determine the real reason for
running away. She wonders if Egwinna were spying for the
Vikings. Lae is astonished to find that Egwinna could not
bear to be separated from Stan. Lae assures Egwinna that she
will not be sent away. Edward's wife and mistress will be
housed in separate parts of the fortress. Given King
Aelfred's orders to rear Stan for the throne of Wessex, Lae
decides that she will have to make up rules as she goes
along. Never had an illegitimate child been groomed for the
throne of the House of Wessex before, so all protocol is
obsolete anyway.

Lae goes for a ride on her horse to clear her thoughts.

Page Six

While she is riding along the river toward the north, another rider on the other side of the Thames races with her. Lae cannot stand to lose or to quit, so she pushes her horse to the limit. Neither rider can win.

Lae's curiosity is such that she stops at a small foot bridge, she ties her horse and walks to the middle. The other rider does the same. It is the Viking who keeps coming in and out of her life. Eiric tries to seduce her, but Lae pulls away. It takes all her determination to leave him for his kiss leaves her wanting him all the more. Lae does not know what to do about her feelings for the enemy, so she visits her mother in Wessex. Her mother comforts her and talks with her. Lae's sister, a nun, tells her that Lae needs to confess to a priest and take the punishment.

Chapter VII

Eiric, intrigued by Lae, does not want to fight her. He goes to his father to plead for peace. They argue until Eiric sees that there will never be peace. Eiric's sister, Olenka, who is not married and lives in their father's hut, tells their father than Eiric is not fascinated by one, but two enemy women. Eiric is so angry with her that he hits his sister. Their father intervenes.

Eiric is told the Danes from all over the island have agreed to join together to fight the Anglo-Saxons.

Eiric takes his three sons fishing. One of the boys

Page Seven

falls in the frigid water. Eiric rescues the child and
worries for days while the child hovers between life and
death. Eiric's sister is a healer and saves the boy's life.
Eiric had promised his gods that if the boy lives, he will
fight the Anglo-Saxons. The child lives and Eiric prepares
for war.

After making preparations for war, Eiric relaxes by
riding. He can't help but think of Lae and how they both
share a love of riding. He sees Lae riding and follows her,
keeping the Thames between them. He lets his horse race,
then when he looks across the river to see if he has caught
up with Lae, he sees a riderless horse. Eiric's curiosity is
so strong that he urges his horse to swim the Thames.

He finds Lae on the ground, unconscious. He cares for
her until she awakens. The two enemies are forced to fight
together as a pack of the ever present wolves threaten them.
After they chase the wolves away, they have to share a horse
because Lae's horse had bolted. Lae has a broken arm and
since they are closer to the Viking village, Eiric takes her
to Olenka to heal her.

Chapter VIII

Olenka and Nissa, Eiric's wife, become admirers of Lae
and she admires them. They become friends, albeit, guarded.
Lae is enchanted by Nissa who is an artist with the loom
weaving wonderful pieces of wool as well as being able to

Page Eight

embroider. Olenka is a gifted healer and miracle worker with herbs. Lae wonders if she can really wage war against the Danes after all.

Messages had been sent to Lae's husband explaining her where abouts. The Viking code would not let any harm come to a guest. However, the atmosphere is tense when Lae's husband, father, and brother come for her. Lae smooths things with her family, and Eiric is thanked for saving her from the wolves.

Chapter IX

Lae joins her brother in leading an army into Beamfleot. Much to her anger after having befriended the Viking women, war has started anyway. While the Vikings are fighting with her husband and her father, the lair of the enemy is captured and burned by Lae and Edward. Lae does spare the huts of Nissa and Olenka. Some women and children are captured and taken to Lundenburh.

The Vikings are sent for to take back their people. Lae goes with her husband, father, and brother to return the hostages. On the trip, she gets a chance to talk with a cousin of Nissa, and she learns that Nissa and Olenka have a tremendous amount of respect for the Lady of the Mercians. This information further saddens Lae because she cannot see how war can be avoided.

The exchange is made and the Anglo-Saxons return home.

Page Nine

As Lae and her men folk gather around the fire, there is more talk of war.

Chapter X

Egwinna has been wooed and won by Edward, again, and he shares her chambers. Egwinna learns that Edward's wife and family are on their way for a visit.

When she accidently meets Edward's wife on the stairway, their exchange is not pleasant and Egwinna is called a whore. In her heart, Egwinna knows the woman is right.

It is Egwinna's expertise in the use of herbs for sheep that helps her to stop Edward's wife's premature labor. The two women have a temporary truce, but of course, it cannot last. Egwinna feels a pang of regret for having been Edward's mistress, but she loves him too much to give him up. Furthermore, she is pregnant and wants to give Edward another son.

Edward's wife finally gave birth to a son, but he was as sickly as her other children. The child is never strong and dies while an infant. Edward has only Stan as an heir.

Egwinna is surprised when Lae bangs through the door into her chambers and announces that the Vikings have sailed up the Thames in the dark of night to attack inner Mercia. Lae is excited that the war has begun in earnest.

Chapter XI

Lae is with her husband and the army as they go after

Page Ten

the Vikings. She is a part of the army and sleeps on the
ground as they do. She hates not having a bath and fears
that she has lice.

Edward and his army are to the right. Her father is
fighting the Vikings in the south. This will be Lae's first
real battle. She rides into the foray as it begins. She
survives through her excellent swordsmanship as well as help
from her foot soldiers. Toward the end of the battle, Eiric
approaches her with his sword down. Etiquette dictates that
she must not take advantage of the position of his sword.
She is upset that she cannot run him through. They talk and
Lae notices that Eiric is as saddened by the fighting as she
is happy.

The Vikings lose the battle and retreat into a fort.
The Anglo-Saxons lay siege.

Lae swims in a river where they are camped. Leaving
troops in siege, the Anglo-Saxons ride back to Lundenburh
to celebrate their victory.

At the dinner, Lae sees red wine in a silver goblet and
it reminds her of bright blood on her sword. She rushes from
the great hall and throws up outside. Her husband tells her
that all warriors have times in which memories cause a
sickness.

Because of Lae's first successful battle and her first
kill, she has the honor of naming her sword. She calls the
sword 'Boadicea' after the queen of the Iceni who tried to

Page Eleven

push the Romans from the island in the first century.

Chapter XII

Lae watches the Viking ships burning in the Thames from her position on her horse. She sees the Vikings leap from the burning ships. Going after Vikings who were hiding along the river, Lae and her men come across a few. Lae is injured and she rides home to have Egwinna sew her cut. Egwinna is not feeling well and confides to Lae that she is worried about the health of her son, Aelfred. He is as sickly as the children Edward had had by his wife. Little Aelfred dies, leaving Egwinna so saddened that her health is affected. She is in the later stages of pregnancy and soon after Aelfred's death, she dies while giving birth to a daughter. Lae is with her and promises to care for the child. Egwinna is missed by everyone in the castle, but mostly she is missed by the tantrum-throwing child who had been loved by Egwinna.

Lae's life is further turned upside down by the news that her father has sent for her. He is dying. Lae and the grandchildren are able to visit with King Aelfred. He dies in 899AD.

BOOK II -- 907 A.D. through 908 A.D.

Chapter XIII

Lae has been approached by a despicable Viking who wants

Page Twelve

to inhabit a deserted area. He stands before her with a ragged band of women and children. Lae grants him a place to live. As she later explains to her husband, it is better to know where the snake lives.

Lae tries to show her daughter, Wyn, by example how to rule. Wyn is a woman, now, but is still spoiled. Lae is concerned that Wyn, who is in direct line to rule Mercia, is not effective at making decisions. Lae is aware that her nephew, Aethelstan, son to Egwinna and Edward, is much better suited to ruling. She hopes that the Houses of Wessex and Mercia will be joined with the marriage of Wyn and Stan. Unfortunately, Wyn hates Stan and Stan hates Wyn.

Lae's husband is bedridden most of the time with an illness that cannot be cured. Lae has run the country single-handedly for several years with Aethelred as a consultant. He had helped teach her to fight and to rule.

When Lae goes to their chambers to tell him about her meeting with the ragged group of people, Lae and Aethelred argued about Wyn's ability to rule.

Aethelred talks to Lae about forming a treaty with Wales and with Ireland against the Vikings to strengthen their country for the war with the Vikings. Lae accepts the challenge and prepares for the journey, taking Wyn and Stan with her. She had been reluctant to leave her husband in his condition, but he insists that she needs the treaties.

When Lae is greeted by the King of Ireland, she is

Page Thirteen

startled by his lack of propriety. She ignores his obvious
attempts to seduce her. They spend time playing chess at
night in the great hall with the contest observed by many
court members. Wyn tries to blackmail her mother by telling
her that she'll tell her father Lae has been unfaithful.

The king in Wales is imposing, but agrees to sign a
treaty against the Vikings. The journey comes to an end when
Lae returns home.

Chapter XIV

Lae stands near the window with a parchment letter from
the King of Ireland in her hand. She tries to spare her
husband the pain of more wars. His health has worsened.

In the letter, Lae finds information that the man who
she has allowed to move into an abandoned fort with his
ragged band of followers, has plans to attack a near-by town
that is under Lae's jurisdiction.

Lae gathers her army and with help from her nephew,
Stan, uses an ancient ploy to surprise the enemy. The clever
trick works and her enemy is captured along with his army.

Later at a meeting with Stan and Aethelred, Lae outlines
her plans for a series of forts to be built along the border
of her country. Her brother, Edward, agrees that this is a
good idea and will help by building a series of forts
himself along the border. Together, they will be formidable.

Lae and her daughter, Wyn, get into an argument. Wyn

Page Fourteen

blurts out that she is going to run away to the Vikings. Lae wonders how her daughter could hate her so much. She also learns that Wyn has felt neglected by Lae since childhood. Wyn is bitter. Mother and daughter fight.

Chapter XV

Wyn does not want to be guarded by her mother and confined to her room. She makes an escape before the men are placed outside her door. She runs to Eiric in Viking territory.

Eiric is not happy to see her, and Wyn sees that the Vikings have fear of her mother. Wyn is surprised at how her mother is perceived by the enemy. Eiric tells her that he will make certain she is returned so that her mother's wrath will not be taken out on his people. Nissa and Olenka tell Wyn that she is not welcome there.

Lae and her army come after Wyn. She expects her mother to ask her to return to Mercia and is surprised when she is told that she is to stay with the Vikings. Wyn is shocked and tearfully begs her mother to allow her to return. Lae allows her to, but reluctantly, promising to all Lae's demands.

Wyn is not home long when she becomes deathly ill. Lae is concerned that she will not rally. Since there is no physician from Arabia at hand, Stan is sent for Olenka.

Page Fifteen

Chapter XVI

Olenka comes because Lae did save her hut and Nissa's. In spite of their being enemies, Olenka cannot bear to see illness. Eiric and Nissa have also urged her to come.

Olenka is at Lae's Lundenburh fortress for several days treating Wyn's illness until at last Wyn is her usual nasty self. Lae is relieved and escorts Olenka back to the Viking settlement. She visits with Nissa and the three women have a bittersweet meeting.

On the trip home, a band of Vikings from the north attack Lae, and a fierce battle ensues. Lae's army wins the battle and in triumph she rushes home to tell her husband of the victory. He is feeling better because of the medicine that she has ordered for him. Lae is happy to be in his arms. She tells Aethelred that she loves him more than anyone else in the world.

Edward comes for a visit to plan with Lae where the line of forts will be built. While he is there, messengers come from several different areas. They tell that the Vikings are amassing a huge army. The thoughts of such a huge battle in the near future frightens Lae, and she breaks down. Her husband helps her overcome her fears. She is ready to lead her first major battle as commander-in-chief.

Chapter XVII

Lae and her nephew, Stan, mount an offensive while

Page Sixteen

Edward fights the Vikings on another front. Lae has never seen such a large army before. Three kings have combined forces to fight the Mercians and Anglo-Saxons. The battle is difficult and there is much killing. Lae wants to kill the kings, but they have eluded her. At the end of the battle, the Mercians are the victors. Although Lae didn't kill one king, all three have been slaughtered. As a tribute to her army and to remind the peasants that they will always be safe, Lae plans to build a fort near the site of the battle. She calls in the master builders and her plan to line her borders with forts is begun.

Lae's fight to keep her husband alive is over. He dies just after Christmas. Lae feels the loss heavily since he had been a part of her life from the time she had been a child.

The elders of Mercia came to see Lae and asked that she not allow Wyn to rule after her. They explain that Wyn is not suited to rule, for she has caused the death of at least one servant. Lae argues with them at first, then agrees that Edward or Stan should follow her rather than Wyn. She asks that their conversation be kept secret until her death. The elders agree.

Lae sends for Stan and tells him that he will not have to marry Wyn. She would like for him to marry for love, not politics. Lae tells him that if he marries Wyn, he would be miserable. She also tells him that to preserve both

Page Seventeen

countries, Edward or Stan will rule both Wessex and Mercia, merging the two countries to prevent the Vikings from controlling either one.

BOOK III -- 916 A.D. through 918 A.D.

Chapter XVIII

Lae has moved to her favorite part of her country, the northeastern part. She's at an outpost called Tamoworthig.

Wyn hates being there because there is nothing to do. While mother and daughter are arguing, as usual, a messenger tells Lae that the Welsh have come into Mercia and attacked an unarmed band of monks. She sends Stan and his army to take care of the Welsh king.

Edward comes to visit, and Lae is very happy. They plan an offensive together with Stan. Lae is to take Deoraby which she does easily.

Riding home after the battle, Lae falls off her horse when he stumbles. She lands on her helmet and is injured seriously. Lae is ill for most of the winter. It isn't until spring that she feels better, although she never fully recovers.

Lae goes for a ride on her horse and feels her appetite return. During dinner it is announced that the Vikings are floating down the river toward them. Lae plans to attack them. Her spirits soar.

Page Eighteen

    The Mercian army is victorious, and the Vikings flee to the woods. Lae orders carpenters to cut down the woods to flush out the Vikings while she and her army wait at the other end of the woods. The enemy is killed along with their king.

Chapter XIX

    Lae meets with the Scots and Picts to seal a treaty in order to work together to rid the island of the Vikings. It will take one more strong push to get the enemy out. The blue painted Picts arrive with their friends, the Scots. Wyn is horrified at the heathens, but Lae treats them well. A pact is made and they become allies.

    After the treaty has been signed and the delegation has gone, Lae awakens with a raging fever followed by chills. She never gets well.

    The Lady of the Mercians dies after extracting a promise from Stan that the will erase her name from the English Chronicles so that Wyn will have no claim to the Mercian throne.

APPENDIX FOUR

QUERY LETTER TO AGENT

Jane Smith
678 Myrtle Street
Cleveland, OH
(222) 555-1011

Ms. Cynthia Sterling
Lee Shore Literary Agency
440 Friday Road
Pittsburgh, PA 15209

Dear Ms. Sterling:

I have just completed a 450-page horror novel entitled, NIGHT OF THE DEAD IGUANAS, which is approximately 90,000 words long. It is about the terror that ensues when a community of human-like iguanas (the result of secret governmental testing) attack the residents of a small town in New Mexico.

I would like to send you the manuscript for your review. If you are interested, please send me your submission guidelines if available, or a request to see the novel.

Thanks very much for your consideration.

Sincerely,

Jane Smith

APPENDIX FIVE

MEDIA FILE CHARTS

MEDIA FILE
For Radio and TV

STATION ADDRESS PHONE/FAX	
HOST	
SHOW	
CONTACT/ PROGRAM DIRECTOR	
DATE(S) CONTACTED	
COMMENTS	

MEDIA FILE

For Publications

PUBLICATION NAME ADDRESS PHONE/FAX	
INTERVIEWER	
PUBLICATION SECTION/ FEATURE TITLE	
CONTACT NAME	
MANAGING OR SENIOR EDITOR	
DATE(S) CONTACTED	
COMMENTS	

APPENDIX SIX

MEDIA CALENDAR CHART

MEDIA CALENDAR
For Interviews

STATION/ PUBLICATION NAME ADDRESS PHONE/FAX	
INTERVIEWER	
TIME AND LENGTH OF INTERVIEW	
CONTACT NAME	
DATE OF INTERVIEW	
COMMENTS	

PROOFREADING SYMBOLS

∧ = inserts

∧, ; ∧. ; ∧: = insert comma; period; colon

∨' ; ∨" = insert apostrophe; insert quotation marks

?∧ = insert question mark

⊖ ; ⊼ = insert hyphen or dash

= insert space

ℓ = remove space

⊂ (th⊃e) = close up space

|← = move left

→| = move right

(?) ; ?what? = query to author; author's meaning not understood

ℍ ; no ℍ = new paragraph; combine paragraphs

SP = correct spelling

SP out ; S.O. = spell out word or number

2(seth) ; tr = transpose

ital; ———— = italic type

bf ; ⌁⌁⌁ = boldface type

reg. type = do not use italic or boldface

lc ; ℬ = use lower case letters

≡ ; cap = use capital letters

/ ; | (in/the) = separate words

stet = let it stand; ignore editor's remark

I.A. = indirect antecedent

A.I. = authorial intrusion

POV = point of view

POV shift = point of digression

⊥/m = dash (em-dash)

awk = awkward phrasing or structure, unclear meaning

agr = check agreement

& = and

conf = confusing

frag = sentence fragment

red = redundant

tense = check tense

trans = transition needed

w/ch = reconsider word choice

ℓ ; del = delete

INDEX